THE REAPER CLINIC

I'm not dead! I made my right hand into a fist.
"Subject shows no sign of male pattern baldness,

A GATHERING
EVIL

THE OLDER CLINIC

...we will attempt to preserve the scalp intact as we go in after the brain."

I straightened my hand again and slapped it against the table. There, she has to hear that.

"Doctor, his right hand moved," I heard Andre tell her. "I think he is still alive."

"Andre, I think you are right. This is a complica-tion."

Had I the ability to do so, I would have smiled.

"Quickly, Andre, over there, the cabinet."

Good, get something to fix me.

"Here?"

"Yes, Andre, you idiot, do what she tells you to do."

"Yes, Andre, bring them to me."

"Is this enough?"

"Four? I suppose, but bring a couple more, just to be sure," I heard her pat the instrument table. "Put them here. Whenever one is alive there's always more blood. You can never have enough towels."

A WATHERING
EVIL

A DARK
CONSPIRACY novel

A GATHERING EVIL

Michael A. Stackpole

To Michael Stanton,

This book points out why
Phoenix Might Not be A place for
Retirement in The future.

Best
wishes
Michael
Stackpole

DARK CONSPIRACY™

GDW

This novel is set in the universe of **Dark Conspiracy**™—GDW's roleplaying game of modem horror.

A Gathering Evil is an original publication of GDW, Inc. This novel has never before appeared in book form. Any similarity to actual persons or events is purely coincidental.

Cover: Dell Harris

GDW Books
A Division of GDW Games
P.O. Box 1646
Bloomington, IL 61702-1646

First Printing, Summer, 1991
01 02 03 04 05 06 07 08 09

Dark Conspiracy™ is a trademark of Game Designers' Workshop, Inc.

Printed in USA. Made in USA.

To Dennis L. McKiernan
I know this should be something clever but you'll
have to settle for my thanks. You're a friend and an
inspiration.

Acknowledgments

The author would like to thank Frank Chadwick for letting me play with his universe and his understanding during this project, Loren Wiseman for answering questions nights and weekends, Liz Danforth for listening to this work in progress and Richard Mulligan for reading it over and helping me make it make sense.

The author also thanks GEnie Computer Network through which the manuscript passed to the publisher, and editorial questions and answers were exchanged with the author.

A GATHERING
EVIL

Awakening in a speeding ambulance, with the scream of its undulating siren ripping your brain apart, is not a pleasant experience. It becomes even less so when you realize you're in a body bag zipped up tight and you can't move. Trapped in suffocating darkness, with the rubberized canvas pulling at your flesh, you realize that if this is death, eternity in a grave will be hell itself.

The strap across my chest and another just above my knees bound me tightly to the gurney. They kept me with it as it crashed around in the back, jouncing up and down or smashing side to side with the fast turns. The driver, mercilessly pushing the whining engine to its top end, sadistically pounded his way through potholes as if on a divine mission to crush them all.

The irritating stink of rubber and the lingering scent of decayed meat filled my nose. I tried to breathe through my mouth, but I could not make my lips part. I fought against the paralysis locking my jaw and quickly discovered the condition extended to my whole body. I could still feel the straps dig into my flesh and the slick roughness of the bag against my fingertips, but I could not make my muscles work. Try as I might, I could not even open my eyes.

It took no genius on my part to know I was in severe trouble. Being in a body bag meant the ambulance folks thought I was dead—and that conjured up all sorts of horrible images of premature burial or a seriously distasteful cremation. I started to panic, then fought against it because a clear head was all I had to get myself out of this situation.

And getting out of it was even more important that

wasting brainsweat on figuring how I'd gotten into it.

The siren snapped off and the ambulance began to slow. I heard the crunch and ping of gravel beneath the tires, then felt the jolt as the gurney clanked against the inside of the ambulance as we rolled to a stop. The sound of passenger doors opening and closing cut off the static from the radio, then I heard the doors in the back open. I rolled forward, then landed hard on the ground.

"Take it easy, Jack."

"The stiff won't care."

"Yeah, but Harry will charge us for damage to the gurney." I tagged this speaker as Gruff-voice.

Jack hacked out a cough. "So, we take it out of petty cash. This guy was loaded. His cards will be worth something."

"No need to spend what we don't have to." Gruff-voice took a couple of steps away from the ambulance, his footfalls moving from my feet toward my head. "Where are they?"

"They'll be here." Another hack. "See, there they are."

Both men fell silent as I heard another vehicle drive up. Its engine had a nasty ticking sound and the door slid open. I immediately imagined it to be a van or delivery truck.

Jack greeted the newcomers. "Evenin', tulmen."

"The last batch was unsatisfactory." The voice had no compromise, and even less humanity in it.

Jack managed to keep fear out of his voice, but he radiated it so palpably that I could feel it from within the bag. "I know, and I'm sorry about that, but look, this one will make it up to you."

I heard a pair of clicks and the pressure on my chest and legs went away. I felt a tug near the top of my head, then heard the rasping sound of the zipper being undone. For a half-second the air rushing in felt cool; then it turned hot and very dry. I smelled dust in the air and the sharp scent of burned-out engines and steaming radiator fluid. My nasal passages dried out immediately and I could feel myself desiccating as they stood there.

Gruff-voice tried to let laughter override his anxiety. "Look, he's mid-30s, clean and in good shape. No scars. You can get kidneys, a liver and a heart out of him. His eyes should be good, too. Hell, you could even take his lungs and give them to Jack, here."

Panic again surged through me. *They're selling off my parts, but I'm not even dead yet. They can't do this. I have to let them know I'm still alive!*

"Why? He'd just ruin them as well." I felt fingers poke and prod me. Hands slipped beneath my right shoulder and lifted me enough to get a brief glimpse of my back. My head fell back, opening my mouth, and I gasped aloud. Jack and Gruff-voice jumped back, with one of them clunking against the ambulance.

"Jesus!"

Yes, there, now they know I'm still alive.

The inspector laughed harshly. "Come now, aces like you know gasses build up in corpses. Only time you'll see this deader again is in your nightmares."

My heart sank.

"Well, we don't spend as much time around them as you Reapers do. We generally get them before they become spare parts."

"So you do. Still warm. Good. Looks clean. Where did you get him?"

I heard Jack swallow hard. "Call came in an hour ago. He was in a squat-shack hotel in Slymingtown. Setup looked staged, like he had been dumped there. No one was asking questions, but Scorpion Security was on its way, so we snatched him and called you. How much?"

"A meg, plus 10% of anything unusual we get."

"A meg? Are you kidding? I could get three megs piecing him out, and still get a point on DNA applications."

Jack had sounded angry, but the Reaper called his bluff. "If you can, do it. You'll find it is a buyer's market, Jack, not a seller's. I could see going 1.5 megs, but you'll drop to 7% for exotics."

"With two points on DNA aps?"

"One, and only because I've forgotten how the last two maggot-ranches you gave me weren't fit for dog food. Literally, we left them in the desert and the coyotes wouldn't touch them."

"And we keep the effects?"

"Yes, Jack. We care not for his earthly possessions." I felt a hand grasp my forehead and work my head side to side. "Good bone structure and no cranial damage. I think we can save the brain. This is good. Do we have a deal?"

"Done. Always enjoy doing business with you Reapers."

"You lie poorly, Jackson, but we tolerate you because of your product." The Reaper snapped his fingers. "Gord, Kenny, red tag this one and put him in the back. We want to do him quickly, before he spoils any more."

The zipper closed again, shutting me away in the stuffy world of rubber and stale flesh. I sagged into a U-shape as two people grabbed the handles at my head and feet. I swayed between them as they carried me along, then I heard the rumble of a roll-away door sliding up into the truck's ceiling.

"Which side do we put him on?" one voice asked thickly.

"You sar him; he's vanilla."

They rocked me three times, then I flew up into the truck and landed solidly. Something shifted below me and I half expected to be buried beneath an avalanche of corpses. I slid a bit sideways, but nothing crashed down on top of me. The door slammed shut and the engine coughed to life. Gears ground and we lumbered forward.

I heard another sound in the back of the truck above the ticking idle of the engine. I first caught it as a cyclical pinging and noted it remained constant. I wondered what it was, but not for long: I felt a chill nibbling at my toes and fingers. The logic of icing down a truck full of corpses did not surprise me, but the reality of it sent a jolt of adrenaline through my body.

The cold and adrenaline combined to do what all my willpower had been unable to manage. I started to shiver. My limbs trembled uncontrollably. I found myself no longer locked in the grasp of paralysis.

I tried to move my hand under my conscious direction, but still found myself unable to do so. *Too ambitious,* I decided. I tried to open my eyes, but realized, in the dark, in a body bag, I could not tell if I had been successful. I made an attempt at breathing through my mouth, but found I still could not open it.

Despair opened its jaws wide to swallow my spirit whole, but the hope inspired by my shivering saved me. *Before you can run, you must learn to walk. Before you can walk, you need to shiver. Shivering is good. Shivering is progress. Think cold. Make your body want to do what you cannot make it do.*

I abandoned myself to cold and panic, repeatedly having to overcome unconscious efforts to control myself. I knew each burst of adrenaline that pumped into my system was helping, yet I felt constitutionally averse to admitting panic. It represented a total loss of control, and that spelled disaster. It felt as if part of me believed that by admitting I was in serious trouble, I would not find a way out of it.

Though I knew I should have been paying attention to the motions of the truck, I decided against it. I knew it would have been simple—a child's game—to keep track of twists and turns. By counting slowly and estimating speeds, I could have easily cataloged our journey and had an excellent chance of backtracking it. I had done it before, but not knowing where we had started, and unsure if I ever wanted to return there, I let it go.

I also found, for the brief time I did keep track of things, that the driver was doing his best to take us through a very evasive and difficult-to-follow route. We changed levels several times and traveled both city streets and highways. We made no more stops, which I pridefully saw as a reflection of my own value, and ended the journey with a long downward slope.

My shivering stopped instantly as the truck door opened. I felt all my senses come alive as if I were trying to project my mind outside the bag to see where I was. I could not, of course, and my attempts were interrupted by the jerk on the handle at my head. My body limply slithered over other corpses, then I slid free of the truck and my legs slapped stiffly on the ground.

"Key-ryest, Gord, don't let the legs hit!"

"Geez, Kenny, the guy ain't complaining."

"But the doctor will. Soft tissue damage, she calls it."

There was nothing soft about the way my legs and heels felt as Gord hefted me up. Hitting the ground had hurt and I would have screamed had my jaw not been locked. Anger twisted my belly up and burned like fire. I wanted to let it run wild like I had the panic, but I immediately shunted that energy away and calmed myself.

Then I noticed that the rage—or pain—had caused my fingers to claw inward. They felt stiff, but they had moved. One by one I willed them to straighten out again. The paralysis fought me, but the commands got through. On my right hand, my little finger snapped to attention first, then the ring finger and the index. I reissued the order and the middle finger complied.

My left hand responded more sluggishly, but it did

respond. I tried to curl my toes inward and they also worked. Concentrating hard, I forced my fingers back in again and the right hand got almost all the way down into a fist. The left hand tried, but failed. The fingers did straighten out again on command, and I managed to flex all the muscles in my right arm, which gave me great cause for joy.

So concerned was I with regaining the use of my limbs that I was unprepared for Gord and Kenny dropping me on a table. I smacked the back of my head on the surface and saw stars in front of my eyes. As they sizzled off like Technicolor comets, I heard the bag being unzipped, then I was tipped right and left so they could whisk it from beneath me.

They left me lying naked on a cold metal table. Despite my eyes still being closed, I could see a golden glow from outside my eyelids, and I could feel the warmth of the lights on me. I brushed the fingertips of my right hand across the surface and felt a shallow groove running from beneath me toward the edge of the table.

A door opened and I heard a woman's voice. "Oh, this is a fine specimen. Thank you, tulmen. Andre, roll tape on this one. We want to document him."

"Yes, doctor."

I heard a wheeled cart roll closer to the table. The clink of instruments accompanied its arrival and I did not like how close to my head it all sounded.

From right above me I heard the woman's voice. "Subject is a white male, six feet tall, approximately 175 pounds, moderate body hair which is dark in color. He is in excellent condition, with no visible signs of trauma. Fluids will be drawn and toxicology run to determine cause of death."

I'm not dead! I made my right hand into a fist.

"Subject shows no sign of male pattern baldness, so we will attempt to preserve the scalp intact as we go in after the brain."

I straightened my hand again and slapped it against the table. *There, she has to hear that!*

"Doctor, his right hand moved," I heard Andre tell her. "I think he is still alive."

"Andre, I think you are right. This is a complication."

Had I the ability to do so, I would have smiled.

"Quickly, Andre, over there, the cabinet."

Good, get something to fix me.

"Here?"

Yes, Andre, you idiot, do what she tells you to do.

"Yes, Andre, bring them to me."

"Is this enough?"

"Four? I suppose, but bring a couple more, just to be sure." I heard her pat the instrument table. "Put them here. Whenever one is alive there's always more blood. You can never have enough towels."

The whirring buzz of a bone-saw hovered over me like a malevolent wasp and wrung the last ounce of adrenaline out of me. As the saw descended, my eyes snapped open. The doctor brought the instrument down with both hands, but my right arm shot up on a desperate collision course. Forearm to forearm I blocked her, then shoved back with all my strength.

Her grandmotherly face disappeared in a red mist as the saw-blade bridged the gap between her eyebrows. She flew back out of sight with her stool clattering metallically against the tile floor. I scissored my legs left over right and pitched myself off the right side of the autopsy table, then half-collapsed as my legs buckled beneath me.

I thought that a disaster, but it turned out to be more fortuitous than I ever could have imagined. As I sank toward the floor, the snap-kick Andre had aimed at my head missed cleanly. From below I posted my left leg up into his groin, and that took all the fight out of him. He doubled over, moaning. Grabbing a handful of his hair, I accelerated his face into the tile floor.

I sagged down beside him, almost as limp as he was, and felt as if I had been de-boned. My limbs moved as if they were made of lead and powered by the wind, but I gathered them beneath me. Inch by inch, I climbed up one leg of the autopsy table and hauled myself back upright. I glanced over at the doctor. The only sign of life there was the cutter still whirring away in her right hand. Andre was out for the count, if not the rest of this incarnation, which left me safe for the moment.

Now, without knowing where I am or how many

people exist outside, I have to escape. Oddly enough, quantifying the problem in that way, I did not so much find it impossible as annoying. It was a time-consuming complication. Those who had inconvenienced me would pay.

I stripped Andre of his pants and donned them, despite their being three inches too short. I likewise appropriated his shoes—nautical-style loafers that fit after I loosened the rawhide lacings—and white lab coat. I pocketed the four scalpels on the instrument tray, then picked up one of the white towels Andre had dropped.

Crouching next to the doctor, I looked around the room. Aside from a certain amount of mildew on the grout between the tiles, the room could have passed for a hospital emergency ward. The glass-fronted cabinets housed small drug ampules and stainless steel implements. Over on a filing cabinet I saw three glass jars with various organs preserved in them, and noted on a table back in the corner that four others were open and ready for filling. The back wall had three rows of small, squarish doors that I assumed held deaders in various states of harvesting.

I swished the towel through the doctor's blood puddle, then pressed the dripping cloth to my head. It obscured enough of my face that I believed I could pass as Andre, so I crossed to the door, yanked it open, and slumped in the doorway. "We have trouble. He was alive!" I shouted in a voice that matched Andre's with surprising accuracy.

People throughout the warehouse-like structure reacted. Four steps away a man drew a pistol and sprinted forward. As he closed, I flipped the towel over his head and snatched the pistol from him. I snapped the automatic's safety lever down and pumped a round into his stomach at point blank range.

The two large men who were unloading bodies from

an ice cream truck onto a cart had started to run toward me, but the gunshot brought them up short. They clawed beneath their jackets for weapons, but never got a chance to complete their draws. Cutting to the left, I snapped off a shot that sent the one on the right to the ground clutching his throat. I hit the other in the shoulder, slowly starting him to spin to the right, then dropped him with a shot to the middle of his back.

I glanced at the gun to confirm visually what I already knew about it by feel. *Colt Krait. Ten millimeter ammo, muzzle brake, open sights. Fourteen in the clip, could have had the first one in the chamber. I'm running four shy of full.*

Above me I heard the hollow clank of a boot on a catwalk. I dove forward in a somersault, then let my legs splay out to stop me. Craning my head back, I saw a woman with a machine pistol sweep a thunderous line of fire back through where I should have been. Our eyes met as I pumped one round into her chest and sent her flying back off the other side of the catwalk.

His black trenchcoat flying open, a slender man leapt from the driver's seat of the truck. He pointed at me and yelled in a voice I recognized. It was the Reaper who had bargained for me. "Shoot him, but not the head. Save the head!"

What is it about this guy and my brain?

I dropped the Krait on his outline and sent two rounds into him. They both hit high chest and sent him tumbling backward. Off to my right two men ran round a corner, each with a submachinegun in hand, but they discounted the sight of me because I was in a lab coat. A head-shot put the first man down and a gut-shot jackknifed the second man to the slick concrete floor.

I sprinted across open ground to the ice cream truck. The keys were still in the ignition, so I dropped into the driver's seat, shifted the pistol to my left hand and

cranked the engine. It sprang to life, still ticking like a
bomb. I jammed the clutch down and forced it into first.
The truck lurched forward and I started it turning in a
large arc toward the ramp and the big doorway that
would take me back up to street level.

*Have to get out of this charnel house. Fresh air. The
sky. Life!*

In the rearview mirror I saw bodies tumbling willy-nilly
from the back. I also saw two more men with pistols
come running into the area. They triggered off shots, but
I knew that unless they were even better shots than I was,
they had no chance of hitting me. Punching the gas, I
upshifted and steered straight toward the ramp.

I started up the ramp at 30 mph when the Reaper in
black appeared in the driver's-side doorway. Blood
bubbled from the lung-hits he'd taken, but he stood
there, clutching either side of the doorway as if he'd not
been hit at all. He opened his mouth to hiss at me like a
cat and a thin, bloody mist sprayed out. His left hand
grabbed at the wheel and jerked it toward him.

I had no clue as to what this pasty-faced lunatic
wanted to accomplish, but I had plenty of ideas how to
discourage him. I shoved the Krait in his face and stroked
the trigger. His visage disappeared in a cloud of smoke
and fire. He hung in the doorway for a second, then fell
away, anchored to the speeding vehicle by his left hand's
deathgrip on the wheel.

I pressed the Krait to his wrist and fired. The body
dropped away with a thump, but it had hung there long
enough to pull the truck over to the left side of the ramp.
Sparks shot up as I sideswiped a railing, then I jerked the
wheel back to the right. Oversteering, I pulled away from
the railing, but managed to hit a girder stanchion on the
other side at the top of the ramp.

The airbag deployed as the girder crushed the right
front quarter of the ice cream truck. I bounced forward

then back as the vehicle slewed around to the left in a fishtail that sowed half-frozen bodies all over the ramp and the landing. The truck hit the closed doors going backward, which slammed me back into the rear of the driver's compartment, then I rebounded into the steering wheel. With a screaming crunch, the roll-away door snapped off the supports at the top and flowed out into the street like a metallic carpet.

Shocked and battered, with blood leaking from my nose, I scrambled back through the truck, over the bodies and out into the street. Once clear, I turned back and emptied the pistol into the truck's gas tank. It went up in a boiling, orange-black ball that rose toward the sky, but never actually got there.

One hundred feet up the fireball flattened against a construct of black panels, steel girders and tangled wires. In its wake it left ablaze a small structure that looked like a bird's nest built beneath the eaves of a house. In this case, however, the nest was large enough to house humans and the eaves were part of a roof over the whole city. The fire's smoke rolled across the underside of the panels like a dark thunderhead, then started to descend like a malevolent fog.

They roofed over the city! Something inside me crumpled. The claustrophobic feeling of being inside the body bag flooded back like a recurring nightmare. The sky and the sun and the moon meant freedom to me, yet I found myself trapped like a cockroach beneath a black steel bowl. *How can people exist like this?*

I felt a tugging on my pant leg and saw the Reaper's hand had become entangled in the fabric of Andre's pants. Revulsed, I shook it free of my leg, then kicked it back into the blaze choking the doorway into the Reaper's sanctuary.

All around me the shadows began to move. People wearing multiple layers of clothing despite the stifling heat, slowly crawled out of the surrounding tenements. They shuffled forward, mesmerized by the fire. The reds and golden yellows provided the only color in this world, and people stared at it as if it were some mysterious avatar coming to liberate them from their gray homes.

Where in hell am I? They murder people for their organs here. They have a roof between them and the sky. These people are mindless creatures. Why am I here?

As that quandary struck me, an even more horrible question followed in its wake and left me hollow inside. My chest tightened and it drove me to my knees in the stinking street.

Why do I care where this is or why I'm here when I don't have a clue as to who I am?

I awoke with a start from the nightmare spurred by the day's events, barely remembering any of it. I had wandered dark, oppressively hot streets. Behind me a roaring conflagration attracted firefighting equipment the way an open flame attracts moths. Faceless and weary, with the empty gun tucked in my waistband, I staggered through the streets and trash-strewn alleys. With each step I felt the paralysis reassert control over my body until, stiff-legged and lock-jawed, I stumbled face-first into a phalanx of garbage cans.

Now, sitting bolt upright, the sheet covering my sweat-slicked chest slipped down toward my lap. I found myself lying on an overstuffed couch with crocheted doilies on the arms and back to hide the spots where the cloth had been worn shiny and bare. Over in the corner I saw a television and wondered why there seemed to be so much cabinet and so little picture tube. The rabbit-ear antenna hid within a collection of a dozen black-and-white photographs arranged on top of the TV and a blocky, black rotary phone sat atop a dais of thick phone books on a table next to it.

I shivered. I felt as if I had awakened in the first reel of a 50-year-old *cine noir* classic film. That impression deepened as I looked over at a chest of drawers built into the wall and saw a huge radio with a yellow light softly glowing in the little window showing a portion of the tuning wheel. Faint strains of monotone Spanish music with tinny horns and castanets clicking like the hungry mandibles of a giant cockroach came from its speakers.

Over on the wall, between two windows with the shades drawn against the night, I saw a clock. What first struck me as unusual about it was that it was analog, not digital. That was not an overwhelming problem. I glanced at my wrist, where my watch should have been, and knew whatever I wore there normally had both a digital and analog readout, so I could decipher the meaning of the hands and their position. What struck me as absolutely odd was that, instead of numerals, there were little words at the positions of the clock.

Those words were what made me uneasy. It took me a second or two to see why. They were in Cyrillic and corresponded the number at that position on the clock, which made sense. What baffled me was why whoever owned the house would have a Soviet clock on the wall.

No one buys Russian if they can avoid it.

In any language, the clock reported it was 11:30.

A giggle caused me to spin and look behind me. A little girl with bright brown eyes looked at me, surprised and delighted that I saw her. She clapped her hands to her mouth, then went running back down the dim hallway to a back bedroom. From my vantage point I could see the foot of a bed onto which she leaped, then scampered up toward the headboard. I heard voices but could make no sense of what I heard.

The bedsprings creaked, then a man of slender build and average height filled the doorway. He wore a tank-top T-shirt and was in the process of zipping up a pair of canvas work pants that were covered with splotches of brightly colored paints. As he approached, I saw that the girl's coppery complexion and dark hair could well have come from him.

He gave me a smile that showed he still had most of his teeth. "*¿Cómo está usted?*"

"*Bien,*" I answered fluidly. "*Buenas noches.*"

"*Buenos días.*" The man scratched at the thin growth of beard on his chin. "You have slept for a day and a half. It is 11:30 in the morning, Señor..."

I concentrated, but still could not recall my name. "I'm sorry, I'm afraid I don't know who I am. I don't even know where this is."

"You are in Phoenix." He came around and pulled a chair away from the wall. My lab coat and pants were folded on it. The Krait rested on top, but the clip had been pulled from the gun. "I am Estefan Ramirez. The little girl is my daughter, Maria. My wife, Consuelo, is still in bed." He set the clothes and gun on a TV tray and sat down.

"Phoenix?"

What the hell am I doing in Phoenix?

Somewhere in the distant reaches of my mind I knew there was an answer to that question, but it was beyond my ability to recover it. "How did I come to be in your house?"

Estefan gave me a lopsided smirk. "*Los Reapers son muy malos.* Word got around fast that someone had chewed on them real good and many folks thought it was Coyote. I did not think so, but I went to check anyway, and I found you."

"Why did you help me?"

He shrugged. "Five years ago I came up here and someone helped me. 'You don't pay back; you pay forward,' he told me. I pay forward."

Off to my left, at the opposite end of the house from the bedroom, I heard a knock at the kitchen door. Estefan smiled, but after what I had been through, I did not feel optimistic. I reached for the Krait and he produced a loaded clip for the gun and tossed it to me. I knew, in the easy way he did that, he trusted me. As I slid the clip home and snapped the slide back and forth, I hoped that whoever I was, I was worthy of his trust.

When Estefan returned to the small sitting room, he brought with him the tallest man I had ever seen. Ducking his head to get through the doorway, the African-American man smiled, then straightened up to his full height. At least seven and a half feet tall, his loose-fitting shirt and faded jeans covered a body with enough muscle to rob him of the string-bean physique expected of someone so huge. Bearded and balding, he gave me a wide, white smile and offered me a hand that would have swallowed both my right hand and the Krait if I hadn't shifted the gun to my left.

"I'm Hal Garrett. From what Estefan has said, you're a mystery man."

The name Hal Garrett rang a bell somewhere, but I could not place it. "You have me pegged."

"Anyone who can anger the Reapers is a friend of mine." Garrett appropriated Estefan's chair and the master of the house retreated to the bedroom where he closed the door. "If possible, I'd like to help you with your problem."

As with Estefan, I sensed in Garrett's booming voice and easy manner a basic trust and willingness to aid me. I found this very gratifying, but likewise suspicious. Still, when alone in a foreign land, any alliance is a benefit. "What do you want to know?"

His shoulders heaved like mountains in an earthquake as he shrugged. "Anything you can remember that will give us a place to start."

"Us? Is that 'you and me,' or are there other elves who will become involved in this quest to find my memory?"

"For now it's you and me, but I have friends who might be able to help solve the puzzle." His manner hardened a bit, and this pleased me. I decided Hal Garrett was a man proud of his own abilities, but not so vain that he did not seek out assistance when he needed it. "Not many folks wake up in a Reaper packing house and live to tell about it. That alone makes you remarkable."

"Fair enough. I actually woke up before the Reaper chopshop. I found myself fully conscious but unable to move any voluntary muscles. Whatever I had been hit with, adrenaline seems to help throw it off, and I had plenty of that coursing through my veins when I heard they meant to sell me off in job lots."

Garrett nodded easily. "I can see that."

I closed my eyes and found the memories came easily, which frustrated me because they only went back, at best, 36 hours. "I was in an ambulance. One of the two men was named Jack or Jackson. I was not the first person they had sold to the Reapers. A recent deal including two bodies proved unsatisfactory. The name Harry came up as someone who might be a supervisor with the ambulance company. The ambulance crew said they found me in Slymingtown."

"That's 24th and Camelback—the Esplanade and Build-more district. That's north of here a bit."

"Jack said they found me in a squat-shack in a room that looked like a setup. They said Scorpion Security was on its way, so they took me and called the Reapers. Within an hour of pickup, they'd sold me off. The drivers sold me for 1.5 megs, 7% of exotics and 1% of any DNA applications from my body. Should I have been flattered?"

"You don't look like a wastoid or twink, which means your insides should be useful. You could probably earn that many dolmarks in a week if you wanted to turn yourself out as a slumming corporator's night-thrill, but that's a fair price for a worm-buffet." Garrett again gave me one of his disarming smiles. "You've given me some real basics, so we can probably track down the drivers. I'll make some calls."

"Good. Part of their deal was that they got to keep my effects, which means they might be a shortcut to solving this thing."

"I hope so." He stood and we shook hands again. "So, listen, Mr. Mystery, I've got to go to a local gang pow-wow. I won't be able to help you track these ambulance dexters down, but I'll send over another guy who will. His name is Rock Pell. Estefan knows him. He'll get you around so you can find them—and he can be convincing if they fan on your questions."

I smiled. "Thank you. One thing."

"Yes?"

"Are you this Coyote Estefan mentioned?"

Hal threw his head back and roared out leonine laughter. "No, no I'm not. I am, however, acquainted with him. We have many parallel goals and I am pleased to help him when I can."

"And will helping me help him?"

"I don't know. I have not heard from him concerning you, but I suspect your situation will intrigue him. Rock is another of Coyote's associates, so he may have other news. I will see you later, I hope."

"I look forward to it. Thanks."

Garrett let himself out and Estefan stayed in the back bedroom, which gave me time to think. Something Garrett had not mentioned, but something I was certain he did not miss, was Jack having said he felt my "death" had been a setup. It suggested I had one or more enemies and because of my current memory loss, I had no idea who they were. This did not bode well for my continued survival.

As Garrett had required of me in recalling details about the ambulance, I concentrated to see what I could postulate about myself from my experiences. I apparently was, at the very least, bilingual because I understood and spoke both Spanish and English—though some of the street slang Hal had hit me with I caught only from context. I had no idea what a "twink" or "wastoid" was, but I assumed they were derogatory in some form or another. Coupled with my shock at Estefan having a Soviet-made clock, radio and television in his home, I suspected I did not often frequent this socio-economic strata.

Whatever had been used on me to simulate death was not a natural thing. Most animal or plant toxins that paralyze the neuromuscular systems cause death by suffocation when the diaphragm stops working. I knew of none that had as its specific or recommended treatment a dose of adrenaline. Whatever had been used on me was very special stuff, specifically designed to paralyze voluntary muscles but not the autonomic nervous system.

That special toxin, and the setup remark, again pointed to my having some special enemies. By the same token, my familiarity with the Colt Krait and my ability to shoot well at extended pistol ranges suggested I could take care of myself. Even the kick that disabled Andre had been more reflex than thought, which told me I'd been trained in martial skills. Taken with my feelings about Estefan's possessions, I could see myself as having been a corporate security specialist or something equally bizarre in the corporate world.

There were still some loose ends that made no sense. In the Reaper area I had only heard Andre say a couple of things, but I had pegged his accent and had been able to mimic his voice convincingly enough to trick at least one guard. That might have been a natural gift, but surely one that had been honed by practice. My surprise and despair at seeing a roof over the city told me I was not at all familiar with Phoenix. If I *was* a corporate security specialist, I had been brought in from outside to deal with a problem.

That problem, quite likely, had cost me my memory and almost cost me my life. Without knowing who I was or what mission I had been given, my chances of survival were slightly higher than those of a blind man doing a freesprint across the Autobahn. And, like it or not, those long odds were what I was betting my life on.

Estefan reappeared, bringing with him his daughter and a very shy wife who looked barely, if at all, out of her teens. Without saying a word she went directly into the kitchen and started clattering pots and pans. Maria took up a position in the doorway leading to the kitchen so she could watch me and her mother at the same time. Estefan again took his chair.

I kept the gun hidden beneath the sheet that had been draped over me. "Garrett said he is sending another man, Rock Pell, to help me find the men who sold me to the Reapers."

"*Señor Pell es un hombre bueno.* If those men can be found, he will do it. My wife, she makes us some lunch." He pointed to the clothes on the tray. "Those do not fit you. Señor Pell will be bringing other clothes that will. *Con permiso,* I will get rid of them."

"Please, and if you can get money for them, keep it in exchange for the inconvenience I have been." I glanced back toward the hallway. "*¿Dónde está la ducha?*"

Estefan glanced down. "We don't have a shower, but that is the bathroom and you can clean yourself up there."

"*Muy bien, gracias.*" Wrapping the sheet around me like a toga, I padded across throw rugs to the bathroom and closed the door behind me. I hung the gun by its trigger-guard from a hook on the door, then draped the sheet over it. As I looked the bathroom over, a depressing wave of nostalgia hit me again.

All of the fixtures looked old and the pipes supplying water were not built into the wall. Over beside the low-water-use toilet I saw a hand crank sitting atop three feet of pipe. From it led another pipe to a shunt valve that let water flow to the toilet or up into the newest device in the whole room: a storage tank that had a heating element on one half of it.

Below the storage tank, so gravity would feed the water, was the rust-stained sink with dual faucets—both of which leaked. Off to the right, next to the door and the interior wall, a claw-footed tub dug its talons into tile mosaic floor. The floor, which once had some sort of logo as the central feature of the design, had been patched with so many different sizes and colors of tile that the original pattern had been all but lost.

I reached up and flicked the switch to start the water heater working, then I sat on the john and bided my time cranking water into the tank and the toilet. I would have found that task tedious in the extreme, but after having lost complete control of my muscles, having them respond for me in this menial task provided its own satisfaction. Besides, in the desert, pumping water was as close as it got to chopping wood, so it was the least I could do for Estefan and his family in return for my room and board.

Despite the decrepit conditions of the bathroom, Consuelo had attempted to make the best of it. The single window had been framed with frilly curtains. Little pictures of insufferably cute angels—likely the front half of old Christmas cards—had been framed and hung on the wall facing the toilet. A little wall rack held four magazines, but all of them were in Spanish and three dealt with soap operas, so I refrained from reading them. The spare roll of toilet paper hid beneath the skirts of a knitted doll.

I took a quick glance at myself in the medicine chest mirror hanging over the sink. While my face looked familiar and my black hair seemed a bit long, I did not have a quick flash of insight that provided a name. I rubbed a hand along my jaw and the black bristles lurking there, but I saw no razor on the sink and didn't want to go digging around in the Ramierez medicine chest.

Besides, I thought, *if someone is out to kill you, adopting a beard might make target recognition and acquisition a bit more difficult.*

Kneeling in the tub, I pressed the rubber stopper down into the drain and turned the water on. Like the sink, the water came out of two faucets, so I scooted back a bit to avoid getting scalded by the hot water. I really hadn't needed to bother—in Phoenix the water seemed to come in "warm" and "a bit warmer than that." The hardness of the water made it a bit difficult to get good lather out of the soap, but I managed to clean myself up fairly easily and dried myself with a threadbare towel that once belonged to a hotel.

Wearing the towel like a kilt, I returned from the bathroom and found Estefan talking to a clean-shaven Anglo roughly his size, with blue eyes and a buzz-cut crop of red hair. "Rock Pell, I assume?"

"Fully-on, tulman." He tossed me a thick packet just slightly larger than the Yellow Pages beneath the phone. "These are some clothes. They should fit you fine. If they don't, Coy-man said I can drop a couple of aught-aughts getting you tripped out in gutter-ware."

When Pell said "aught-aughts" I saw Estefan's face light up. I assumed Pell had meant $100 bills which, given the way the house looked, would be a vast fortune to the Ramierez household. At the same time I sensed from Estefan a fear that Rock would offer him money in return for the kindness shown me, which Estefan would refuse—despite desperately wanting it—because he did what he did for me to return a favor Coyote had done him long ago.

I also got from Pell the feeling that he *would* offer

Estefan money—not because he lacked feeling for Estefan and his family, but because it was easier than actually figuring out another way to help them. I looked at my host. "Estefan, did you go out and buy the bullets for my pistol after you'd brought me here?"

"*Sí.*"

"So you paid street prices for them." I shifted my gaze to Pell. "If you think Coyote can spare it, you might want to repay him for the ammo. I will take the gun with me and I would like the rest of the bullets. Fifty should cover it, right, Estefan?"

Estefan started to protest that he had not paid that much, but Pell never heard him. "$50, Estefan? Man, they sold you a grande line of dookey, you know?"

"I don't think it was a buyer's market, Rock. He was in a hurry, and I'm happy he did get the bullets, because I was out."

Pell pulled out a wad of bills and started to peel them off, one at a time. He stopped at three Reagans and four Lincolns, then folded them over and gave them to Estefan. Again my host tried to protest, but I shook my head. "Putting me up was your favor to Coyote. Buying bullets for me was your favor to me. I have yet to pay forward for you, but this will show my good faith."

"*Gracias, señor.*" Estefan pocketed the money and handed me a nearly full box of bullets.

"*De nada.* Be with you in a minute."

I retreated to the bathroom and pulled the plastic wrap off the package I'd been given. Pell had brought boxer briefs, which I found I did not like, but put on anyway, and a pair of white tube socks with blue stripes at the top. The jeans fit perfectly, though were brand-new and still starchy-stiff. I pulled on the black T-shirt and had to wonder what the true meaning of having "Rollerblades does slalom" emblazoned on my chest portended, but I was in no condition to complain.

Dressed, I returned to the front room to find everyone had retreated to the kitchen where Consuelo was serving beans and rice with tortillas. Pell had taken a place at the table and eyed the food hungrily. A quick glance at the pots on the stove told me the Ramierez family would go hungry if they tried to feed all of us, and I knew they would make the attempt.

"Rock, let's go."

He looked up at me as if I were mad. "It would be impolite to refuse…"

"I know, and I hope Estefan and Consuelo can find it in their hearts to forgive me." I made a show of tucking the Krait into my waistband at the small of my back. "It just occurs to me that if someone was out to kill me, having me here puts them in danger."

Pell hesitated as his hunger fought with what he thought was best. He finally nodded, then stood. "Besides, we need to get you some real shoes."

"Among other things."

"Right."

I turned to Estefan and shook his hand. "*Muchas gracias, mi amigo.*"

He smiled. "*De nada. Hasta luego.*"

"*Adiós.*"

Pell led the way from the house and I got my first good look at Phoenix in the daytime. Of course, given the solid ceiling 10 stories above us, separating day from night was difficult. Unlike when I made my escape, I did feel an incredible amount of heat radiating down from the roof. Sprayed on the underside of the panels I saw the letters APS.

"Rock, what is over us?"

"It's Frozen Shade, courtesy of Lorica Industries and Arizona Public Service—better known around here as Another Public Screwing."

"Fascinating. So what is it?"

"Solar voltaic cells, man. The city's covered with them to produce power."

I squinted my eyes and took a closer look at Frozen Shade. Massive steel girders, rendered black either by design or thick coats of soot, supported the panels on either side of their centerline. The panels themselves looked to be about a quarter of a mile on each side. In a couple of places I saw little shacks built onto the girders or bridging the gap between a girder and a nearby building. I also saw, nestled like a bubble of shadow, cylindrical housings attached to the panels near the top of each girder.

"The panels can be moved?"

"Yeah. When a dust storm comes through and coats everything with dirt, APS tips the panels up about 20 degrees and washes them off with a sprayer system built into the panel itself. That's the only time it ever rains down here in Eclipse. The only other time they crack the panels is if the air gets thick enough down here that it starts leaking up into the citadels."

We reached his car, and he punched the keycode into the lock on the driver's side. I found the vehicle an improbable white. Only the barest dusting of soot had settled on it. He opened the passenger door on the Ford-Revlon Elite sports coupe. I pulled the Krait before getting in, then shut the door and let the car adjust the safety restraints.

"A sadist designed these belts, eh, Mysterioso?"

I smiled politely as he started the electra-glide engine, and we set on our way. Thinking to stash the pistol, I opened the glove compartment. A huge drawer slid down, revealing a perfectly organized cosmetics tray. At the same time, my sunvisor flipped down, and the twin spotlights on either side of the mirror temporarily blinded me.

"Is this factory-standard, or did you special-order it?"

"Standard. Ever since Revlon bought in, they've really done the glove box up right. You know the joke, right? 'I had to get a new Elite because my lipstick was used up.'" Pell chuckled to himself until he noticed his mirth was not, in my case, infectious. "I never use that stuff, of course, 'cept maybe some of the black nail polish and some mascara when I have to go into Drac City."

"Drac City?"

"Bunch of skanky hippy witches and vamp-punks from the '90s decided to settle in Scottsdale and breed. They turned 'The West's most Western Town' into a little slice of Transylvania. They go for skin bleaching and canine implants. Got a weird Christian sect there, too, that claims Jesus rose from the dead because he was a vampire—you know, 'He shed His blood for you and now He wants it back' kinda thing."

"I see," I said when I didn't. Even though I had no real idea who I was, I knew I had nothing in common with the world Pell was describing. "Look, I need a couple of things: Some proper footwear, a shoulder holster, some spare clips for the Krait and a bullet-proof vest. Do you think Coyote will spring for that?"

"Are we looking for your identity, or are you going to war?"

"Could be both, dude. Glad you're along for the ride?"

Pell didn't answer, so I settled back in the plush seat to watch the city go by. Above us I could see the seams of the solar panels running down the middle of the street. This made sense if, as Rock had said, the panels were able to vary their pitch enough to let water and debris run off. Beneath the panels, buildings varied from old sprawling ranch-style homes to a variety of tall and short apartment complexes. Strip malls and convenience stores dotted the corners of intersections, and occasionally whole huge blocks were taken up with open malls.

In this land of always night, colors appeared muted, if

at all. Some bright neon signs flashed on and off to lure customers into this bar or that video rental center, but the thickness of the air seemed to leech the life from the lights. Racing through the city in Pell's Elite, I felt like a cockroach scuttling across a kitchen floor in fear that someone would turn the lights on and squash me.

"How did the city ever get the populace to agree to putting this thing up?"

Pell shrugged stiffly, and I immediately assumed anything he said would be half-fabrication. "Phoenix City Council lost some public referendums in the late '80s. They decided that was not the way anything could get done. Working with the Feds, they had the Environmental Protection Agency sue the city because, with the ozone layer going wonky, there was an increased incidence of skin cancer. Then they also inspired some trouble out at the Palo Verde Nuclear Plant. Pinned some sabotage on an eco-terrorist group they called Blue Thunder—fried a couple of people because of it.

"All of a sudden, every tree-hugger and anti-nuke freak pushed for an alternate power source. The city threatened to annex large parts of the desert to the southeast of here to blanket with solar panels, but the same environmentalists protested. In a brilliant compromise, the Sierra Club and other groups that live *outside* the city agreed to let the city build the solar collection panels *above* the city. We used to be known as the Valley of the Sun, which is still true up *there*, but down here we're the Valley of Midnight."

"Incredible." As we continued on, I noted, in places, a parallel road system approximately 40 feet above us. "What's with the dual roadway?"

"In Phoenix, you can't dig down because the ground is baked hard. The upper roads connect some of the citadels with each other, though only contract labor uses them. Notice how they don't have any exits, just run on straight lines?"

"Yes."

"That's so regular Mikes like us can't get on them. You enter and exit only at corpvils like Lorica or Honeywell & Koch. Or City Center—as if we'll ever see the inside of *that* place."

I decided I did not like Rock's attempt at including me in as "one of the boys," and I heard some bitterness in his voice when he mentioned City Center. I did not know who or what I was, but I knew I was not the same as him. Even so, I could see how Coyote could find him useful. The man had an open face, but used it well to conceal a scheming mind. Pell had correctly seen that he had not made a good impression on me, so he sought to change it. While he failed, his chameleonlike ability would make him very useful as a go-between with different groups.

Rock pulled into a parking lot and honked the horn. A garage door in the side of a warehouse opened up, but only barely enough to let the Elite squeak through. Rock hit a button on the dash that retracted his antenna, then pulled forward. "Watch yourself in here. These neo-Nazi freakos are truly bad, but they know their stuff. Be careful; these bleach-brains have no sense of humor." He frowned. "Knew I should have driven the Benz."

Rock let the Elite roll forward into the lightless warehouse, and that started my palms itching. Behind us I heard the door roll shut, then suddenly two dozen arclights flooded the place with light. Instant white-out for me, but as I squinted and shaded my eyes, I saw Pell had pulled on a pair of mirrored sunglasses.

Okay, Rock, if these are the games we will play...

Rock opened his door and got out. I did the same, moving slowly and easily to make it obvious to the silhouettes behind the lights that I was unarmed and very nearly blind. Throwing his arms wide, Rock greeted a short man with long, blond hair, exchanging back-slapping hugs. "Heinrich, you son of an Alsatian bitch, you look great!"

Heinrich, who looked about as healthy as an albino mushroom farmer, grinned broadly. "Stein, you have not changed. What can I do you for today?" He snapped his fingers, and three-quarters of the lights died.

Rock nodded toward me. "He needs some boots, a vest, maybe a jacket."

Heinrich came around the front of the Elite and looked up into my face. "Gut, they are green."

"Pardon?" I knew the German expression I wanted to use was "*Verzeihung*," but I felt disinclined to use it for two reasons, the primary being that his German and his accent had undoubtedly been learned by watching too many Nazi wet-dream war movies.

"I said your eyes are green, and this is good. That means there is no blood from the mud people in you."

I smiled. "Or it means my contact lenses are green." I thoroughly detest race-hatred, and I was starting to get angry that Rock had brought me here.

Heinrich leaned close to get another look at my eyes, but Rock slapped him on the back and laughed. "He was joking, Heinrich."

"We in the Warriors of the Aryan World Alliance do not take racial purity lightly. I have heard he spent the night with a beaner."

"Just sleeping, Heinrich, not swapping blood." Rock gave me a frown, then draped his arm over Heinrich's bare shoulders and steered him deeper into the warehouse. "This is business, remember?"

"Heinrich, would it make a difference if I were 'tainted?'"

The little man turned and nodded slowly. "It would cost Herr Stein more, and get you less. Your attitude may accomplish that yet."

"Easy, Heinrich, you owe our mystery man here. He dusted a Reaper lab. Who knows what they were harvesting and selling for transplant."

"*Ja*, good point." Heinrich turned back and led Rock into the maze of wide shelving units running from floor to ceiling.

Their departure gave me a chance to look around. Aside from the obligatory portraits of Adolf Hitler, Evan Mecham and Tom Metzger, the place actually looked fairly normal. This section of the two-story building had no second floor, but a catwalk ran around the walls at roughly 12 feet. Armed guards roamed along the catwalk, carrying submachineguns and practicing truly disdainful sneers.

All of the Warriors I saw wore the same sort of uniform Heinrich had sported. Gray jodhpurs were tucked at the knee into gleaming cavalry boots. Black suspenders held the pants up, and only three of them wore anything more on their upper torso. Those three—one man and two of the five women I saw—sported gray T-shirts with a Nazi eagle emblazoned across the chest like a super-hero insignia.

The Warriors appeared to me to be uniformly lean. They wore their hair very short, with the men favoring the high and tight cut of special military forces or corporate security teams. The women tended toward longer hair or more stylish cuts, but none of them let their hair get beyond shoulder length. And, yes, of course, everyone had their hair bleached white blond.

The odd thing about all of them—and it took me a moment to catch it—was that they had undergone some very subtle cosmetic surgery. On the men, the haircut almost hid it, but I could see how implants had been inserted beneath their scalp to give their skull more height. It literally made their foreheads look larger, which would have made them look smarter if not for the piggish ignorance in their eyes.

The guns they carried were impressive. I don't know

how I did it, but I identified them as Honeywell & Koch MP-7s. Like my Krait, those guns took 10mm ammo in their 30-round banana magazines. Heinrich had worn a sidearm instead of one of the MP-7s. I did not get a good look at it, but I guessed it was an antique Walther he kept more as a memento than because of its firepower.

Rock and Heinrich returned quickly with the items I needed. The Bianchi shoulder holster fit perfectly and Heinrich had even strapped two loaded Krait clips into place on it. The Kevlar vest they showed me looked sufficient to stop anything this side of a big-game round. I grunted and tossed it on my seat.

They brought me two pairs of boots, which was probably Rock's idea. The first was a pair of standard punk-issue Doc Martin's. I rejected them *a priori* and opted for the more appealing Schwarzkopf boots. They fit snugly, and I laced them up. As I did so, Rock wandered off and left me there with Heinrich.

"You know, my friend, you should not think so harshly of us." He opened his arms and took his brethren in with one generous gesture. "We are here protecting what our people have earned in this world. You are not a stupid man. Being in that den, even for one night, would have told you what kind of people they are. They dilute us and drag all mankind down to the level of beasts."

I finished knotting off my second boot, then stood slowly and towered over Heinrich. "By no stretch of imagination am I your friend. What I saw in that home was a loving family doing its best to eke out an existence by any means possible. They are less a threat to you than, say, I am."

I let my words hang in the air between us. Heinrich concentrated hard enough to make me combust by an act of his will, but I just got chills looking at him. A couple of his roving guards stopped to watch us, and the tension built as if we were in a crash-dive on a sub. I watched his eyes and read his desire to draw his gun and shoot me, but he knew I'd make him eat it.

Rock arrived and folded his arms across his chest. "I go to make a phone call, and you two are at it again. Whatever am I going to do with you?"

Heinrich stepped back and Rock tossed me a black windbreaker. "Good day, Stein. You need not bring this man back here again."

"Chill, Heinrich, he's new in town. He has to learn the lay of the land." Rock reached into his pocket. "What do I owe you?"

The Nazi rubbed the thumb of his left hand across his right palm in irritation. "$150, and the clips with bullets are my gift to you, mystery man." He accepted a handful of bills from Rock. "I hope you become smart enough that you do not need all of them."

"Don't worry, Hank," I said as I winked at him. "I'll save the last clip for you."

Once Rock had the Elite back on the road, he flicked the air conditioning on high, looked and me and shook his head. "Now I know why Hal turned you over to me. He saw you as trouble from miles off."

I pulled off the shoulder holster and followed it with the T-shirt. "I find it curious that the same Coyote who could inspire loyalty in Estefan or Garrett could condone your trading with racists."

"Do you?" Pell's face took on a stern expression. "If you're so sharp, tell me, what did you learn while you were in there?"

This is a game of one-upsmanship you will lose, Pell. "Well, we can start with the dozen neo-Nazis I saw armed with some of the latest in military hardware. They were not wearing body armor, so they feel very secure in their hideout there. I further note that Heinrich would not have had the time to load the two clips in the shoulder holster, which means he pulled them from a bin somewhere. The Warriors of the Aryan World Alliance are very well financed and ready for a war. How's that?"

Pell blinked twice, then doubtlessly put my observations down to luck. "Close enough for my purposes. If you saw that much, you know I'm very Protean. Coyote uses me to keep different groups happy. You saw what you saw, but I got into their armory and can write up a report on everything they have. If there's going to be a war between them and the Blood Crips, Coyote will be able to handicap it perfectly."

Somehow I doubted "handicapping" gang wars was Coyote's purpose in Phoenix, but I said nothing as I pulled the Kevlar vest on and fastened it snugly over my chest.

"Okay, you are a scout, and trafficking with the Warriors keeps them happy. Just because you're comfortable with them, don't expect me to become Heinrich's best buddy."

"Hey, splash him for all I care. I've known Enrico Vitale since childhood, and I don't think he looks good as a blonde." Rock turned left onto 40th Street and headed north. "Look, that phone call I made was to another of Coyote's people. She's a whiz with computers and pegged your people as Carl Jackson and Billy Harris. They work for the Wheel of Life ambulance company. Their unit handled a call to Slymingtown two nights ago."

I smiled grimly as I pulled my T-shirt back on. "How do we find them?"

Pell let a triumphant grin twist the corners of his mouth up. "Jytte pulled Jackson's financial files and saw he spends a lot of time at the Du Drop Inn. He runs an open tab on his Digital Express card and happens to have opened one a half hour ago. A mile past Thomas and we're there."

I nodded. "Excellent."

"Look, when we get there, let me handle things. The Du is not a bad place."

"No, they obviously cater to only the finest body snatchers."

"Okay, okay, I can sense this hostility, and I understand it, but work with me. It's mostly a beer and billiards place, see? The folks there don't react well to violence."

I narrowed my eyes and nodded. "It's your game, but I want results."

"Good." Pell brought the Elite to a stop in front of what had started life as a squat triplex about four decades earlier. At one time I decided it must have gone for a western motif because of the broken wagon wheel on the exterior wall and the aged boardwalk leading to the door. If not for the Harleys chained to the hitching rail, I could have been on the set of a billion western mesmervids.

As we got out of the car, the heat hit me like a punch. I tucked my T-shirt and the tails of the vest into my jeans, then pulled on the shoulder holster. Rock saw me do that and grimaced, but I ignored him. I retrieved the Krait from the glove box, checked to see that the safety was still on, then slid it into the Bianchi holster. Despite the heat, I shrugged the windbreaker on and let it hide the pistol.

"You won't need that."

"Then I won't use it."

Walking in behind Pell, I saw the bar's interior had not substantially changed from its early days, and that included an exchange of atmosphere. The smoke in the air softened everything, but coiled neon lights doing a python around rough-hewn pillars and lots of glittering silver streamers did give the bar back a bit of an edge. Tiffany lamps advertising beers no one had heard of in a quarter century provided the light for three pool tables over in the far corner. I drifted toward them, remaining in the shadows as much as possible, while Rock crossed to the long bar and spoke to the bartender.

Most of the clientele hovered somewhere between blue-collar workers and white trash looking to cadge drinks. The waitresses, all two of them, had once been pretty women, but working here had clearly hammered any lifejoy out of them. The petite one wheeled and glared at a man who patted her rump, while the blond Rubens woman made a great show of bending over and flashing her cleavage to encourage tips. The drink of choice looked to be a cut-rate Mexican beer, but shooters of whisky or tequila also made their way down lots of throats.

The bartender gave Rock a big shrug about the same time I heard Gruff-voice groan over the click of balls and say, "Nobody coulda made that combination."

A guy about an inch or two shorter than me smiled and

answered him. "Wrongo, Billy, I just did."

Something about hearing those voices again let the terror of my night in the body bag just pour through me. All of my muscles tightened at once, as if to prove to me that the toxin could not longer control me. I watched the two of them for a moment, assessing their every move and applying it to what I thought was their threat level. Aside from the pool cues in their hands, I saw nothing to indicate they would give me trouble, which meant I was free to make trouble for them.

Deep down inside I hungered to make them as scared as I had been.

As Jack bent over to line up another shot, I stepped up behind him and slapped the butt end of his cue-stick with the palm of my left hand. He miss-hit a table scratch and spun around angrily. He started to shout something, then he saw who I was. His face went ashen. "Jesus Christ."

"You got that half right." I grabbed double handfuls of his jeans jacket and hoisted him up onto the table. I perched him on the corner of the table, with his butt right over the hole. "He returned from the dead, too, but he was more forgiving than I am."

Gruff-voice started to come around the table, but I stared him back. "Finding out you're being sold for party favors can really piss a guy off, Jack. Lucky for you, I can take a joke." I smiled and Jack aped me while nervous sweat beaded up on his forehead.

"What do you want?"

I reached over and picked up the 8-ball. "I want you to think about what I would mean if I called '8-ball in the corner pocket.'" I pressed the cool ball against his lips. "You can keep the money you got off the Reapers because I don't want it, and they won't be asking for a refund." I let that sink in for a minute, then continued. "You kept all my stuff, my 'effects.' I want my things back."

Jack didn't make much sense trying to speak around the 8-ball, so I pulled it away, yet held it up by his left eye so he'd remember I still had it. "I don't have your cards and stuff—I sold that stuff off quick."

I frowned, masking my true feelings. While the identification and credit cards would have been an easy way to find out who I was, having them in the hands of others could be a blessing. With someone out to kill me, and this Jytte having shown how easy they were to use in tracing someone, having a whole host of folks using different cards all over the place was good.

"And my cash?"

"You didn't have much. Only $200, half in dolmarks and the rest in Lorica scrip."

Dolmarks were coin of the realm, more or less. Officially the currency in North America was still the dollar, but their worth generally fluctuated based on the exchange rate with the Deutschmark, so folks knew they played the float with any cash they held. Corporate scrip, on the other hand, was based on the corporation's net worth and tended to be more stable. Furthermore, corpscrip could be used at company stores, which meant it was the hardest currency most folks could get their hands on.

Generally, though, only corp employees or black marketeers had that sort of scratch. *Did I work for Lorica?* "I'll take the cash. What else have you got?"

"Nothin', nothin', honest."

"Nothin' honest kinda sums up our relationship, doesn't it, Jack?" I looked over at Pell. "Rock, buy this lying remo a beer because he's going to want to wash this 8-ball down right quick."

Pell was a quick enough study that he nodded and ordered one in a loud voice.

"Don't hold out on me, Jack, because I'm in the mood to run the table, and then I'd have to rack you up. I don't think you'd like that." I looked up as Gruff-voice again moved toward me. "Trust me, Ace, he's not *that* good of a friend."

"Jack, the wallet. You kept his wallet."

Jack looked like a video preacher who'd gotten a suspended sentence. "Yeah, I have your wallet. It was new. I kept it." His hand dived inside his jacket, but I slapped it away. He looked at me with hurt in his eyes, then he swallowed hard as he figured out what I had assumed he was going for.

I let the 8-ball bonk-bounce across the table as I opened his jacket. Sitting in an interior pocket I found a wallet that felt more familiar than it looked. I opened it and started dropping card after card of his from it to the floor. In the cash compartment I removed everything except the $200 he said I'd had and tossed it into the air. I poked around in a couple of other pockets of the thing, grunted, and slipped it into my back pocket.

"Thanks for the game, Jack." I gave him the coldest smile I could imagine. "I hope we don't play again because next time it will be sudden death." Shaking his hand, I also pulled my watch off his wrist, though I doubt he noticed the loss for at least a week.

I walked out of the Du without looking back, though I found myself preternaturally aware of everything happening behind me. It is difficult to explain, but I felt as if I could see the fear and awe and suspicion of everyone in the room. I know I got some of it from the stunned looks on certain patrons' faces, and other clues from whispered oaths, but there was something more there. I felt like a shark isolating the signals from a school of badly scared fish, and what's worse, I found myself viewing most of them like prey.

Rock remained in the Du for a second or two longer than I did, no doubt basking in the respect he would get by being associated with me. I had, after all, spoken to him and had called him by name. Given the way he worked, the Du would provide him with both customers and information. For the foreseeable future, this was one habitat in which that chameleon would not have to change colors to blend in.

I, on the other hand, had unconsciously downshifted into a personality that overpowered the habitat. Walking in, I had been more than content to have Pell handle the whole encounter. Had the bartender pointed Jackson out to him, Pell would have bought the man a beer, spun a tail about wanting paper on me, and would have dropped enough of Coyote's dolmarks to buy what I had extorted. I couldn't tell if I'd acted to embarrass Pell for his failure in getting the bartender to help, or if I just wanted to return to Jack a bunch of the fear I'd known when he sold me. I suspected it was more of the latter than the former, but seeing the shocked look on Pell's face had felt good.

Rock left the Du but said nothing until we were sealed in the Elite's air-conditioned cocoon. "He'd have given you his wife *and* his mistress if you'd asked."

"Probably." I pulled the wallet from my hip pocket and opened it again. I slipped my fingers in behind the piece of plastic securing the picture and card holder in the middle of the wallet. I felt a stiff piece of cardboard and pulled it out. The purple bit of cardboard had a number printed on it and a serrated edge that told me it had been torn from a larger piece of cardboard. I flipped it over. "Do you know where Ernesto's Upstreet is?"

Pell cast a sidelong glance at the valet check I held. "You were at Ernesto's?"

"Is that a problem?"

"No, just I didn't take you for a snorter. You musta been there for the games in the back." He gave me a half grin. "Of course, you could have been there for dinner, I suppose."

"Do you *suppose* you know where it is?"

"Yeah, 36th and Indian School, on the second level."
He pursed his lips together. "I'll drive over to a Build-
more access point. That should be good enough to get
us in, though they might only let you go up."

"Let's do it, then."

"Okay. Find anything else useful?"

I nodded. In the cash section of the wallet, stuck to the
inner lip, was a small piece of flexible plastic that had
been sewn into it by the manufacturer. It was designed for
holding spare car keys or house keys, but held neither in
this case. Flipping it up, I slid out a small, flat key with
blocky grooves gnawed out of the lower edge. "Safety
deposit box key. Probably for a hotel, but maybe a bank.
It has a serial number."

"That's interesting." He grinned. "Hidden treasure."

"Maybe." I returned his smile and let Rock daydream
about untold wealth. I sat back and just hoped that the
treasure was the solution to the question, "Who am I?"

The Build-more checkpoint reminded me more of a secret military facility than it did any sort of urban subdevelopment. Walls ran from the ground right up through Frozen Shade above us. Sections of it reminded me of pictures I'd once seen of the old Berlin wall, with building fronts as part of the wall with their doors and windows bricked over. Graffiti decorated the walls in a few places and tattered handbills in others, but the Build-more corporate logo predominated.

We tried to enter it at 32nd Street and Camelback but the Build-more security guards refused to give Rock access to the drive-up ramp despite his having the valet ticket and a nice car. "Here, this is the number for my phone," he said handing me a preprinted card. "You'll have to go up there yourself and use the Ultra-shuttle to take you to Ernesto's. When you get your car, head back here and drive down. If you have trouble, call me."

"Got it." I popped out of the car and shoved my wallet into my back pocket again. I flashed the valet slip to one of the guards who had refused us earlier. He took it from me and, resting his Armalite Stormcloud on his right shoulder, carefully scrutinized it. He turned from me and held it under an ultraviolet light. That caused a green barcode to glow on the face of the ticket and a red laser-beam flickered across it to read it. Seconds later some data came up on a small video display.

"Checks." He took a pass from his desk and pushed it down into his timestamp machine. "This will get you on the second level, sir. The Ultra-shuttle will be along in 15 minutes or so."

I smiled and accepted both the valet slip and the travel

pass from him. "Thank you."

"Sir, one thing." The guard leaned in close to me. "I know you execs find playing in the shadows down here exciting, but I do not recommend it. Every so often, one of you doesn't make it back, if you know what I mean."

Yeah, I have a vague idea. "Thanks for the warning, Bud. I'll remember it."

He pointed me toward an elevator marked "Transient," and I stepped into it. In accordance with the verbal instructions the elevator gave me, I inserted the travel pass into the slot, and it immediately climbed to the next level up. The door opened and directed me to the transit station on my right.

Being 40 feet up gave me a different perspective on the city. From here I could see the labyrinth of upper level roads very clearly. They appeared positively deserted compared to their counterparts below. They also looked clean and well maintained. They avoided repetition of the grid pattern used on the streets below, but from what Rock had said, I gathered they only went to places of importance, so they did not have to go everywhere.

Looking out over the city, on a level just about 15 feet above most of the streetlights, I could see a number of tallish buildings, but they all stopped before they hit Frozen Shade. They looked like little seedlings languishing in the shadows of the massive corporate citadels. Looking south I could make out, in the distance, the Lorica complex and more to the west, the solid wall that formed the City Center.

Consulting a sign I saw, the circuit that would take me to Ernesto's had an estimated transit time of 15 minutes. I stepped over to an autovend newsstand and shoved a Lincoln into the slot. I mulled over the selection, noting for the first time that it was the middle of June, and finally chose a *Phoenix Metro* magazine. *If I'm stuck here, I might as well know something about the place.*

I collected the magazine and the two copper Columbus dollar coins the autovend offered in change. Thumbing through the magazine I recognized a face from a picture. In a column called "Where Are They Now?" I saw Hal Garrett surrounded by smiling kids. I read:

> When Hal Garrett walked away from a 5.5 million dollar one-year deal, most folks figured he'd end up in the State Hospital at 24th and Van Buren. "It was quite a large amount of money to pass up, but I felt I was past my prime." Garrett, who had averaged 28 points per game with the Phoenix Suns the previous season, appeared to be set to play well into his 40s, so his refusal to play another year stunned most bystanders.
>
> Garrett, today the CEO of the charitable Sunburst Foundation, says he misses basketball, but not the big leagues. "When I have a chance I go down to the park and play with some of our kids. Sports can be a way out from living in the Eclipse, but it's for the lucky few. Our kids have to learn to stop killing each other, then to get a job, if they want to make life better for themselves than it was for their parents."

I gathered from context that the Sunburst Foundation helped get kids the materials or training necessary to complete their educations. The article noted that living at 36th Street and Palm Lane was not that far from his former home in City Center, but that Garrett said he felt far more at home now than he did during his playing days. Reading that brought a smile to my lips for reasons I could not fathom, but I let the smile remain anyway.

The blue and yellow Ultra-shuttle arrived with brakes

squealing. The doors opened, and I stepped aboard. I ran my pass through the reader beside the driver, and my destination appeared on a little screen on her right. She snapped the doors shut and started the vehicle forward before I found I seat, but I defied inertia and sat without mishap.

The article about Garrett put some things into perspective about this Coyote and his organization. I knew from Estefan that Coyote had 'helped him when he showed up in the city. It seems equally likely that he noticed Garrett's efforts with Sunburst and created a liaison so they could share resources and avoid duplication of effort. Rock Pell, on the other hand, was useful as a gadfly who could flit between various groups and gather information. That, in turn, could be used by Coyote and Garrett to head off trouble.

My piecing together those bits of the puzzle helped ease my mind. Lurking in the back of my brain had been the nagging question "Why are they helping me?" The answer, it seemed to me, was that they were helping me because I was in trouble. I also suspected that they would want me to help them in the future. That harkened back to Estefan's "paying forward" remark. Because they both helped other unfortunates, I knew I had not been singled out for special treatment, which dulled my feelings of paranoia.

In another squealed brake symphony, the Ultra-shuttle let me off in front of Ernesto's Upstreet. It looked like a nice restaurant and, if the line of very expensive automobiles parked along the side was any indication, one patronized by some of the city's more successful mid-level management. The building's facade had been done in faux marble, with smooth Doric columns and a down-scaled copy of Michelangelo's *David*, modestly augmented with a figleaf.

The doorwoman waited with her white-gloved hand

on the door's handle, but I shook my head and walked over to the valet's station. I handed the ticket to the pimple-faced kid sitting inside the tiny shack. "It's been here for the past two days. I was detained."

The kid shrugged his shoulders and set down a comic book. He flashed the ticket through a reader similar to the one the Build-more guard had used. "Not a problem, it's still here. Gonna have to charge you for the storage, though. $27.50."

I pulled three Reagans from my wallet, and he dutifully passed the coded end of them through the barcode reader. "Keep the change," I added.

The kid looked unimpressed, but ran off to get my car anyway. I glanced at the screen but I could not decipher any of the coding except where it totaled my charges. I suspected somewhere in that jumble of numbers and letters I could have learned a great deal about my life, but I was blind to it.

I was not blind, however, to the car the kid drove up. Fire-engine red, the General Dynamic Motors Lancer looked less like a car than it did a shark cruising for pedestrians. Sure, it was of domestic make, and probably had been put together in GDM's west Phoenix plant, but could smoke the international competition with ease. I dimly recalled seeing a street sprint evaluation of the Lancer up against the Mitsubishi-Ferrari Kamikaze that might as well have been the Battle of Midway II.

The smile on the valet's face came not from the Reagan I offered him, but from driving the car on the short run from the parking lot. "I took good care of it."

"And I appreciate it, believe me." I slid in behind the wheel, and he closed the door behind me. I fastened the lap belt, but before I did up the double shoulder straps, I popped open the glove compartment. It was not as large as the one in Rock's Elite, nor did it have cosmetics, but it did contain something that was more valuable to me than gold.

I pulled the rental receipt and unfolded it. *Paydirt!* I smiled as I read the car had been rented to Mr. Tycho Caine. I didn't recognize the name, but I rolled it around in my mouth a couple of times and it worked okay. *Cool name, cool car. Find out who wants you dead, and you could be in good shape.* I refolded the paper and slipped it into my windbreaker's pocket.

Locking in the shoulder restraints, I slipped the car into gear and eased it out onto the road. The Lancer rode as easy as water gliding across ice. On the upper shot of 32nd Street there was no traffic in front of me, and I felt sorely tempted to wind the car out. Glancing in the rearview mirror for Scorpion Security vehicles—which I realized I could not have identified anyway—I noticed a Chrysler LeBoeuf pull in behind me and come up fast.

Somewhere in my head a part of me started to calculate the rough odds of someone coming after me so immediately. In a metropolis that boasted over 3 million people, the odds started long, but became short fast. The last place I was known to have been was at Ernesto's. Clearly I left there with someone else, or not under my own power. I was moved down to Slymingtown and left for dead. If whoever had wanted me dead had looked for an obit on a John Doe, he would not have seen it. If he then heard about the problem with the Reapers, he might set up a stake-out on my car to see if I claimed it.

I felt my heartbeat quicken as I decided I was being followed by people who knew something about what had happened to me. The chase made my blood race and my nostrils flare. I felt the same energetic jolt I had when I confronted Jackson. The urge to stop my car, pull my Krait and start shooting nearly overwhelmed me.

At the same time as bloodlust rose up in me, I shunted those feelings aside. As I made a quick right turn onto Camelback heading east, I knew there was only one way to determine if these folks were following me or not. At 36th I took another right and the LeBoeuf stayed right on my tail. Furthermore the driver decided he'd been spotted, so he hit the accelerator and pulled into the left lane. A hand with a gun appeared through the driver's side window.

I tapped the gas and the Lancer's engine roared loudly. The car lunged forward, and the LeBoeuf surged ahead to catch up. As I hit the brakes and dropped the car out of gear, the Chrysler rocketed past me. The passenger pulled the trigger on his pistol as fast as he could, but tracking my car while his sailed on was well nigh impossible.

I yanked up on the hand-brake, immediately kicking the Lancer into a bootlegger's turn. As the LeBoeuf again appeared in my rearview mirror, I hit the foot brake, jammed the car into first and popped the clutch. The Lancer bucked a bit, forcing me back into the driver's seat, but it shot off like an arrow. At my first intersection, I cut right and left the Chrysler behind.

As I entered this narrow side street in the limited network of roads above the city of Phoenix, I realized that one important factor in evading pursuit is having a better knowledge of the battleground than your enemy does. I clearly did not have this, or I would not have entered a street marked "Dead End." A hundred yards later, as I brought the Lancer to full stop just before the roadway came to a full stop, I wondered if that sign might not have been prophetic.

The Chrysler filled the street at the far end, offering me no chance to get around it. Its headlights flashed in tandem off the guard rails lining the elevated roadway. It came forward slowly as if a mechanical beast stalking prey.

I popped my restraining belts and stepped out of the Lancer. Moving a couple of paces toward the LeBoeuf,

I pulled my Krait and flicked the safety off. Dropping to one knee, I held the gun in both hands and sighted carefully.

Something about being under fire causes most folks to panic. The LeBoeuf's passenger, to forestall that happening, leaned out of his window and aimed back at me. His first two shots wounded the tarmac to my left. I returned his fire, and when he flopped limply in the window with a lot of blood leaking over the rest of the car, the driver decided I was his.

In his position I could see his thinking. As I discovered when I shifted over to target him, the LeBoeuf had been specially fitted with bulletproof glass and puncture-resistant tires. The body had been armored too, so all I managed to do was strike sparks from the hood or spatter lead on the windshield.

The driver hit the gas. I swapped out my spent clip for a new one and triggered two shots as I stood. The car, its engine howling demonically, charged straight at me. The driver corrected as I took one step to my right, lining me up with his hood ornament. At the last second he even began to ease off on the gas as he did not want to sail on into my car and off the upstreet.

I leaped back to the left, barely avoiding the dead passenger's flailing arms. The driver started to apply the brakes, but I triggered off three shots that stabbed through the open passenger window. I don't know where they hit, but they did, and he lost control of his vehicle. As I crammed myself up against the guard rail, his LeBoeuf slammed my driver-side door shut, then started my car tumbling.

The Lancer rolled perfectly, with fiberglass side panels shattering and flying off into the air. The windscreen and rear window both blew out, sending sparklies of glass hail down into the streetlights' halo below. With a hideous cracking sound, the Lancer flattened the wooden barricade marking the end of the road and plummeted out of sight.

The Chrysler, its frame sparking as it scraped over the edge, careened after my Lancer.

I threw myself to the ground as the fireball from their final collision lit up the street. Debris pelted me and a secondary explosion shook the roadway. When I looked up, little fires burned like votive candles to mark the cars' passing at the end of the roadway. Flames from below licked up as if yet hungry for more and, in the distance, I heard the keening wail of sirens.

I tucked the gun away and jogged along the roadway until I came to one of the concrete stanchions holding the roadway up. The concrete relief decorations on it made climbing down simple enough, and the added light from where two cars had crushed a chiropractic office and set it on fire provided all the light I needed to see where I was going.

I found a 7-Eleven and dropped a copper Columbus coin in the slot. Fishing Rock's card from my pocket, I dialed him up. "Rock, this is your mystery man. My car was a Lancer."

"Was? What happened?"

"Nothing much. Pick me up, and I'll tell you about it."

"How will I find you. Where are you?"

"I'm not sure," I laughed, "but I've set a signal fire. You can't miss it."

I hung up the phone and found my hands were shaking. I knew it had to be the physical aftereffects of the adrenaline rush I'd felt up on the overstreet. As I looked at the fire burning a block distant I also knew I felt afraid. A fraction of a second slower and I would have been jammed between both of those cars. I would have been roasting in that fire and that realization sent a shiver up my spine.

I sincerely hoped my shots killed both men before their

car went over.

Scorpion Security cordoned off the area fairly quickly and their firefighting arm came in and had the blaze smothered in no time at all. When Rock rolled up, fire marshals had started picking through the steaming, foam-covered wreckage. They repeatedly looked at the half-melted cars, then back up at the upstreet and at the wreckage again.

"Roger," Rock said into his car phone as I sat down and pulled the door shut. He glanced at the flaming wreckage and winced. "If I ever offered to let you drive one of my cars, forget it."

A weak smile lightninged across my face. "My name is Tycho Caine. The Lancer was a rental."

"Glad you know your name." Rock pulled a wide U-turn in the road and headed us away from the fire. "I talked to Hal. He heard from Coyote. You're in for a big palaver with a bunch of us. Coyote has decided your problem is our problem."

Rock drove me to what looked like an abandoned executive garden office building. A chainlink fence topped with concertina wire surrounded the place and had signs on it that threatened prosecution of trespassers. The windows facing the street had been boarded up and a couple of walls had been decorated with graffiti. When Rock drove up, he punched a code number into a keypad beside the gate and it rolled back automatically. Once we were in, it shut again.

Rock took us around back and parked the car in some covered parking. Using another security code, he let us in through the back door. Once he made sure the door had closed, he pulled a nasty little Nambu automatic from an ankle holster and set it on the table in the anteroom. He glanced at my holster and I reluctantly did the same with my Krait.

I followed him into another, larger and more well-lit conference room with a big table in the middle of it. "Everyone," Rock announced to the five other people in the room, "this is Tycho Caine, the man with many enemies and no memory. Hal Garrett you already know."

I nodded and shook Hal's hand again. "I hope your meeting went well."

"As well as can be expected."

Rock pointed to a well-dressed Hispanic man. "This is Alejandro Higuera."

Higuera offered me his hand, and I shook it firmly. He looked similar enough in build and features to me to have been Estefan's cousin, but there was a world of difference between them in culturalization. Alejandro was clean-shaven except for a thick moustache. His hair had been professionally styled, and his suit cost easily three times what Estefan made in a good month. A gold Rolex watch glinted on his left wrist as he adjusted the knot of his tie, and a diamond-encrusted ring flashed on his little finger.

"Charmed."

"As am I, Señor Higuera."

Rock pushed on and pointed to an unlikely pair of individuals in the corner. "These are Natch Feral and Bat."

Natch Feral, I gathered, was the girl's street name. At first I thought her sloppily groomed, but then I noticed her long, kinky hair had been bound and stuffed down the neck of her leather jacket to make it difficult to grab in a fight. Her eyes had a hint of almond-shaping to them, but her hair and cafe-au-lait complexion suggested more than just oriental blood in her mix. Small and undoubtedly quick, she wore fingerless gloves that exposed daggerish fingernails painted black. Her bright blue eyes shot old Heinrich's racial heredity theories down in flames.

Bat, on the other hand, looked like an ancient, square-jawed socialist hero statue that had come to life. He was not as tall as Hal Garrett, easily surrendering eight inches in height to him. On the other hand, Bat had to outweigh Garrett by at least 25 pounds, tossing him up into the 325+ pound class. From what I could see beneath the plain white T-shirt he wore and through his short-cut black hair, that weight had been distributed 90%/10% between muscles and scars. Bat carried his fists balled, and I saw thick lines of scars on his knuckles. Whoever this man was, he had been in a lot of fights and, by the look of him, he'd won more than his share.

"Hello," I offered.

Natch squinted at me, then grunted. Bat let her answer serve for him as well.

The next person in line offered me her hand. "Hello, I

am Marit Fisk, Mr. Caine."

I smiled broadly, and I saw reflected in her blue eyes her pleasure at her effect upon me. "Tycho, please, Ms. Fisk"

"Then you must call me Marit."

"As you wish." As I took her hand and shook it, I sensed some anger from Rock. I glanced in his direction and saw the tightness around his eyes, but I did not care. If he had a problem with Marit, that was for him to deal with. I did not know if they were lovers, had been lovers or, in Rock's dreams, would be lovers, but I could not fault him for his taste.

Tall for a woman, Marit had broad shoulders that tapered to a slender waist. Her long black hair covered her shoulders and went to the middle of her back. Obviously athletic, she was one of the very few women who could successfully wear a Spandex bodysuit and not suffer for her audacity. The two-inch heels on her boots accentuated the length of her legs. Her smile brightened a beautiful face and, as she directed it at me, I realized I had met the woman with whom I wanted to spend the rest of my life.

From the corner of my eye I caught Natch smiling at me.

"Where's Jytte?" Rock snarled.

"Right here. I had work to complete."

Something about the woman appearing in the room's other doorway shocked me. At first glance I would have called her beautiful. The long locks of golden blond hair cascaded in waves over her shoulders and nearly reached her tiny waist. Though the jeans jumper she wore was hardly stylish, she did belt it in the middle, allowing the dress to hint at a very appealing body beneath. Her striped blouse was not quite the height of chic and she wore it buttoned down at both wrists and up at the throat as if to hide as much of her bare flesh as possible.

As she stepped forward into the light, I saw what had set off unconscious warning bells in my head. Her face had absolutely no animation at all. She looked to be wearing more of a mask of beauty than the real thing, though all I saw was her flesh. Her dark eyes did not match the blond hair or her fair complexion, and while she was statuesque, she moved with a coltish awkwardness that reminded me of the herky-jerky motions of a manual transmission car driven by someone who's not yet gotten the hang of the clutch.

I extended my hand to her. "Hello, I am..."

"Tycho Caine, I know." When I looked shocked, her eyes tightened a millimeter or two. "Rock reported the crash, and I managed to tap into the Scorpion site commander's datafeed. Tracing the car tag numbers and identification numbers got me the rental record. I have your financial file, and I even have your Digital Express bill. The Mizuno Sheraton in City Center still has your room and is racking up charges each day."

Marit rested her right hand on my left shoulder and, in a husky voice, introduced me. "This is Jytte Ravel. She is our communications coordinator and, lucky for us, one of the better computer empaths in the world. It was probably more difficult for her to hide her tracks than it was for her to get any of the information she's compiled."

I knew computer empaths were what once had been simply called hackers. Using an uncanny amount of intuition and frighteningly competent programming skills, they were able to burrow into computer networks. Clearly this Jytte had the run of the city's computers, which made her very valuable. I gave her an appreciative smile and acknowledged her skill with a nod.

Jytte seemed to warm up beneath Marit's praise. I extended my hand to her, and she took it after a moment's hesitation. Her flesh felt cool to the touch, and her arm oddly light. She held my hand rather gently, and we shook once before breaking.

Hal moved to the chair at the head of the table. "Jytte, any information on the two bodies Tycho here put down?"

The blond automaton nodded slowly as she took a seat toward the middle of the table. "I have caused one to be identified as Tycho Caine, and I sewed enough discord in that file to keep it that way for a couple of days. The other is Paul Gray. He was a private investigator who worked mostly for Lorica Industries. He used a man named Wallace Griffin on a lot of his contracts, so I suspect this is who the other body was. The LeBoeuf was a Lorica fleet car."

I think her face made an attempt to frown as she added one other point. "Mr. Caine used his own credit card to secure the rental car, but the bills were going to a Lorica dummy corporation. Someone on the 101st floor was picking up some of his bills."

I took a chair opposite Hal, and Marit seated herself at my right hand. Natch sat across from Jytte, Alejandro sat next to her and Rock sulked in a chair between Jytte and Hal. Bat remained in the corner with his massive arms folded. "Lorica was paying my bills? Why would they put someone on me, in that case?"

Hal shrugged. "Perhaps whatever you were supposed to do had a time limit, and you missed your deadline. Someone might have wanted to take their retainer back out of your hide." He glanced at Rock. "Anything juicy going down with Lorica?"

Rock shook his head. "No beheadings at board meetings, if that's what you mean. The Witch has fully consolidated her power since the takeover two months ago. Nerys Loring does not look like that much of a change from her father, Nero, but the way she ousted him was a work of art. He might have been old, but not that old. Engineers get a lot of use out of their experience, and the man who planned Frozen Shade and the maglev circuit should have had a couple more projects in him."

Natch made a clicking sound with the corner of her mouth. "Word on the street was that some loyalists retired Daddy to Casa Vacío real fast. She doesn't know where he is, and wants him found." She looked at me with an evil grin. "You good at hide and seek, Caine-man?"

"I don't know." I put my hands flat down on the table. "So far I've only been good at shooting things and starting fires."

Everyone grinned except for Bat.

He chuckled.

This did not make me feel good.

Marit patted my hand, then left her fingertips touching my wrist. "Hal, looks like a double tie back into Lorica to me. It occurs to me that if we could get Mr. Caine into the Lorica Industries reception in City Center tomorrow night, we might be able to shake something loose."

The big man smiled broadly and nodded. "Good idea. Can we get him in?"

Alejandro nodded confidently. "I have an invitation to go."

Marit grinned like a predator. "Good, we can make it a threesome." When Hal's head came up, she added, "You don't think, Hal dear, they would even try to keep me out, would you?"

Again Bat chuckled, and Hal shook his head. "No, I don't suppose they would. Good, your being there will unsettle things enough that we might get very lucky."

"Jytte, can you alter the Mizuno files enough to move Mr. Caine to another room if someone checks?"

Jytte nodded an affirmative answer to Marit's question. "You will want me to change the door combination to the room his things are in, correct?"

"Yes. If you do that, we can get his things back." Marit looked over at Hal. "Depending upon what he has in his room, we may have to buy him some new clothes for the reception."

"Go to it, Coyote said he has carte blanche."

Jytte confirmed Hal's statement with a nod. A phone began to ring in the room she had come from, so she got up to answer it.

Rock leaned back in his chair. "Okay, sport, after we get your stuff at the hotel, I know a place we can get some crush'n duds for you."

"Accent on the dud there." Marit slipped her left hand through my right arm. "I'll take him to his hotel, then to buy clothes. This is a party in the clouds, Rock, not some Eclipse soirée where the highlight is crushing beer cans on your forehead."

Her remark stung Rock deeply, but before he could reply to it, Hal cut him off. "She's right, Rock. Besides, I need you here. I want a full report on what you saw in the Warriors' warehouse. I got the Blood Crips to hold off from a major offensive, but I'm going to need you to use your charm on WAWA and the Zombies." He looked at the rest of the group. "Keep your eyes and ears open. If you hear anything odd going down with Lorica, call in to Jytte. She's coordinating with Coyote for us."

As if summoned by the use of her name, Jytte reappeared in the doorway. "Mr. Caine, Coyote would like to speak to you." She held out a solid lump of a black phone to me.

I took the handset and brought it up to my ear. In the background I heard a humming sound as if some electrical device was causing light interference. "Hello?"

"Ah, Mr. Caine, how good to speak with you. You have been a busy boy since you came to our city."

"Apparently."

"Indeed." He paused for a second, and I realized I found his voice a touch mechanical. *No doubt machine altered to make it difficult to identify.* "Mr. Caine, my people and I will do all we can to solve the mystery of your identity. I know we will succeed, but I have one thing to ask in return."

I smiled. "Paying forward, you mean."

"Precisely." I heard a bit of laughter in his voice. "I'm glad you are so quick because, you see, one of the people in the room with you is a traitor. I would like you identify and deal with him before he succeeds in killing you."

Strapped into Marit's GDM Ariel, I remained silent as she sliced through traffic on the Squaw Peak Parkway. She drove quite well for someone bent on doubling the speed limit, and the low sports coupe clung to the roadway as if its wheels were made of Velcro. The roadway itself went up and down like a rollercoaster, providing me an occasional glimpse of upstreet facilities from a downstreet roadway.

I kept a smile on my face so Marit would view my silence as mute approval of her driving, but I also used it to hide my confusion as I mulled over what Coyote had told me. I had only just met his people, and I was coming to trust them, when he sent a cruise missile through my confidence window. Immediately I began putting each of his aides into a box and examining them for motives.

The basic problem I had, of course, was that I did not know enough about them to start making any judgments. Rock Pell was easy to put on the list as the top candidate because he could have used his car phone to alert Lorica that I was going after my car. Then again, I'd already rationalized a workable explanation for why they were waiting, so the only mark against Pell was that I found him self-centered and uncaring, but if that was a capital crime, I'd run out of bullets long before dispensing justice to all who deserved it.

Coyote had not said how he wanted the situation dealt with, but I had no doubt he expected me to kill that individual. Oddly enough, that didn't cause me any problem, which helped convince me I was a trouble-shooter that corps brought in to deal with problems. I just found myself hoping I could uncover the traitor before he or she got a chance to do me. I also hoped Coyote's problem wasn't bigger than he imagined, because a second or third traitor in the group would severely confuse any effort to find one of them.

"Cover your eyes," Marit directed me.

"What?"

"Cover your eyes, we're leaving Eclipse." Marit signaled and pulled the Ariel into the right exit lane. Above us I saw a sign announce: "You are entering City Center. Unauthorized vehicles are subject to confiscation ,and the owners will be prosecuted."

"City fathers have no sense of humor, eh?"

"No." She hit the gas as the car started up a steep incline. "For nearly 20 years they did everything they could, from having festivals to sponsoring a Grand Prix to get folks to come to downtown. The harder they worked to get folks down here, the more folks went out to the hinterlands to watch ostrich festivals and medieval fairs. It was only when they restricted access to the sort of uppercrust clientele they wanted anyway did the rush to rediscover City Center begin."

"Forbidden fruit?"

"Exactly, now cover your eyes."

I got my right hand up just in time as her car nosed its way over the peak of the incline and into daylight. The sunlight hurt my eyes at first, but they quickly adapted, and I lowered my hand. "My God, that's beautiful."

"From Tartarus to Olympus we are bound."

City Center looked like a shining crystalline city of the future that had risen through a glossy black ocean. The base of the urban island spread across the western horizon for almost five miles and extended upward for about five stories. A dozen towers stood like mountains above that, with three extending over 100 stories into the air. Copper trim and rosy marble blended with mirrored silver towers to create a jewel of a city floating in the photovoltaic sea.

Off to the right I saw the gray supports for what looked to be a magnetic levitation train line running into City Center at the southern edge. I looked back along the line and saw two more smaller man-made islands to the south. "What are the little ones?"

"Directly south is the Sumitomo-Dial citadel and back southeast is the Honeywell & Koch complex. One maglev circuit connects all seven of the satellite citadels with each other, while others connect them with City Center. If you live in the towers, your feet never have to touch the ground."

The roadway sloped back down, and I saw it ran straight into the middle of the island approximately eight stories above the Frozen Shade. We passed through the mirrored glass walls, and I suddenly found myself inside what could have been seen as a massive mall. Above me, covered walkways and peoplemovers crisscrossed the sky to move bodies from one tower to another. Below, descending for another two very tall stories, escalators took people to an incredible labyrinth of white marble corridors and stores of every description possible.

Marit pulled off the roadway at a valet parking area. We both got out, and a fresh-faced kid got into the Ariel. He handed her a ticket and she tipped him $5. As we stepped up on to the curb, he headed the car down a narrow roadway that led to a tunnel.

"Where's he taking your car?"

Marit slipped her left hand through my right arm. "We're currently four levels above Frozen Shade, which is roughly 18 stories above the ground. Level Five, the one just at Frozen Shade is a vast parking area. When we get set to leave, they will bring the car to whichever road exit we have chosen."

I frowned as we walked forward and got on an

escalator going down. "City Center is a rather big place. How do we get around without a car?"

"All around the outside of Level Six, and at crossing points on Level Seven, shuttle-coaches will take us wherever we need go to." With her free hand she pointed diagonally across the wide plaza. "The Mizuno Sheraton's lobby is on Level Seven, otherwise we would take an elevator down to Six and go around."

"Let me see if I have this straight: Level Five is a parking garage and Level Six has a train."

"A train and shops. Down there are mostly department stores like Comrade Montgomery Ward or bookstores, newsstands and drugstores. Anyone can go down there, and that's where we have theaters, arcades and restaurants that are best suited to kids. Level Seven has some fine restaurants and some of the finer specialty stores. Mostly European or top-of-the-line Latin products available there. Level Seven even has the new Mercado, which looks just like a Mexican Village. It's delightful, you'll love it."

As she spoke and we slowly ascended through Levels Eight and Nine, I saw some familiar store names. Clearly prices escalated as one ascended in levels, as did items of quality. Level Eight might as well have been sliced out of Tokyo and flown over. Level Nine seemed to cover most of the German manufacturers and some of the very best American companies, with the latter's stock in trade being fine weapons.

"If access is restricted, who gets in?"

Marit gave my arm a reassuring little squeeze. "Those who work in the shops and the offices here take up Levels One through Four. They seldom spend time outside work above Level Six, but they are allowed. Many folks, I am told, celebrate anniversaries or special occasions by attending functions up here. The executives or career folks live in the various towers—offices tend to start at

Level 15 and work up. The ultra-rich, like Nerys Loring, live above the clouds. Folks between her and the normal working folks also live out in Paradise Valley, if they can afford it, and commute in. Eclipsers cannot enter City Center on their own, but they can come here as guests."

"So that means seldom, if ever."

"'Cept when they look like you," Marit grinned.

We left the escalator and started walking through the crowds toward the Mizuno Sheraton. It did not look familiar to me, but then nothing had, so that was not a big shock. The crowds were not that big, but it was easy to see, from the gawking and pointing, who were the *untermenschen* who had come up to see City Center and who were the folks who spent too much time here to be impressed. Despite the fact that they looked clean and well-fed, I felt a certain pity for them. They seemed less people than hamsters trained to wander through a maze to amuse their master.

At one point in the big mezzanine, I saw a whole city park that had been transplanted upward. A cute little white picket fence bordered it, and toy boats floated across a central pond. Nannies in uniforms watched little boys and girls playing ball or using the swing-set. The children all wore very fine clothing, with shorts, knee-socks and white shirts predominating among the boys and frilly dresses, gloves and bonnets among the girls. I looked around for a sign to indicate this was some sort of play or costume drama, but every indication I saw suggested what I was looking at was real.

"Do people actually make their kids dress like that to play in this oversized terrarium?"

Marit nodded solemnly. "Burton Barr Park is only for those who can afford it. They want their children to have the best of everything. You're looking at a breeding ground for the people who will someday control City Center and the corpvils surrounding it."

When we finally arrived, two young women greeted us at the hotel doorway. We smiled politely, and Marit laughed as one girl whispered her name to the other. Without pausing, we swept through the lobby, and Marit directed me to the correct bank of elevators. Having gotten the information on my room from Jytte while I spoke with Coyote, she led the way on our quest.

"Four-three-three-seven," she breathed as she punched the combination into my door. The red LED shifted to green, and the door clicked open. She waited for me go through the doorway first, and I obliged her. I hoped against hope that something in the room would seem familiar enough that it would spark my memory.

No such luck.

The room had a west-facing window in it, which gave us a breathtaking view of the setting sun, but other than that it was unremarkable. It was, after all, a hotel room and allowed no room for personalization. Moreover, aside from some change in an ashtray, it hardly looked as if I had been here at all.

I sighed audibly. "Time for a careful, methodical search."

Marit agreed with a nod. "I'll start with your closet." She opened the door and whistled appreciatively. "You have good taste. Italian, I think, for the suits. The shoes are definitely Bucci Imports."

I smiled as I opened a dresser drawer. There I saw four pairs of jockey shorts all folded neatly. Beside them were four pairs of colored socks, likewise neatly folded in the middle. The next drawer down had four shirts. Three were white and the other was a light blue. Each looked freshly laundered and well starched.

"This is odd." Marit had taken one of the suit jackets from the hanger, leaving the pants hanging over the hanger crossbar.

The jacket looked like a normal black, double-breasted

jacket with dark buttons on the front and sleeves. "What's wrong?"

Marit frowned and pouted delectably with her lower lip. "I know this is an Armando suit—one of the last photo shoots I did had a man modeling this design."

"And?"

"This one has no tags." She opened the jacket so I could see the lining. "The designer label, washing instructions and size tags have been cut out."

I glanced back at the shirts in the second drawer. "Same thing here. Do you think that suit has been worn?"

"Perhaps, but not folded up in a suit bag—no way."

I crossed to the bathroom and flicked the light on. Arrayed neatly on the counter I saw a shaving kit that purportedly belonged to me. The toothpaste tube had maybe one squeeze gone from it. The toothbrush looked new, as did the blade in the razor. The can of shaving gel might as well have been brand new. The bottle of aspirin had not, in fact, been opened.

Returning to the room puzzled, I saw Marit had shifted from the closet to my dresser. She'd opened the other top drawer and had appropriated the sunglasses therein. "Serengeti Vermillions, very nice. Christian Dior sweater, an Iceberg sweater and a nice set of gold cufflinks set with a diamond. Whoever bought these things for you has good taste, and was probably getting a kick-back from the merchants."

I shook my head. "I don't follow you."

Marit lifted up the sweater that, while it had no labels, I trusted to be made for Christian Dior. "This is your size, and even a style that would look good on you, but this powder yellow is not your color. You have such gorgeous green eyes and strong features that you'd not want a soft color like this. And the cufflinks—none of your shirts have french cuffs. I suspect the buyer got a gift in exchange for taking them off the merchant's hands."

"What are you saying?"

"What I'm saying, my sweet, is that this might have been your room, and you might actually have stayed here, but this stuff was in here and waiting for you when you arrived."

I glanced back at the closet. "Even the suit bag and suitcase there?"

She smiled. "Not even the remnant of an airline baggage stub on them." She shrugged. "If this room has any secrets, they're going the be the devil's own to unlock."

"Unlock." I slammed the heel of my right hand against my forehead. I reached for my wallet and fished out the safety deposit box key. "Maybe the secrets are locked away in their vault.

With the key in hand, getting whatever treasure I had locked away in the vault was not a problem. A perky young woman at the concierge desk required me to sign my name on the signature card they had given me when I put things into the vault. I found it very easy to forge my own signature. Satisfied, the girl took the key and returned from the back with an aluminum attaché case.

I thanked her, then Marit and I walked through the hotel lobby. Before we stepped out into the central mall area, I excused myself and retreated to the nearest men's room. I checked the stalls, then chose the last one and locked myself in. Seating myself as comfortably as possible, I pulled the case into my lap.

The case had two latches, each with a three-digit combination. Looking at it I realized I had no idea what the correct combination was, and I did not think I had time to experiment with all the various possibilities. Most folks, when setting such a combination, will chose a number or date significant to them so they would not forget it, but I'd forgotten who I was, so that was of no use to me.

I knew, from everything I had seen in my unconscious activities, that I was a very methodical person. The lack of memories did not destroy my underlying personality. I still functioned the way I normally would, but I did not know who I was. I needed to let myself run on autopilot to figure out the combination.

Given the way I reacted to things, I doubted sincerely I would have opted for a personal date or significant number. That would be easy to crack if someone got a line on me. Chances were I used a random selection of numbers when setting the combination. If I did that, I either memorized the result, or had a gimmick for remembering it.

Mnemonic tricks are an interesting phenomena. Roy G. Biv is one that recalls the different colors in visible light by grouping their first initials: red, orange, yellow, green, blue, indigo and violet. I knew I remembered the difference between *port* and *starboard* because *port* and *left* have the same number of letters in the English language. I knew that whatever mnemonic trick I used, it would be something simple, like the left/port examples and just as constant.

Staring at the combination, a possible solution struck me. *Down* and *even* have the same number of letters. If, in locking the case, I took the correct combination and moved all the even numbers down one position, then moved all the odd numbers up one position, the mnemonic would likewise solve for the combination. As long as I tested that down-even/up-odd theory using odd numbers for position changes, the formula would reverse itself.

Smiling, I set to work. Somewhere, in the back of my mind, I worked out that the key number had to be 1. Tycho Caine has 10 letters in it, which reduced to 1 when you add the two digits. Keying things to my name worked well because, except in weird circumstances, no one forgets his name.

And, if you are careful about picking an alias, you can vary your security procedure on each job.

That thought hit me like a slug right between the eyes. *Maybe I'm not Tycho Caine after all.*

I applied my thumbs to the latch buttons, and the case popped open. I carefully lifted the lid and chewed my lower lip. *No wonder the Krait felt so comfortable.*

Inside, nestled in a bed of black foam I saw a number of things. The first was a Colt Krait. The only difference between it and the gun I wore in my shoulder holster was that this automatic was blued-steel, not bright, and a florescent orange pip marked the front sight. It was loaded and ready for action, with two spare clips in a foam cut-out by the grip.

Above and around it I saw all the pieces of an Armalite M-27 "Keyholer" sniper rifle. It fired a copper-jacketed 7.62 NATO round, and I had three clips of 30 bullets each and one small clip of five bullets that looked to have been drilled and patched to make them explosive. The receiver had been fitted for an Allard Technologies Espion UV laser scope. Pressing the battery check button in, it showed it was ready to go and had been sighted out to 750 meters. The rifle, I knew, had a midrange trajectory variable of +2-inch at the sight's focal distance, but could hit a target at a klick and a half if the shooter was good enough.

Somehow I knew I was good enough.

Aside from the weaponry I found four stacks of $100 bills bound in 10 meg packets. I slipped one of them into my pocket. Another small hole in the foam yielded 10 gold eagle coins, each worth approximately 600 dolmarks in a bank, or roughly double that on the black market. Lastly, a slit in the foam produced a passport and driver's license for me in Tycho Caine's name.

I carefully closed the case and reset the combination as per the mnemonic.

Marit smiled sweetly as I rejoined her. "Did you learn anything?"

"I think so." I slipped on the Serengeti sunglasses from my room. "I am Tycho Caine. And as nearly as I can tell, I'm not in Phoenix for my health, nor anyone else's, for that matter."

"So you're not a doctor? So much for my mother's dreams of me marrying one." Marit again took my arm and led me from the Mizuno Sheraton. "What is it you would say you do, exactly?"

"I don't know, *exactly*. I appear to be a troubleshooter who specializes in retirement." I let my reluctance to discuss the matter bleed into my voice. "I am, however, now well financed. Given that packing up and formally checking out of the hotel would likely set off some alarms somewhere, I will need some new clothing and other essentials."

"And you need something for the reception tomorrow night."

"In fact, I do." I pointed out into the tree-lined mall area with the case. "Please lead on."

Marit had not struck me as the type who would shy away from shopping. We ascended to Level Eight and started wandering the broad walkway encircling the open mall area. Marit laughed and pointed to various window displays. She paused for a moment or two to study a rainbow collection of sequin-studded shoes, then pulled me in the direction of another store. "If I look too long, I'll just have to buy a pair. I can no more resist them than someone else could resist a puppy in a pet store window. Here we are."

I glanced up at the sign and read the *kana* symbols. "You have to be kidding."

She frowned. "No, The Gentleman's Wardrobe is probably the best men's clothing store and haberdashery in City Center."

I read the English name of the store for the first time

as she said it and laughed. "Do you know what the Japanese name for this place is?"

"No."

"*Dansei no ningen.* That means 'virile man.'"

"Trust me," she giggled, "you can pass."

"You know how to flatter me."

The men working in the store recognized Marit almost immediately and, when assured I was her friend, they became very attentive. Roger, a man I would have guessed as being a year or two younger than me and of a similar slender build, whipped a tape measure from around his neck and set to work. As he figured dimensions, he announced them to one of two aides standing behind him, pen pointed and pad ready.

"Will Caine-*san* require just a suit, or are we looking for a whole change of image here?"

Marit smiled coyly. "Mr. Caine wishes a complete wardrobe. Good looking, but a bit conservative. He will require formal wear for the reception tomorrow, two business suits and four days of casual wear. He'll also need underwear, socks, and a full shaving kit."

"Understood, Ms. Fisk." Roger stood and lifted my arms away from my sides. He looped the tape measure around my chest. "And should we account for both the shoulder holster and bulletproof vest, or just one of them?"

"Just the vest, I think, Roger," I replied. He grinned as I added, "Conservative on all the clothing except, perhaps, what I will wear to the reception tomorrow. I want to make an impression."

Roger rolled his eyes to heaven. "If you are with Ms. Fisk, you will. Still, I think we can accommodate you." He turned from me and started giving numbers to his assistants. One of them scurried off to gather up the items he had ordered, while the other continued to faithfully record everything Roger said. At the end Roger took the pad and pen from his aide and dispatched him with a wave.

Roger flipped the page on the pad over and squinted at me. He sketched something on the paper, frowned, then added heavier lines. He looked at me again, made one last adjustment on his picture, then smiled and showed it to me. "Here, what do you think of this? It has traditional elements and will be in style, yet is different enough to get you noticed. You'll also note, cut this way, we could easily conceal the holster if you still wish to use it."

I studied the drawing for a moment, then smiled. "And you can have this ready for tomorrow night?"

"You'll know it was a rush job only by the price you pay." Roger raised his left eyebrow. "The boy-mayor may have to attend in last year's suit, but no one notices him anyway."

"You do very good work, Roger."

"So kind of you to say so, sir."

I reached into my pocket and pulled out the $10,000 stack of bills. I saved ten of the Trumans for myself and handed him $9000. "Let's put this on account. You have my measurements, and you can do custom work. Tip your staff generously for their help. I will have more for you to do."

Pocketing the meg, I turned to Marit. "If you're hungry, we can get something to eat, then pick up the off-the-shelf stuff later."

She shook her head. "Roger, just have it delivered to my apartment. We can get it there, later."

"Very good, Ms. Fisk. Mr. Caine, it has been a pleasure."

"Nine meg poorer and nothing to show for it," I laughed as we walked away from The Gentleman's Wardrobe.

"You can trust Roger. He'll gouge you on the price of the suits, but he's honest otherwise." She looked out across the vast open gulf between one half of the mall and the other. "Do you like Japanese food?"

I shrugged. "I don't know."

"Feeling adventurous?"

"Marit, I've been living an adventure for the last 36 hours. I've been shot at, chased, and nearly dissected. What could a restaurant offer that could worry me?"

Without answering me she pointed to a restaurant a quarter of the way around the mall from our present position. "*Osome*, you'll love it. C'mon."

I offered her my elbow, and we set off. "I have this impression, Marit, from the hotel and the store staff, that you have a bit higher profile than most of the other people I met today. Am I correct, or has my amnesia begun to slop over into my reasoning?"

"I'm more notorious than I am famous, I am afraid." Her right hand swept up over her head as she tucked hair behind her left ear. "There was a time when I would not have been allowed access to City Center—just like everyone you met today except for Alejandro and, maybe, Hal. Like the others I grew up a Mike..."

"Mike?"

"Ah, bureaucratspeak. Marginal Income, Knowledge Exiguous, Sterile. MIKES was a classification used by United Nations bureaucrats to classify various populations in the newly freed Eastern Europe in the 1990s. They were the ones that were judged to be able to maintain a minimal existence without government handouts, yet their chances for advancement in the society were seen as non-existent. The term has bled over into popular use." She looked toward the people crowding City Center. "To the folks here it retains its original meaning and is something you threaten young, misbehaving children with becoming. The folks in Eclipse, on the other hand, cling to it defiantly. Every time something in their lives improves, they've beaten the margin and take pride in the victory."

We arrived at the restaurant and removed our shoes at the door. After we put on slippers, we were taken to a low table by a Japanese woman in traditional dress. The tables were cunningly arranged over a pit into which people could put their legs if they could not tolerate kneeling throughout dinner. I put my case down in the leg well and knelt.

Marit watched me and pouted slightly. "Now we can't play footsie."

I smiled, but shook my head. "Very poor manners in a fine restaurant like this. You're a big girl, you should be able to behave yourself for a little while."

"A little while, perhaps. I'll save it up."

The waitress came, and we ordered sushi a la carte. Marit also ordered a whisky sour, but I refrained from getting a drink. "Marit, you were saying you grew up a Mike?" I kept my voice low as I asked the question.

She nodded. "My parents owned a small store at Oak and 36th Street. That's fairly near the Lorica Citadel, so we got some traffic from the Proles working for them. I made it through high school, then someone mentioned that Lorica was hiring candidates for their security forces. I applied and, because of some complicated quota formula put together by Nerys Loring, I was accepted as a cadet. I trained and, after six months, was put on the force. That was five years ago."

"How did they train you?"

"Weapons training, both handguns and long guns, unarmed combat, antiterrorist tactics and crowd control. We also took courses in proper manners for parties, how to be discrete, and some very basic detective skills. For the most part we were trained to be seen but not heard, to protect our execs and keep folks from unauthorized access to the citadel."

"Interesting." As she spoke I cataloged information on the potential threat level of opposition at Lorica. "Still, that's not the sort of duty that's likely to make you infamous."

She smiled shyly but her blue eyes sparked mischievously through a thin veil of black hair. "No, no, it isn't. I had been with the security force for just over a year when Lorica decided it needed a corporate video to instruct their executives how to act in various security situations. At times the gang wars in Eclipse threaten the citadels, so we wanted our people to know what to do in that sort of emergency. I was picked to be one of the security people in the video."

She fell silent as the waitress brought our food and her drink. Marit broke apart her chopsticks and rubbed them together to get rid of splinters. I aped her, unknowing if I knew how to use them. As I tried to imitate the way she held them, the chopsticks dropped perfectly into place in my right hand. I picked a single grain of rice from my plate and ate it.

Marit nodded her appreciation of my dexterity, then continued. "Back in those days, I was not much to look at. My mother belonged to a rather repressive church, so cosmetics and clothes like these were seen as the devil's tools. I guess I'd grown up figuring that I'd meet my Prince Charming when he off-loaded beer flats into my father's store, so I never set about dolling myself up as bait."

"So Cinderella awaited the cinematic fairy godmother's touch?"

She smiled. "Ugly Duckling tale from beginning to end. When they got through with me, I couldn't recognize myself in the mirror. All of a sudden I looked beautiful. In shock, I think, I did everything I was told to do on the set and the video became a hit within Lorica. I'm told copies have even showed up in rental shops under 'Action/

Adventure—Do It Yourself' headings.

"That video brought me to the attention of the market-
ing department in Lorica. All of a sudden I found myself
shucked out of flak-suits and stuffed into slinky gowns so
I could 'smile and point at the product.' An agent found
me, and I signed a modeling contract, though Lorica
hired me exclusively. Suddenly I found myself one of the
Nomenklatura."

"A gnome." I spread some *wasabe* on *tekka-maki* and
smiled. "Such success leads me to find your spending
time in Eclipse rather odd."

"Oh, the first year was wonderful. I moved my parents
into the Lorica Citadel, and I bought a place of my own.
I traveled, I attended parties and even had a couple of bit
parts in films shot in Hollyweird. I was on top of the world.
I had just turned 20, and I was definitely an *enfant
terrible*." She sipped some green tea. "As they say, 'Pride
goeth before a fall.'"

"Actually, it's 'Pride goeth before destruction, and an
haughty spirit before a fall.' Proverbs 16:18."

My correcting her brought her head up. "You are rather
amazing, Mr. Caine." She smiled. "Of course, with that
name, why should I be surprised at your quoting the
Bible."

*Why, indeed? A man with a killer's name and an
assassin's rifle quoting the Bible. Is that irony, or some
inside joke I missed until now?* "So, how far did you fall?
From *enfant terrible* to *enfant perdu* ?"

"Not quite that badly, I think. A highly placed Lorica
executive decided that since Lorica owned my contract,
they owned me. When he tried to press his claim, he
discovered that Lorica's security training is very effective. I broke his perfect smile and severely dented his self-
image. His wife made his life a living hell after that and
her mother, a substantial stockholder, made Lorica get
rid of me. News of a scandal was leaked to the tabloids,

and they managed to wedge it onto the front pages between stories about UFO baby-eaters and a man who impregnated his grandmother to give his father the brother he never had."

"That sounds horrible."

"It was, for a while. My agent got me some work in Japan, so I lived over there for a year. When I returned here everything seemed smoothed over, but there were still ripples. Through friends of a friend I met Rock and bought a handgun. Rock introduced me into Coyote's circle and I, in turn, was able to get a number of people to patronize Alejandro's gallery down on Seven. It's part of the Mercado."

"I would like to see it at some point." I reached across the table and caressed her left hand. "So, for the past two years, you have given Coyote entré into the City Center society."

"More or less. Coyote does not have me introduce him to people. I've only met him twice—and that's if you care to define meeting as talking to a shadow in the middle of a dark warehouse. Most often I get instructions through Jytte or by phone, just like you did today. Coyote generally describes a problem to me and asks if I think there is a gnome who would be willing to help with it."

"Gnomes would help with a problem in Eclipse?"

"Sure, if it's presented to them in the right way." She dipped the tip of her index finger in her drink, then licked the liquid off. "Most gnomes are good people, but they are very wrapped up in their lives and careers. With some you appeal to their sense of fairness, especially if you know of a parallel from their own life where they could have used some help. Others get caught up in the delicious danger of dealing with someone from Eclipse. Others act because they want to exact revenge on someone in City Center and the best way they can hurt them is to screw up some sort of power play going down in Eclipse."

Marit smiled impishly. "I just do my job and collect information, rumors and lies that I funnel to Coyote. Then, when he needs me to do something, I do it."

"Like help me?"

"Exactly."

I squeezed her hand. "Jytte seems rather different. What is her story?"

Marit shrugged uncomfortably. "Jytte is very private, but she has told me something. Do you mind if I don't violate her confidence?"

I shook my head. "I'd be upset if you did. I just want to put her into perspective. She's clearly had body augmentation surgery. I gather it did not go well."

Marit took a sip from her drink. "Every so often you hear rumors about someone or something that gets tagged with the name *Pygmalion*."

"Like the sculptor from Greek mythology."

"Right. It's said he likes bringing beauty to life. He kidnaps people who are not beautiful and changes them. I think this would be a good thing, *if* he actually asked the people he worked on if they minded."

I nodded. "From the job done on Jytte, this Pygmalion could make a great deal of money with his skills."

"Ah, but that would necessitate two things: his doing what the client wants and his willingness to let his clients leave. Jytte escaped and, in the process, has blanked out much of what she endured at his hands. She has no idea who Pygmalion is. There are other times when a beautiful corpse gets dumped in Drac City or Boxton and Eclipsers just assume it is one of Pygmalion's failures. Most of those are suicides. I guess some folks can't stand being made pets."

"I can't blame them."

"Nor can I." Marit smiled. "Jytte is slowly coming to terms with herself, but she feels much more at home with her machines. I can't remember when I last saw her outside the meeting place."

We spent the rest of the meal eating in relative silence because the tables filled up around us. In many ways I think we would have run out of things to talk about anyway because Marit was better at getting information out of people than she was sharing it. Despite her having been open about what had happened to her, she had been detail-vague, so that I would have had to work hard to attach names with people. I suspected that might be a natural defense mechanism, especially after having been up so far and then having fallen so low, but I also felt Coyote would have encouraged that tendency in her.

Of course, had the discussion turned to me, it would have ended soon enough. So far in the day I had discovered I could read Japanese, could quote the Bible and had excellent taste in weapons of individual destruction. I doubted those revelations would have made for good table conversation. That went double for my excursion with the Reapers.

I paid the bill and tipped well, but left the money on Marit's side of the table so the waitress would remember her and not the boy-toy escort she'd had. Marit noticed what I had done and laughed loudly enough to draw attention to herself, and that triggered a host of whispers that covered me with anonymity as we left the restaurant.

Marit led me all the way around the mall to the elevator bays between the Goddard Towers. One stood not as tall as the other and she, naturally, pressed the button for the larger, grander of the pair. "Where are we going now?"

"You'll see."

A bit uneasy about venturing off to a mystery destination, I let myself take solace in the fact that in the briefcase I had enough hardware to hold off almost anything this side of a heavy weapons squad of security guards. As the elevator doors closed, Marit inserted a coded card into a slot on the wall.

"27th floor selected. Thank you, Ms. Fisk," the elevator intoned.

"Cute."

She smiled. "It gets better."

She was right. The elevator took off swiftly enough to put a bend in my knees. "Thanks for the warning."

"*De nada.*"

As we reached the 27th floor, the back of the elevator opened, and we stepped into another box. Marit pushed the "Close Door" button. The cage shut itself up, then sent us hurtling along sideways. It eventually slowed and moved to the left before stopping. When it did, the front of the cage opened up, revealing the foyer of a sprawling apartment.

"Welcome to my home."

I stepped from the transversor box, and the doors clicked shut behind me. The foyer, which was easily the size of Estefan's living room, opened on to a living room and dining area that could have accommodated his whole house. The wall I faced, which looked out to the south, had a full view of the Sumitomo-Dial corporate citadel and, beyond it, to South Mountain Park. With nightfall all I could see was the black outline of the mountain against the stars and the red beacons atop the broadcasting towers there.

The rooms themselves looked like layouts from a home decorating magazine. The living room featured white leather couches and chairs, with glass tables and track lighting arranged to illuminate the abstract pictures hanging on the walls. The dining room was a bit more traditional with a cherry wood table and matching chairs that were so polished they all but glowed. A hutch and some smaller wooden pieces contained crystal and china. A gold and crystal chandelier hung over the middle of the table, ready to impale the bowl of fruit that served as a centerpiece.

Marit pointed to the right and the shorter half of her apartment. "That way is the kitchen. Anything you can find in there you can eat. I don't really know what I have, but Juanita and Anna never seem to complain about the food when they are here during the days."

Pointing off in the other direction she indicated the doors on the right side of the long paneled hallway. "Those are the guest bedroom, my office and my media room. At the end of the hall is the master bedroom. The doorway on the left is the guest bathroom."

I frowned and set my briefcase by the wall. "I don't see the things we bought earlier."

Marit thought for a second, then shrugged. "Roger probably had one of his boys hang the suits in a closet and put the other clothes away for you. We might have given Roger the wrong impression." Her smile slowly grew. "Of course, we do have to figure out where you *are* going to stay tonight."

I don't think I'd been making any assumptions, but that question had never occurred to me. Clearly going back to the hotel was as potentially dangerous as retrieving my car—perhaps more so after Paul Gray died trying to kill me. Similarly, returning to Estefan's home would be unwise. Not only would it put him in jeopardy, but it would make me easy to find again. Estefan might like Coyote and feel that he owed him, but that did not mean his neighbors had not seen me or could keep their mouths shut if they had.

"The hotel and Estefan's place are out." I looked down angrily. "And, without credit cards, all the money in the world will not get me a hotel room."

Marit shook her head. "You misunderstood me. I always assumed you would spend the night here. I was just trying to determine if you would have the guest room all to yourself or, if, perhaps, you felt adventurous."

I raised an eyebrow. "Do you mean, Ms. Fisk, you would give me the master bedroom?"

She came to me and slid her hands up over my chest and around my neck. "I could do that or you can consider this: You can remember, what, the past 48 hours?"

I brushed her lips with mine. "Approximately."

"And during all that time people have been trying to kill you?"

"It seems that way."

She slipped my jacket off and let it fall to the floor. "Then why don't we spend time tonight ensuring that tomorrow, when you think back on your life, you will have something to smile about."

Awakening in a dark typhoon, with its deafening winds shrieking, is not a pleasant experience. I sat bolt upright in the bed, clawing the sheets with my right hand to find Marit, but she was gone. Sweat poured off me as if it were blood and my throat had been cut. I tried to swing my legs off the bed, but I met resistance. As I looked down I saw the lower half of my body had been wrapped in a gray silk cocoon.

When the wind's howls changed from sound so keenly sharp that it made my teeth buzz to colors no less painful or vibrant, I realized I was dreaming. Even so, the knowledge that I was trapped in a dream did not drain the fantasy of its power. Instead the rainbow winds became a vortex that focused itself beyond the window looking east and eclipsed the dawning sun. The whirlwind flashed with crimson and a neon green, then pulsating, electric blue tendrils climbed up through it like ivy assaulting a wall.

I hate dreams and always have because here my mind creates problems it knows I cannot solve. It confronts me with situations I would avoid. Like an ancient oracle, it poses riddles that it calls answers, then leaves me to agonize over meanings that are trivial at best and drawn from experiences I do not really remember.

Dreams drain off the mental strain that would drive the sane mad.

This dream, however, was different, and I recognized it instantly. While it did not surprise me that I might feel this dream alien, given its womb was made of memories I had no way to access, I felt this dream came from outside. This was not a dream of *my* making, yet it imposed itself on me and used the symbolism I would use. Like a cancer, it masked itself in things I recognized so I could not escape it.

The sizzling blue tendrils hooked over the vortex's event horizon as the plane of the dream shifted. I saw the tentacles thicken as whatever they were attached to pulled itself up out of the hole that now lay parallel to the floor. As the thing neared the top, the tentacles lost their suppleness and hardened into a thin blue outline-chitin with spikes and bumps and horns kinking its flesh. The creature itself, to my eyes, became a thing visible only as a thick, smoky-gray translucence that leeched light from the sun it eclipsed.

Talons and elbows appeared first, with two arms becoming four as it heaved its bulk out of the hole. I could not see its face, but atop its head I saw a crown with seven spires surrounding one grander tower in the center. I could not tell if this was something the creature wore, or was part of it.

One pair of legs appeared, then another to clutch the edge of the hole. The creature remained perched there like some arachnoid gargoyle watching me from the roof of a church. One arm stretched out in my direction, each segment of exoskeleton telescoping out like an antenna. Three talons, each set at a 120-degree angle from the other, reached for me, and I heard the chitin click as they met and missed barely a millimeter from my nose.

"The pet no longer wishez my carez?" The creature spoke in scents and colors, but I heard words form in my brain. "Iz the pet infirm?"

Behind me, suddenly, where nothing could stand or be, I sensed another presence. When this one spoke, I actually heard the words with my ears. I wanted to turn to look at him, but I found myself held even more rigidly than I had been in the toxin's grasp. *This is a dream. Your body is asleep. Not moving is natural.*

Somehow, knowing that, I still panicked.

"So you use the term *pet* to define slaves?"

The creature looked up and focused beyond me. "If your power matched your audacity, you might be ztrong enough make a zlave of me."

"But never a pet, I think."

I felt hands on my shoulders. I moved my head enough to glance at my right shoulder and there saw a shadow hand with a golden ring on the appropriate finger. The ring had a design that looked to be, at first, the Egyptian Eye of Horus, but it was different as well. Still, the green eye stared back at me, and my panic began to drain.

The creature again reached for me, but I managed to jerk back enough to avoid the second swipe. "Do not interfere with my pet! It belongz to me. Give me what is mine."

"Your pet belongs to himself. He is not yours, nor is this place yours. Be gone."

Golden lightning played through the blue outline, sparking gold from the crown's spikes. The thing reached back with a hind leg to grasp the far edge of the hole, but missed, and the whole beast swayed as it fought to regain its balance. Throwing all four pairs of arms wide, it braced itself like a huge mechanical crane, but its limbs trembled with the strain.

"You zmall creaturez zo revel in zuch inzignificant victoriez." Its voice started to distort as if the creature was both close and far at the same time. "Yoooouuuur raze izzzz owwwuuurrrrzzzz to devouuuurrrr aaazzzz we will it." It looked down at me. "Come ttttoooo mmeee, my pet. I willlll rewaaarddd your fiiiideliteeeeee."

"Be gone," repeated my guardian.

"I *will* come again." The creature struggled against the vortex, then, like a diver who surrenders to gravity in the midst of a dive, it straightened its limbs and slipped from sight. The light at the edge of the hole brightened, but only because the hole itself started shrinking. I sat up taller in bed and saw it tightened down from the size of a truck tunnel to a pinpoint, then it vanished.

Behind me I heard mild laughter. I turned to look, but only caught a fleeting glimpse of a human silhouette. It evaporated instantly as the sun's rays poured through the master bedroom's unshaded window. I glanced back and felt the light skewer my brain, then my arms collapsed, and I dove nose first into a pillow.

"*Dispénseme, señor.*"

Squinting I looked toward the corner of the room just beyond Marit's vanity table. Pretty, despite being a bit heavy, a woman smiled at me. She wore a gray dress— a uniform really—that buttoned up the front and had been trimmed collar and sleeves in white. "Señorita Fisk, she say to let you sleep, but Señor Garrett will be here in a half hour to speak with you."

I nodded and rolled over on my back. The cocoon I had dreamed enfolding the lower portion of body was, in fact, one of the lavender silk sheets on the bed. It probably ended up being good that I'd wrapped it around myself because—despite having triggered the dream—I was naked beneath it, and it saved me some embarrassment in this encounter. "Juanita o Anna?"

"Juanita, Señor."

My stomach growled. "What time is it?"

"Noon. Señorita Fisk said to fix you breakfast when you woke up." Juanita smiled. "I have put fresh towels in the bathroom for you, and I can make food while you shower."

"Good. Just a sandwich, I guess."

"*Bueno,* señor."

"*Gracias,*" I said to her retreating back. I freed myself from the sheet and wandered into the bathroom. Shutting the door behind me, I saw myself in the triptych mirrors and realized I'd not shaved for at least three days.

My beard was coming in black and gave my lean face an edge. *Maybe I won't shave it all off.*

Unlike Estefan's home, here I did not need to pump water up to a holding tank. The oval tub was set diagonally across one corner of the room and was almost big enough to have given my ill-fated Lancer a good washing. I stepped in and thought for a moment that I might need a ladder to climb back out again. Pulling the curtain shut, I turned the water on and began washing.

Freed of any important tasks, my mind started mulling over the dream I'd had. The only vivid symbol, aside from the monster, was the strange design on the shadow man's ring. It had been formed by melding the letter R with the Eye of Horus design. I could not remember having seen it before, but it could have been something floating to the surface from before I lost my memory. I made a mental note to ask Hal about it.

The presence of the monster and its referring to me as its "pet" did not really surprise me, especially after Marit used that term to describe Pygmalion's victims. I was not in control of my current situation and, in many ways, it did feel like others were toying with me. The shadow man was clearly a metaphor for my hidden identity or Coyote. It seemed obvious to me that the message of the dream is that with help, I would be able to put all of this behind me.

I smiled. *Dreams are* never *that simple.*

I turned off the water and dried myself off. Using the electric razor in the shaving kit Roger had sent up, I removed all of my beard except for a narrow band running the line of my jaw to my chin and on up as a moustache. While I knew that would be insufficient to fool anyone who was hunting for me, I liked how it made me look.

Back in the bedroom I scouted around and discovered my clothes had, in fact, been placed in the master bedroom. I matched a blue button-down shirt with my jeans and boots. I wore the vest beneath the shirt and ended up adding a navy blue sweater. Marit kept her apartment cold.

I found Hal waiting for me in the living room. He stood and gave me a warm smile. He wore gray sweats with the Suns logo emblazoned on his chest. "You look better and better each day. How do you feel?"

"More myself?"

Garrett laughed, then joined me as we walked toward the dining area. I saw Juanita had set two places and an open beer stood at each one. "Hope you don't mind. Juanita offered, and I can't remember ever having turned down a meal."

I took the place at the end of the table, facing the windows. "By all means. I'd rather have someone to talk to while I eat."

Hal sat at my left hand. "Marit is out making some arrangements for a little problem Coyote has to deal with. She will be back in a couple of hours to start getting ready for this evening."

I nodded to Juanita as she set a plate in front of me. "This problem, it has to do with the Warriors and the Blood Crips?"

Hal picked up his turkey sandwich and held it in both hands with his elbows on the table. "The Warriors are looking to expand their territory or, at the very least, reclaim some turf they lost two years ago. They are pushing the BCs east, which is backing people right up against Lorica. The BCs don't really want the area the Warriors seem determined to take, so I've been trying to negotiate a solution. It's tough going."

"I imagine." I crunched a potato chip. "Anything new in my situation?"

The black man wiped a little mayonnaise from the corner of his mouth. "Jytte says you're still dead as far as any official sources are concerned. The funds you gave Roger have been pushed aside into an account named Uriah Thompson just to keep the fiction of your death intact. Roger knows, and the change was made before anything showed up on his computer anyway. We have even dummied an inquiry from San Francisco from a relative of yours inquiring about obtaining your remains from the crash."

I thought for a second as he attacked his sandwich again. "Roger works for Coyote?"

Garrett's eyes hardened a bit as he swallowed. "Coyote helped Roger at one point, same as me, same as all of us. So, yes, he reported on you to Jytte." Hal glanced over at where I had left the case I had gotten from the hotel's safe. "And, no, Marit has not told me what is in the case, but she did mention you had it so that Jytte could erase any notice of its having been recovered."

"How did he recruit you?" I lifted my own sandwich to my mouth and bit down.

Garrett smiled in spite of himself. "One night I got a phone call. I had been on the fence about retiring from basketball. I felt the attrition rate on highly paid players was getting a bit high, and the law of averages and I were on a collision course. I had already formed the Sunburst Foundation, but thought I could spend my last year in the NBA plugging it and get more money to fund it.

"This caller, who was calling on my unlisted home phone, identified himself as Coyote. I'd never heard of him before, but he told me that if decided to play that season, I would have my left hand broken in the 10th game of the year. I would come back in time for the drive to the playoffs, but I would die in a seventh and deciding game against the Nicks."

"Hmmm." I nibbled at the edge of my sandwich. "In your shoes, I would have taken him as a madman, or someone being paid frighten me."

"Oh, he did frighten me, but I knew, just listening to him, that he was no threat to me." Hall took a pull on his beer. "Somehow he managed to add my fax number to an owners' network, and I saw enough stuff coming through that I knew the season was being scripted in a way that certain teams would make the playoffs and, while there would be a winner, their victory would be, at best, pyrrhic. The sum and total of the season would be grimly disappointing."

"You opted out."

"Right. I threw myself into the Sunburst Foundation. Anonymous donations filled up my war chest and now even the southside gangs will hold off on making war long enough for me to try to find a more peaceful solution to their problems." He smiled. "Every so often Coyote tips me when something really strange is going down, so I can forestall it. Gang violence is down over 30% from five years ago."

"Now Heinrich and his boys want to make it a growth industry again."

"You got the picture."

I thought about the sniper rifle in my case. "If he becomes an obstacle, let me know."

Hal shook his head. "You and Bat think the same way. The solution to this situation is figuring out what Heinrich wants and then figuring out some way to get it to him without making the other gangs lose face or their temper."

"That is not an easy line to walk, my friend." I picked a brown chip from among the others. "Some folks will listen to reason and," I snapped the chip in half, "some folks need killing."

Hal leaned back in his chair. "That's pretty cold coming from a man who woke up in a body bag."

"Truer than either one of us wants to know." I reached out and plucked the pen he had clipped to the collar of his sweatshirt. Smoothing out my napkin, I drew for him the symbol I'd seen in my dream. "Do you know what this is?"

His hand descended on the paper like a giant brown tarantula and spun it around. "I can't recall seeing it before. What is it?"

I shrugged. "I don't know, I saw it in a dream. You want another beer?" He nodded and I called out, "Juanita, *dos cervezas, por favor.*"

"A lot of people believe in dreams, but not me."

"Why not?"

"Because all I ever see in them are the shots I missed."

Juanita appeared from the kitchen with a beer in each hand. She set the bottles on the table, then saw the napkin. "*El Espectro!*" She quickly crossed herself.

I grabbed the napkin and held it up to her. "You know this?"

She held her hands out to shield it from her eyes. "*Por favor, Señor, por favor.*" She turned and fled.

Hal and I exchanged confused glances. "What did she mean by 'the ghost?'"

Garrett shrugged eloquently. "In Eclipse there have to be about a billion 'ghosts.' I've heard stories that 'real' vampires live in Drac City, or that some weird *brujo* is waging war against demons and devils on a daily basis. I've also heard mutant wolves and other monsters roam the countryside, and after the tinkering with the Palo Verde Nuclear Plant, who knows. As far as I'm concerned, it's all fiction."

I raised an eyebrow. "Which is what others might say about Coyote."

"There's a difference with Coyote."

"And that is?"

"He's real. I've seen him, talked to him. I know when he has gone to war, and I know the people he's helped—through me or through others. Marit is one, for example, and Estefan another."

I crumpled the napkin. "You're right. We'll leave ghosts to fight dreams." I patted my vest. "And I'm content to let Coyote handle reality."

After we finished lunch, Hal headed back down to the Mercado on Level Seven to make arrangements with Alejandro concerning the Lorica reception that evening. I offered to go with him, but he said no. "You're dead right now. Jytte says she can keep you in the grave until tonight, at the very least. Tonight your unanticipated resurrection might shake some folks, and that will help us unravel the whole thing."

"Works for me." I shook his hand. "One last thing, has there been any word on Nero Loring?"

"None."

I didn't let his hand go. "Was Coyote involved in getting him free of his daughter and corporation?"

Hal tightened his grip a little. "If he was, he did not involve me in it."

We broke our grip by mutual assent, and Hal retreated into the transversor. I saw by the red readout of a digital clock that it was already 1 p.m. I had no idea when Marit would return or when the reception was, so I wandered down to her media room, found a remote control and started a survey of the television landscape.

Television, despite having 178 channels available, proved more desolate than South Mountain's Desert Preserve. Aside from premium channels that started racking up special charges when I flitted across them— as denoted by the total accumulating in a small LCD panel down in the corner—the vast majority of stations were only transmitting in black and white. With a wall-mounted HDLCD unit from Sony like the one Marit had, that was the rough equivalent of using a professional Cuisinart to process dried out dog food. I expected television to be banal, but having one whole channel devoted to rebroadcasts of 40-year-old Soviet grain harvest films was a bit excessive. Still, I did imagine they looked very good on the Soviet sets that most folks owned.

The city's public-access channel did provide a bit of insight into the nature of Phoenix. Programs on it alternated between promotional videos that featured an incredibly optimistic artist's rendition of what Phoenix would look like in five years, and utterly bizarre fare in five- and 10-minute bites that reflected the sharp split between City Center and Eclipse. Chiropractors and naturopaths diagnosed problems and offered back adjustments for those patients who would press their backs against the screen. Psychics warned of hideous calamities and conspiracies that no one but they knew about. Members of every bughouse club from Arizonans for the Preservation of the Black Scorpion to the Phoenix Skeptics did their bit to proselytize their causes, filling the airwaves with an unending stream of contradictory and confusing "facts."

"The city could call this channel the good, the bad and the ugly," I muttered as Heinrich's face appeared on screen.

His program was called "People of Purity." In it he read report after report of crimes committed by people of color while videotape copied from news reports played in the background. At the end, while a video of him and his "honor guard" kicking the life out of a black youth played, he said, "People of Phoenix, come to us. Take back your city. The phoenix is destined to rise to greatness from the ashes. Mud people are the ashes of humanity. Join us, and reclaim your heritage!"

Unconsciously I sighted down my index finger and brought my thumb forward like the hammer falling on my Krait. "Some day, Heinrich."

Behind me I heard clapping. I spun around in the capsule chair and saw Marit standing in the doorway. "I didn't hear you come in."

"This room is soundproofed. I like your taste in targets. Getting to know your foe?"

I shrugged. "Hal doesn't think a 180-grain bullet whizzing along at 3000 or so feet per second would improve Heinrich's disposition, so no hunting permit." I turned my left wrist over and looked at my watch. "It's six now. What time does the party start?

"Depends." She gathered her hair back into a ponytail and fastened it with an elastic band. "I'm going to start getting ready as things officially kick off at 7:30. We won't arrive until an hour after that, but why rush? I'm taking a shower. Want to scrub my back?"

The television started showing a Phoenix Skeptics tape proving bodies found in the desert definitely were *not* trolls. "Garbage in, garbage out." I hit a button on the remote control, and the screen went black. "After watching all that stuff, I definitely need a bath. Lead on, m'lady."

Two hours later I stared at my image in a trio of full length mirrors. I wore black shoes and socks, black slacks with creases sharp enough to shave with and a heavily starched white shirt with onyx studs and cufflinks. At the collar I wore a large, silvery, rectangular-cut hematite stud and no tie. The collar itself, which had no lapels, pressed uncomfortably against my Adam's apple.

"I feel like a wolf in priest's clothing."

Marit glanced up from her vanity table and looked at my reflection in her mirror. "Pleased to meet you, Father Caine. Would you care to minister to my spiritual needs later?"

I gave her a smile. "You say that only because I look neither pious or holy."

"Oh, I'd say you look like a holy terror to me."

"You're not the one I need to impress tonight."

"Coming back from the grave, you'll look like an *un*holy terror to them."

"Amen." I slipped on the Bianchi holster and settled the blued Krait beneath my left armpit.

Mascara brush in hand, she paused. "Do you think that is necessary?"

"I hope not, but you know the saying: 'Praise God, but pass the ammunition.'" I pulled my jacket off the hanger in the closet. "Will they let me keep it?"

"Normally, no, but I trained with the guy heading up the security detail on this reception. I told him I was bringing a bodyguard along. He'll let you pass."

"Good."

I pulled the jacket on and smiled broadly. Roger had put together a jacket that did triple duty. It was appropriate for the gathering, stylish enough to get noticed, but not weird enough to be laughed at—and it concealed the gun perfectly. As I had seen in his drawing, he started from a basic waist-cut jacket, then had flipped over and extended the left lapel of it so it attached on a diagonal that ran from my right shoulder to just past the midline at my waist. In effect I had a black asymmetrical double-breasted jacket with enough room in the left flank to mask the presence of my gun. Furthermore, because Roger had left a gap in the velcro that closed the jacket, I could reach inside with my right hand and draw the Krait without being forced to open the suitcoat at all.

I tugged at the waist and looked at myself in the mirror. The slight dip in the jacket's fabric at my throat left the hematite visible. The jacket hung perfectly and felt comfortable on me. Even the trace of beard on my jaw fit with the image the clothes had created, that being someone who could quite possibly be as dangerous as I was afraid I might be.

Marit walked up behind me and kissed my right ear. "If I tell people you're a priest, you'll have women wanting to confess and convert all evening."

I winked at her reflection. "Tell them I take my vow of celibacy seriously."

"Ha! Fuel thrown on the fire, that would be." Her darkened eyes narrowed. "That tale might even attract the attention of the Witch herself."

"Nerys Loring?"

Marit's nostrils flared. "She Who Would Eat Her Own Young." She shook her head. "I don't even want to think about her right now." Taking two steps back, she held her hands out. "Well, tell me how beautiful I look."

Turning around, I did nothing to hide my look of pleasure. Marit wore a strapless crimson leather minidress which clung to her somewhat tighter than oxygen clings to hydrogen in water molecules. Her lipstick matched her dress, as did the pair of two-inch stiletto heels on her feet. She bent over to smooth her white stockings, then innocently glanced up to see if the sight of long legs had affected me in the desired manner.

I cleared my throat. "Do that at the party, and I'll be forced to shoot."

She giggled and straightened up. She added a ruby pendant and matching earrings to her outfit, then pulled on a black jacket that had been cut high enough to reveal the lower edges of her breasts. "We're a pair. I'm dressed to stun, and you're dressed to kill."

To get to the party we took the transversor to the elevator, then descended to Level Nine. From there we walked to the Civic Center Tower and boarded an express elevator to the 45th floor. Because of the tower's height, the elevator shafts could not run all the way up to the top and, under normal circumstances, our car would have moved sideways into another shaft to take us the rest of the way up to the party.

The circumstances surrounding the Lorica Industries Reception, however, were nothing even close to normal. We stopped at 45, and the doors opened slowly. Bright video lights blasted into the box and bleached all but the brightest color from us. I raised my hand to shield my eyes, but Marit reacted to the light like a plant seeking the sun.

Flash strobes went off like explosions in an air raid and left tracer-like afterimages on my eyes. People in the crowd called Marit's name, and she turned toward their voices, smiling like a fox eluding hunters. Lorica security guards cleared a path for her through the press of reporters, and I followed in her wake. A reporter asked who I was, but Marit waved the question off with casual disregard.

A security man guided us to a short corridor that led to an express elevator to the top of the tower. Marit preceded me through a metal detector, then turned and spoke to the security force lieutenant seated at the desk beside her. "Hi, Charlie. This is Günter, my bodyguard. I told Captain Williams about him."

The white-haired older man stood and motioned for me to step around the barricade. I did so and opened my jacket. He reached in and pulled the Krait from the holster. Hitting the thumb release, he slid the clip free, then worked the slide and popped the live shell out into his hand.

"I like the Krait, Mr. Günter." He returned to his desk and opened a drawer. He pulled out a fluorescent orange stop-tab and inserted it into the chamber. He closed the gun on it, leaving an orange tab protruding from the open breech about a quarter of an inch. He shoved the clip home, then returned the pistol to me. "Standard procedure. We don't want personal security shooting first. If you see anything strange, you report it to one of us, got it?"

"Got it." I made my voice sound like that of someone I could imagine being named Günter. "Could I have my bullet as well?"

The old man nodded. "Sure."

He tossed it to me, and I put it in my pocket. Closing my jacket, I smiled at him, then followed Marit to the express elevator. A white-gloved attendant pushed the button, and we watched as the numbers in the LED window above the doors counted down from 90.

I jerked my head back in the direction of the other elevators. "Quite a zoo there."

Marit smiled and gave my right forearm a squeeze. "Local press. They want gossip and stars to brighten their newscasts. Local celebrity stuff always goes down well with the folks in Eclipse. It lets them dream about getting to City Center at some time in their lives, I guess. I know that's what I used to fantasize about when I lived there."

The elevator arrived, and we stepped into it. The attendant, a black woman, smiled politely and turned the key that sent the box skyward. We did not speak as we ascended and, as we sailed past Floor 80, Marit did a last minute check of her makeup in the elevator's mirrored walls. "Ready if you are."

The doors opened, and I braced myself for another light show, but none materialized. We stepped into a small lobby that looked perfectly normal, even if the lights were a bit dimmer than normal in commerce. Off to our right, double doors stood open into a reception room that actually occupied both the 90th and 91st floors of the Civic Center tower. The room's floor lay a half level below the lobby and an upper balcony overhung the entrance. The lights, both crystal chandeliers and wall mounted, art deco lamps, were tuned down to low intensity so the room's light would not cause too much in the way of reflections on the exterior glass walls.

As I moved from the lobby to the reception area I saw
the room was, in fact, a doughnut that revolved around
in a slow, almost imperceptible counterclockwise motion. The core of the 91st floor was greater in diameter
than the lobby below it, providing the overhang. I smiled
as I noticed a slight drift in the crowd in a direction
opposite the motion of the room. Without thinking,
people were desperately trying to maintain their position
relative to the landmarks outside.

The windows showed a truly wonderful panorama of
Phoenix. The entrance pointed east toward the Lorica
Citadel. The rising full moon backlit the corporate towers
and made the maglev train tracks look like buttresses on
the exterior of an old cathedral. Blinking red and blue
lights on top of the towers matched the winking of the
stars in the night sky and, in the background, I saw the
distant lights of a plane coming in for landing at the
regional airport southeast of the city.

What surprised me the most was how well the black
panels roofing over Eclipse reflected the stars and
moonlight. As far as the stars were concerned, the
photovoltaic cells could have been a placid ocean and,
without my feet planted firmly on the floor, I would have
had a hard time telling exactly which way was up. The
moonlight—twin slivers outlining the Lorica silhouette—
collected in sharp lines at the seams, but looked no
different than it might have on a dark sea.

Marit stepped into the reception room, and immediately a number of people called her name. She descended into the throng, kissing cheeks or hugging
people. Some of the men held her closer and longer than
she might have liked, and for those she really detested,
she put up a mock protest that immediately darkened
the expression on the face of the man's date.

Before I could trail after her, a man in a midnight blue
suit cut me off. "I'm Captain Williams, Brad Williams."

"Günter."

"Günter, good." He looked over at Marit and smiled. "Look, these are the ground rules: Don't speak unless spoken to. If you spot trouble, you report it to me. If Marit looks like she's trapped in a boring conversation or a situation that is getting ugly, walk over and tell her she has a call. If something weird *does* go down, leave the shooting to us. If you find you have to *extricate* Marit from a situation, try not to kill any of the guests."

"Not a problem."

"Good. No drinking for you, but help yourself to food."

"Thanks." I drifted into the room, leaving him to pick off the next bodyguard and brief him. I spotted Marit working her way around to the right, still in greeting mode. Descending another step, I gave the arc I could see I quick look to spot any potential problems and saw none. Knowing I would not feel secure until I had done a full circuit of the room, I descended the rest of the way to the floor and headed off on the trail Marit had blazed.

The reception itself, while being sponsored and hosted by Lorica Industries, was for the Make-A-Wish Foundation. At a number of places around the room, and on the interior, nonrotating wall, paintings and sculptures had been set up with a small tote board beside each. A Lorica employee stood next to each work and spoke about it and the artist who had created it. I also noticed them accepting small pieces of paper from people and, after reading them, punching numbers in on a small keypad. On the toteboard, beside the pieces, an LCD display flashed up the current bid in what appeared to be a low-key silent auction.

The guests appeared to represent the upper crust of Phoenix society. I easily identified a white-haired, aristocratic-looking man as Darius MacNeal, the man who had created the Build-more Corporation, because of the ads I'd seen on television earlier in the day. I could not, however, place a name on the two young women clinging to his arms, though judging by age, I imagined they had to be his granddaughters. He laughed uproariously at the joke Phoenix's boy-mayor told him, then showed how affectionate his family was by nuzzling one woman's long neck.

Waiters and waitresses wandered throughout the gathering bearing trays of drinks and hors d'oeuvres. I passed on placing a drink order, but did indulge in food when a woman carrying a tray of sushi came within striking range. The *tekka-maki* tasted good enough that I wondered if Osome was doing the catering.

Marit came back for me and linked her arm in mine. "Incoming. You'll want to see this performance, I'm certain."

Without saying another word, she dragged me halfway around the room until I got to where a broad stairway descended from the 91st floor suite to the reception room. We took up a position just upstream of the bottom of the stairs and slowly drifted down toward them. Off to our right I spotted Alejandro, but before I could point him out to Marit, Nerys Loring made her appearance at the top of the stairs.

My instant assessment of her was that she was a strikingly handsome woman. She looked to be in her mid-forties and had a mature confidence in herself that made her actively seductive. She wore her black hair cut to hang just above her shoulders and to frame her strong face. Her dark eyes and brows combined with her incarnadine lipstick to make her face seem almost vampire pale. The bodice of her black, strapless gown sparkled with a decidedly modest number of sequins and hugged her hourglass figure in a most flattering manner. The velvet skirts flared out to hide her feet, yet she did not appear the least bit inconvenienced as she descended the stairs. A string of pearls encircled her throat and a diamond ring glittered from her right hand as she maintained her balance through feather-light finger-contact with the bannister.

She smiled with the pleasure you might expect to see on the face of a potentate being welcomed by groveling peasants. She knew she deserved the homage, but she also welcomed it. Part of me resented her basking in our attention, but I knew that was like the sun resenting the beauty of a flower it nourished. Here was a woman who was attractive, smart and powerful—a nasty and very erotic combination—and she clearly knew that she could use one or all of those assets to get her anything she wanted.

As she reached the same level as the rest of us, people whispered greetings almost reverently. Nerys paid them scant or no attention and headed straight out into the room. I felt Marit pull herself up to her full height and turn her smile on full force as Lorica's CEO homed in on her. She braced herself for what might, in light of her history with Lorica, be a very nasty encounter.

Nerys dismissed Marit with a casual glance, then offered her hand to me. "We've not been formally introduced. I am Nerys Loring." She enfolded my hand in a firm grip and gave me a smile that threatened to swallow me up. "Had I known you were in Phoenix, Mr. Caine, I would have invited you to our party myself."

Even given twice the warning I had, the late Shakespearean actor Mel Gibson could not have covered his surprise at her greeting. I saw my surprise reflected in her eyes, and her grip tightened ever so slightly. I forced a smile and let blood flush my cheeks. I met her black stare, then looked down.

"Forgive me, Ms. Loring. I would have let you know, but I knew you were quite occupied with business." I reforged eye contact. "I also felt it would have been presumptuous of me to wheedle an invitation out of you. Ms. Fisk asked me to accompany her, so I felt this was the easiest solution to the situation."

"Ah, Marit," Nerys said without looking in her direction.

"You are looking quite...fit, Nerys," Marit returned. She leaned forward and kissed me on the cheek. "Darling, I think I'm going to bid on a picture for my place. I'll be back."

She retreated, and Nerys let a satisfied grin twist up the corners of her mouth. "You are an interesting man, Mr. Caine. I understand two of my employees left Lorica because of you, yesterday."

What game are you playing? "Independent contractors, they must have been. They were clumsy and stupid, so I assumed they could not have been yours. I don't like being spied upon."

She slipped her arm through mine, leeching away the warmth lingering from Marit. "I prefer jobs to be supervised. I think of it as quality assurance."

With forewarning, I was able to conceal my pleasure at her admission that I had been hired to perform a job. Given the equipment I found, and the amount of money

I had been given, I felt certain I'd been hired to kill someone. If what Natch Feral had said was true, that Nerys had been looking for her father after a snatch had been put on him two months ago, I thought chances were good that he might have been my target.

I kept a plastic smile on my face as we began to stroll through the party, but let an edge drop into my voice. "If you hire a specialist to do a job, what standards can you use to judge his performance?"

"Please, tell me, Mr. Caine."

"End product." I looked up and out the window. "I think you'll find your problem has just dropped off the edge of the earth."

She smiled appreciatively, but kept a note of caution in her voice. "The world is round, Mr. Caine."

"Only to those who don't know how to find the corners." I patted her hand and gently disengaged it from my arm. "I should not monopolize your time, for you have many other guests."

"You are an interesting man, Mr. Caine. I had not expected to actually meet you. If not for the men who recently left my employ, I would not even know what you looked like." Her eyes narrowed as she looked me up and down. "The cost of a professional specialist is very high."

"But the cost of an amateur is yet higher. Don't worry, your money was well spent."

"As I expected, based on Fiddleback's excellent recommendation." She opened her hands and encompassed the entire party. "Please, enjoy yourself—despite your unfortunate choice of companion—and if you choose to bid on anything, I would find myself in debt to your generosity."

I brought her right hand to my lips and kissed it gently. "It has been my pleasure to be of service to you."

She answered with an elevated eyebrow, then she withdrew and quickly greeted those individuals she had snubbed when she saw me. Their resentment melted like wax beneath a blowtorch, or their spirit died beneath one of her withering stares. Within 10 seconds she had vanished from sight and part of me wondered if she had been there at all.

"La Bruja took to you like a vampire to a hemophiliac." Alejandro sipped a slender glass of champagne. "Did she say anything useful?"

My eyes half shut as I concentrated. "Whatever I was here to do, it was because she was paying the freight. She'd put the two guys from Ernesto's on me, but she made no apologies for their having tried to kill me. I wonder if they weren't working for another faction within Lorica as well?"

"I don't know." He fingered the buttons on his double-breasted, navy blue pinstriped suit jacket. "I do know there is still some factional fighting within Lorica. There have been a couple of purges."

"Is there any chance you can find folks who knew her father before the ouster? Long-time aides who got booted after he was gone?"

The art dealer nodded. "That's easily doable, I should think. Some of them even live in City Center."

"Any in Eclipse?"

"I can find out."

"Excuse me, Mr. Higuera?" A middle-aged woman touched Alejandro on the right sleeve.

He turned and smiled broadly at her. "Mrs. Rosson, what can I do for you?"

She smiled and mouthed the word "Hello" to me, then spoke to Alejandro. "I don't recall ever seeing other surrealist work by Elizabeth Turner in your gallery before, but the piece being auctioned here is being offered by you. Is she another one of your exclusive discoveries?"

Alejandro nodded conspiratorially to her. "I found her two months ago. She's been doing these pieces for years and just sticking them away. I've convinced her to part with some of them."

Mrs. Rosson smiled sheepishly. "I must confess the piece she has here is already too much for me, but I would be interested in other examples of her work. Shall I call on your shop tomorrow?"

Alejandro nodded solemnly. "I have two other pieces I've not yet framed. I will look forward to your visit." As she walked away, he looked back at me. "Sorry, that pays the rent. Anything else from Loring?"

"She used the word 'Fiddleback' as if it were a code-name for someone. Sound any buzzers?"

"No, I'm afraid not."

"Maybe it will with some of those ex-employees, if you can find any."

"We can hope."

Marit came walking over and restaked her claim to my left arm. She wore a big grin on her face, and I sensed her mood had shifted greatly since she departed. "This is wonderful!"

"Yes?"

"There is the most ghastly piece over there—no offense, Alejandro—called 'With a Not in my Stomach,' by Elizabeth Turner. It's, well, it's…"

Alejandro pointed toward the place where the painting had been set up. "You have to see this thing to believe it."

Marit nodded in agreement, so the three of us cut through the crowd to look at this picture. It was a painting of a human form, but it was done in necrotic flesh tones with hints of the green-gray of dead skin. The figure's flesh appeared to be more rubber than skin and had been tightly wrapped up into a ball at the center of the piece. The contorted body's face was hidden in shadows, but it had a mouth, complete with clenched teeth, situated at the figure's right heel.

I shivered. It was truly a horrible vision, yet I could

sympathize with it because I saw myself in it. The hidden face was my lost identity, and all that it would take to unlock the mouth to spout the truth would be a some trigger memory. The flesh being sloughed off was how I felt about trying to shed whatever I had been. Nerys Loring clearly felt she had hired me as an assassin to kill her father, and I might have actually come to do that, but I had no desire to be a murderer.

"It is definitely an expressive piece," I offered.

Alejandro smiled. "It spoke to me when I saw it. Hideous image, but excellent technique and command of anatomy."

"But could you live with it in your house?" I asked him.

He shook his head, and Marit giggled. "That's what is so delicious." She herded us back away from the piece before she said anything more. "I think it is morbid and creepy, but I've placed a bid on it. Nerys immediately topped my bid, so now I have a little war going on with her. She'll win, but it will cost her."

I raised an eyebrow. "How do you know she isn't just bidding you up to stick you with the painting?"

Our male companion shook his head. "Nerys never loses, except, perhaps, when her father overrode her and let Marit out of her 'noncompetition' clause in her contract. That is the soul of their animosity. She will never give in."

"Which means she'll have that thing to look at for the rest of her life," Marit hissed.

Up on the 91st floor balcony, I saw Nerys staring down at the painting, She nodded slightly and a new bid went up on the tote board. With that I saw a satisfaction on her face, but I knew it came from more than her having topped Marit's latest bid.

She, too, identified with the painting and, I felt certain, would enjoy staring at it for hours on end.

The next morning, when the elevator doors opened, I thought certain I had descended into hell. The heat hit me with the force of a punch. I stepped out into it, hoping, expecting that I would pass back into another cool zone, but I did not. The blazing heat remained constant and, as I breathed in through my nose, I felt the air cauterize my nasal passages.

Natch Feral crossed the street. "Welcome back to reality, Caine-man."

"Good evening…," I started to say to her, but I realized it was noon. "I mean…"

"Save it. It's always night down here in Eclipse." She turned and walked away, silently willing me to follow her. "I think we have a line on a dude you'll want to jaw with. Gotta get Bat first, though."

I nodded at her back and quickly caught up with her. At the party Nerys Loring made short work of Marit's bidding war, and Marit, bloodied but unbeaten, made a great show of retreating. Because Nerys had spoken with me for a short but visible amount of time, Marit nibbled on my ear as we left, suggesting Nerys might have won a battle, but the war had yet to be concluded.

We returned to her home, and she apologized most eloquently for having used me so shamelessly to get back at Nerys.

I awoke without remembering any dreams and left Marit to her well deserved rest. In her media room I punched up the Municipal Library's online index service and sought any information I could find on "Fiddleback." The best thing I got was a very authoritative article on the brown recluse spider, which is also known by the name

Fiddleback. While they *are* present in Phoenix, the black widow is much more prevalent, and fiddlebacks are treated pretty much like myths.

Like Coyote.

By 10 a.m., Alejandro called and said he had worked with Jytte to come up with a list of people who fit the parameters of Lorica old guard being retired when Nero Loring was Leared by his daughter. He said the majority of them were in retirement villas around the state, with their bills and "care" paid for by Lorica. He left no doubt in my mind that they were being held by Nerys until any information they had concerning the company had lost its market value.

He did point out that Jytte had uncovered the name of a man who had been with Lorica for as long as the company had been around. Phil Costapain was a black man who had worked as a janitor for his full tenure at Lorica. The reason she added him to the list was because he was Nero Loring's first employee and Nero himself had attended the man's retirement dinner. She noted the two of them always took their vacations at the same time and Alejandro said she thought they might have been very good at keeping their friendship quiet.

"Natch, do you really think you know where Costapain lives?"

She nodded. "I do, but he's real scared of something. Word's been spread that he's dead."

"Dead?"

She shrugged. "There's dead and there's D-E-A-D, Caine-man. Costapain doesn't want folks finding him, so outsiders hear he's dead. I just happen to know better." She glanced at the street, then nimbly darted between the cars. On the other side, she looked back at me and shook her head.

I waited for a bit more survivable break in traffic, then joined her on the sidewalk in front of a concrete bunkerish building. "I'm dying in this windbreaker and jeans. How can you be wearing so much?"

Another shrug elevated and dropped the padded shoulders of her oversized leather jacket. Beneath it she wore a loose striped shirt and beneath that a dark green leotard. Her jeans had been expertly slashed in parallel lines from hip to ankle, revealing black Spandex-clad legs. Her white high-tops looked new and the laces certainly had never been tied.

"Man, I've lived down here all my life. This is only the end of June. It don't get hot for another month. Damned slush duck." She jerked her head toward the bunker door. "C'mon, in here."

I eyed the building with suspicion. "Where is 'here?'"

"Here is 'The Trench.'" Natch jammed her hands in her pockets and headed for the door. "Bat works here."

That little amount of information made me very dubious about the place, and stepping through the door confirmed everything I had imagined, and more. Because The Trench lacked sufficient light, the first thing I noticed about it was the reek of sweat and smoke and blood and beer. Human bodies huddled in shadows, slumped in chairs as if they'd been lashed to them by the shoulders and had their spines removed. The Du Drop Inn was to this place what the Lorica reception had been to my encounter with the Reapers.

Realizing my eyes would only adjust to the gloom in geological time, I followed Natch into The Trench by feel. I caught, in the backlight of a cash register, a glimpse of a bar running the length of the left wall. Avoiding waitresses who looked gorgeous except in the eyes, we plunged deeper into The Trench until we approached what looked like, to me, to be a line of people facing the absolute blackness of the back wall.

Then the lights in The Trench went on.

The bar had taken its name from its most interesting

aspect. In the back a pit had been dug that bottomed out about 20 feet below the level of the floor. The sides had been carved into narrow terraces, each being fitted with a railing that had little holders for plastic cups of beer. At either end, up at floor level, catwalks extended over pit level corridors to let the servers get from the bar to the patrons watching the pit.

The rectangular pit had been fitted with boards and plexiglass walls that looked to me to have been salvaged from some hockey rink. Where the glass had been shattered, chicken wire or strips of chain-link fencing replaced it up to the level of the bar's floor. Above that, secured to the bar's ceiling, more chain-link fencing formed a dome that made the pit a world of its own.

Natch led me along the catwalk on the right side, and a bouncer at the top of the stairs let the two of us past. We descended to the level of the floor and stood in the corridor. Through the blood-streaked plexiglass at the end of the pit, I saw Bat turn and face the last two of his opponents.

Bat had looked big when I'd met him two days ago, but in the center of the pit he looked herculean. Blood dripped from his bare chest and washed over his bare legs, but I knew it was not his. His muscles tensed as one man came in and his whole body twisted as he smashed a pile-driver right hook into the man ribs. I winced when I heard something pop, then cringed as Bat's left fist arced in and nearly twisted the man's head off with a solid punch.

The last man had, at one time, been trained as a martial artist. He flew through the air aiming a kick at Bat's head. Bat, ducked his head out of the way, but held his left forearm up to split the flying man's legs. The collision of bone with groin involuntarily doubled over a number of the spectators and brought an agonized screech from the fighter. But before he could fall to the ground, Bat's right hand closed on bunched muscles at the man's spine, then he took a run at the wall and slammed the man against the plexiglass.

Then he pulled him back and did it again and again and again. When the man hung like a limp rag in his hands, he tossed him aside and began to look around the pit for another victim. The other four men hastened their belly crawls to the door at the far arena end, and Bat encouraged them with brutal kicks. With a wicked smile on his face, he broke the outstretched arm of one man reaching for the doorway, then laughed loudly as the man begged for mercy.

I looked at Natch, and she shrugged. "Amateur night. It's never pretty."

Bat walked back to where the martial artist lay. He picked him up by the waistband of his pants, then dragged him face first through the dirt before tossing him out the arena door like a sack of garbage. Then, alone in the arena, he raised his hands in triumph. Half the crowd roared in his favor, but other people taunted him and threw plastic cups of beer at him. They splashed against the wire to mix with the blood and the dirt in the arena, but left Bat untouched.

As Bat turned to soak in the adulation of the crowd, I saw his eyes. He watched the people surrounding him like a wolf studying a flock of sheep. They were prey to him, and he'd clearly not had his fill in breaking the five who had faced him. Furthermore, and by far the most chilling of my observations, I knew he was not in the pit for the money or the praise or the need to prove himself at the top of the food chain.

He fought because he loved inflicting pain on others.

The lights dimmed again, and Bat left the arena. In the half-light I saw the steel mask of cruelty on his face soften when he saw Natch. It flashed back on his face as he looked over at me, and in that flash of his dark eyes I knew I had an open invitation to fight him any time I wanted.

I shook my head. "If I want a sanity trial, I'll have it in a court of law."

Natch looked confused for a moment, then stepped back beyond the catwalk and opened a door into a locker room. Bat cut immediately to a shower cubicle in which a half-dozen nozzles hit him with harsh spray from various angles. The mud melted off, and the blood ran down the drain. Bat shut off the water, shook his head to flick water from his hair, then stepped out of the shower and went for a locker.

Natch tossed him a towel that had probably once been fleecy and white. Bat doffed his boxing trunks and dried himself off, though he seemed more interested in any blood the towel absorbed than he did getting dry. That made sense in that, in the heat, evaporation would draw the water off quickly enough and summon sweat to replace it.

The towel came away clean, but Bat looked to have a nasty bruise developing on his left shoulder. He sat on the bench beside his locker and opened the door. Whereas I expected to see the sort of pin-up pictures decorating other open lockers, inside Bat's door I saw a drawing of a winged angel bearing a spear, driving a demon off a cloud. Bat touched the picture reverently with his right hand, then crossed himself.

He looked over at me. "Ask."

I frowned. "Ask?"

"What do you want to know about me?" He pulled on some underwear. "Get it over with."

"Okay. Why 'Bat?'"

He shrugged, but Natch answered for him. "His real name is Chwalibog Kabat. It's Polish—his parents came over just before Eastern Europe opened up."

"Bat is easier, and folks don't get it wrong." I nodded, understanding why folks would not even want to try to pronounce his name and risk offending him. His background also made understanding the angel picture easier. "St. Michael?"

Bat nodded.

The patron saint of warriors. Being Polish meant he was probably raised Catholic, and that created a rather strange paradox. Here was a Christian who followed the teachings of the Prince of Peace, yet he worked as a pit fighter because he *loved* hurting people. Thinking back on what I'd seen in the pit, I had no doubt that whoever his confessor was, that priest got hazard duty pay, and Bat got penance that didn't quit.

"One last question: How are you and Coyote connected?"

Bat stood and tucked a T-shirt into his jeans. "I used to fight on the professional circuit. A promoter kidnapped a friend to get me to throw a fight. Coyote freed the hostage, and the promoter died when my opponent flew from the ring and crushed him in his seat."

Natch, perched on the end of the bench, drew her legs up and hugged them to her chest. "After that fight, a Lorica janitor thanked Bat for winning. He'd bet a lot of money on him—money he needed for his wife's medical treatments. She ended up dying anyway, but in a gang drive-by shooting, not from her disease."

I folded my arms across my chest. "That janitor was Phil Costapain, which is why you're coming with us. Costapain trusts you?"

Bat gave me a single nod as he closed his locker. He didn't lock it, but just looking at him told me why he didn't have to. He held out his right arm, Natch grabbed hold, and he lifted her to her feet in one smooth motion. They both smiled at each other, then headed off into The Trench.

I followed, but until we got to the street, I don't think they noticed.

Phil Costapain had managed to choose a hiding place that would have kept him safe from the best trackers in the world. Aside from being thought dead, he had the advantage of living in an area where two mobile home parks had mated and metastasized to all the neighboring areas, including what had once been the Greenwood Memorial Cemetery Park. Interstate 10 thundered through the middle of the community and, just beyond it, twisted through the interchange known as the Stack, but had no real effect on Boxton.

Getting there proved less difficult than I imagined when I learned neither Natch or Bat had a car. We hopped a gypsy bus that angled us across the west side of Phoenix as it dropped folks off and stopped for other riders flagging it down. Big and painted with colors that glowed in the gloom of Eclipse, it lumbered through the grimy streets like a beetle with elephantitis.

The three of us took up a position behind the driver. As Bat boarded, he paid his fare, then stood and stared down at some drugged-out wastrel sprawled across a bench. The guy looked up and saw that his current trip had just veered into the land of bad vibes. Bat waited for him to clear out, then he let Natch and an old black woman sit down.

The guys toward the back looked nasty enough for me to think we might have gotten on a Department of Corrections bus by mistake. Bat grabbed the overhead rail and glared at our fellow riders, which inspired most of them to get off or hang loose in the very rear of our transport. I ended up standing right behind the driver, trying to give the old woman sitting in Bat's shadow a reassuring smile.

The bus' dim headlights hid more than they revealed, but they gave me a strong impression of the nightmare that made up chunks of Eclipse. Buildings that had once been useful now lay in total disrepair. Whole blocks looked like they had been abandoned and had trash barricades surrounding them. Oddly enough, the barricades looked as if they had been put up to keep things *in* that section instead of out. Even more strange was the lack of children playing on or around those barricades.

Because the streetlights in this area of town had been pulled down, shot out or rewired to provide power for squatters living near them, small bonfires had been lit to illuminate the area. The lunacy of starting fires on hot desert days was further compounded by the clouds of oily smoke that hung low, trapped beneath the Eclipse panels. Some of the squatter's nests built on the underside of the panels looked like soot-smudged tumors hanging in place. They could not have been habitable in any serious sense of the word, yet blank faces looked down at us from above regardless.

A passenger jostled me when he came aboard, and I felt my billfold disappear from my back pocket. Before he squeezed past Bat, I drew the Krait and poked him in the back of the head with it. "As long as you have my wallet, you might as well take this, too. You want it in pieces?"

The man swallowed hard, then turned and offered me a picket-fence smile. "Sorry, I'm trying to reform. Really." He held my wallet up, and I took it from him.

He tried to make his way by Bat, but Bat stopped him and grabbed his right hand. He held it up and spread the fingers out by pressing it against his left hand. "You gotta pay the toll."

"Toll?"

"Toll?" Bat's face lost all emotion and his eyes darkened. "Which is your favorite finger?"

"W-what?"

"Wrong answer." Bat's muscles bunched in his shoulder and arm as he jerked the man into the air by his wrist. He smashed the man's hand into the bus's roof, and the fingers broke like dry spaghetti. "There, now you're reformed."

The man screamed, but the mere threat of a cuff silenced him. He clutched his broken hand to his chest and stumbled back, being jostled from seat to seat by the bus's motion and the angry riders he leaned against. Finally, in the back, he met a gang who forced him to "high-five" them with his broken hand before they put him into a seat.

"Thanks, I think."

Bat nodded. "Quick. Good."

I sensed some respect in his voice for how smoothly and swiftly I'd reacted, and that pleased me. Still, I found it disquieting that I felt good about respect from a man who had so casually broken the hand of a man who had done nothing to him. Yet, even as I examined that circumstance, I recalled his religious bent and realized he had only inflicted on the man a punishment for his sin of theft. Within his world, he was being amazingly consistent, and I imagined he would even confess to what he had done here, adding to his burden so he could be absolved of it.

The bus stopped a block from the edge of our destination. Natch preceded me off the bus and crossed the street to where a group of four youths loitered on the corner watching little kids play kick-ball. The youths all wore jackets that had a black disk sewn on the back, and the words "The Plattermen" embroidered beneath it. When they saw her they started preening and moving like lazy snakes. They eyed me suspiciously, trying to figure if I was undercover for Scorpion Security or a mark

to be taken. Bat stepped from the bus, and they sharp-
ened up considerably.

Natch went through an elaborate ritual of knocking
fists, slapping hands and pointing with one of the youths,
then invited me over. "Caine-man, this is Zinger. He was
maxin' in Florence, then he beat the bricks and crawled
back under the Nixrock."

Zinger, a long, lean and languorous black youth kept
his hands in the pockets of his blue jacket. "Caine. Is that
like in *candy* cane?"

I shrugged. "I'm not bent, and it'll take more than you
to lick me, so I'd say not. It's Caine."

"Like the killer," Bat added quietly.

Zinger looked me up and down, then dismissed me
with a sneer. "What chu want, Natch?"

"Paying our respects to the dead."

The youth thought for a second, then nodded slowly.
He turned to a confederate wearing a red bandana over
his head. "Buc will take you."

"Gratz."

Zinger grabbed Natch's shoulder. "If anything happens..."

Like a striking snake, Bat snagged Zinger's wrist and
squeezed until the hand opened like a flower. Natch
turned and stroked Bat's free arm. "It's okay, Bat, no
harm done."

"Not yet." Bat smiled in a most horrifying way,
displaying strong, sharp white teeth. "You were in a
crack, Zinger." He released his hand. "She got you out."

The street boss pulled his hand back but refused to
show it had hurt at all. "Girl, you gotta get that man some
lithium or sumthin'. He needs to chill. Buc, go."

Buc, smaller and stockier than Zinger, walked all
loose and open like he'd been put together with rubber
bands instead of muscles. He didn't say anything and
sauntered along as if he wasn't connected to us in any

way. Other folks on the street called out to him, and he winked or hissed or hooted at them, but never said anything I could decipher as words.

Boxton lived up to its name. Mobile homes and more conventional buildings were stacked up in crenelated clusters that brushed the underside of Frozen Shade at its highest points. Rubbish-choked alleys ran between the trailers, turning Boxton into a rat's warren of twisting trails and dead ends. In the places where the pathways were wide enough for, say, a Scorpion Security vehicle to pass between buildings, the paths themselves doubled back constantly. It took no genius to see the vehicle would be slowed to a crawl and left very vulnerable to antivehicle rockets or automatic weapons fire.

Buc led us into one trailer at the bottom of a pyramid. We entered without knocking and Buc never even acknowledged the family huddled toward the rear of the building. I only saw them in the light of a boxy television, and the slack-jawed look of stupification on their faces led me to believe they never saw any of us. Grandfather, sitting in an easy chair and sucking on a beer, scratched his belly through the thin material of a stained T-shirt. Mom and her eldest daughter both dandled children on their knees, while two other young kids sat on the floor and close enough to the set that I could only see their eyes.

Looking at the reality of the trailer, it did not surprise me that the only spark of life I saw in their eyes came from the TV's reflection. Both stove burners had pots encrusted with what might have been rice and beans, but they'd been there for days and the beans looked like a rat had fed itself at some point. Pizza crusts and grease-stained boxes littered the little table that folded down from the wall. The faucet bled rusty water into the sink, and it coagulated into an orange stain on a plastic plate.

The place stunk of too many people and too much

beer. The sour scent of stale beer managed to cut through the thick, musty odor of human habitation, but near the sink it lost to the sharp smell of whatever was growing beneath the unclean dishes. Mildew fur ringed the base of the leaking faucet and had spread to the plastic splashboard.

We passed through the patio doorway into a trash midden at the center of the pyramid. Buc scrambled up an aluminum ladder and entered through a hole in the bottom of another trailer. Natch followed him and Bat brought up the rear. If not for the additional clue of thick smoke and the exchange of a grandmother for a grandfather, I would have sworn we'd returned to the trailer down below.

Our trek took us through four more trailers; the only cause for hope was that the deeper we went, the degree of decay lessened. I realized, of course, that residents who lived closer to the core of Boxton had gotten there by virtue of either longevity or strength, hence their accommodations had changed hands less often.

The core residents evidenced more life, but only in the fact that they greeted Buc or seemed to recognize Bat. They were neither cordial or hostile to me—they just treated me like I did not exist. Their homes looked a bit less worn down than the fringe ones we'd visited, but even they were leaky, stinky man-nests. Had hamsters somehow evolved to human size, they would have been comfortable in these places—and in most they would have found a layer of newspaper already laid down.

Buc led us through a tunnel that ran beneath the freeway, then down a narrow pathway that took us through a hole in the fence around the Greenwood Cemetery. There, deep in the heart of Boxton, the trailers had only been stacked two high and looked in very good condition. Here, behind the walls of their own transient citadel, the leaders of Boxton had it very good. They drew running water from what used to be the cemetery's sprinkler system, and it looked like they pulled power by tapping the overhead cells directly.

The gang member did not lead us to one of the trailer mansions, but directed us to where a mausoleum had been built into the side of a manufactured hillock. The name above the door read "Freeman." "Inside, cats, you'll find what you want."

In through the dark doorway and down two steps we found a small room with a canvas cot arranged in a corner. A small candle burned on the bottom of an overturned coffee can. Seated beside it, with a pillow under his rump, an old man leaned against the cold, concrete wall. In his gnarled hands he held a paperback book with the cover torn off. Outside we could hear the roar of cars and trucks speeding along the highway.

He tucked his half-glasses back up on his white-haired head and blinked at us. "Who are you?" He put a postcard in the book to mark his place, then set it down.

Natch knelt on the other side of him, putting her back against the cot. Bat tucked himself back into the corner beside the door, and I remained in the shadows near the foot of the cot. Natch gave him her sweetest smile, which bought us some time, and answered him. "We are here to ask you about Nero Loring."

Costapain shook his head slowly. "I don't know nuffin' 'bout no Mister Lorin'."

I dropped down to my haunches to put my head on the same level as his, and he drew his legs up reflexively. "I know you have no reason to believe us, but we know you knew Loring. You were his first employee, and he attended your retirement dinner." I jerked a thumb at Bat. "You know Mr. Kabat, and you know he would not have come if we were going to harm you. Please, this is important."

His voice lost the mushmouth slurrings of an

uneducated man. "Son, I don't know shit about you. Bat's just a pit fighter, and I've seen him work. He doesn't care squat about what happens to me. Natch I've seen around, but she's not from Boxton. You, you look like a Lorica corporator to me. Now unless you want to convince me of something, I've got reading to do."

I nodded and rested my forearms on my knees. "Straight out—I haven't got a clue why, but two bottom-feeders being paid by Nerys Loring tried to off me. I think finding her father and keeping him alive will annoy her, and I'd like to do that. I'd like to do that a lot."

"You won't find him. No one will." He smiled wryly, and his face got a far away look as if he was remembering one of the vacation trips he took with Loring. "I don't even know where Nero is." As he spoke, I saw an unholy red glint play in his left eye.

"Buc," I shouted, "come here, now!"

"Wha chu wa...aarrgh!"

Buc eclipsed the red targeting laser I'd seen reflected in Costapain's eye. As if blasted into the room by the rifle report and not the bullet that preceded it, the youth flew down the stairs and flopped to the floor. His jacket had a small hole midway down the back on his left side, but already a black puddle leaked from beneath him.

Costapain reached out and bodily lifted Natch up. He deposited her on the cot, then got out of line with the doorway himself. As he moved to where I had been crouched, I scrambled up the steps to the outside, then rolled to my right. As I got to my feet again, I leaped back and to the right, then filled my hand with the Krait.

Up on the highway overpass I saw a bleached blond, bare-chested young man lift his rifle and start trotting toward the Volkswagen Kartoffeln van. I ran up the little hill as people streamed out of their houses. I gave the knob below the Krait's rear sight two twists, then dropped to one knee and snapped the safety down. From the top of the hill I aligned the sights with the sniper as he shoved the rifle through the van's sliding door.

I stroked the trigger twice. I saw the sniper pitch forward, but at that range I couldn't have been certain if it was because the bullets whizzed over his shoulders or passed between them. I triggered off two more shots, smashing the passenger side mirror and punching a hole in the door, but the van smoked its tires and slam-merged into a stream of horn-honking traffic.

At the base of the hill Bat eyed the distance from me to the car. He nodded once, then chuckled lightly. Natch and Costapain came up beside him, and the old man had blood on his hands, shirt and tan pants. "Those sons of bitches tried to kill me."

I looked down at him. "Did they?" I pointed with the gun at the clear killzone from the highway to the front of the mausoleum. "I think it was the Aryan Warriors going for a target of opportunity. They saw Buc outside and decided to pop him. I was lucky I saw the laser light. If Buc had moved faster, he could have gotten to cover."

Costapain wiped his hands on his pants. "Could be what you said."

"Could be. Now, tell me, why would anyone want you dead?" I slid the Krait back home in the shoulder holster. "You said you didn't know where Nero Loring was."

The old man's shoulders slumped, and he suddenly looked his age. "Natch, go get me my book. I have a postcard that shows the place we used to go fishing. It isn't signed or anything, but I know it's from Nero. He's alive and well."

"Do you think he's there?"

Costapain shook his head. "That place was an open secret. If his daughter wanted him dead, she'd have him. No, he's not there." He took the book from Natch and flipped open to the postcard. "It is postmarked 'Sedona.' Lots of retirement stuff up there. Pretty country. Best I can do is tell you he might be there."

"Thank you." I walked back down the hill. "I think you should come with us and talk to Hal Garrett about finding another place to stay. The Plattermen are not protecting you."

"What?" He pointed to the overpass. "If I go back out of Boxton, I'll be killed."

"If you stay here you'll die. Ask yourself this: If they meant to keep you alive, why are you in a place where a straight shot from the interstate can kill you? They've got you on ice, but accessible." I looked over at Buc's body. "Likely they were waiting until Nerys Loring got agitated enough to offer a good price for you."

"Is that so?" He folded his arms across his blood-stained chest. "And do you think this shot was a drive-by, or aimed at me?"

"As I said before, likely a drive-by."

"Yeah, as likely as your calling out to Buc was to get him *safe*."

Bat, I could see in his eyes, knew. Natch didn't want to know, and the old man knew the truth didn't matter one way or another. "Mr. Costapain, you're more valuable to me alive than dead. You know things and can remember things that might be useful. If for no other reason, I'd like to keep you as a resource."

The old man looked at me, then scratched the back of his head. "That's probably as close to honesty as I've heard in some time. I'm getting damned tired of sitting on my ass with people hunting me. I'm not up to fighting back myself, but if you need a hound to point you to the fox, I'll join the hunt."

We retraced our steps out of Boxton and got to a small convenience store where Natch used a pay phone to call Jytte. She gave Jytte a fairly full debriefing and when she hung up, told us that Rock was on his way to give us a ride. I bought some soda for the lot of us and Costapain snagged a pack of cigarettes.

His hands shook so badly that Bat had to help him light the coffin nail. The old man looked up and saw me watching him. "Nasty habit, I know. I quit 10 years ago."

I shrugged and looked the street over. "Stress will do that to you. The nicotine will calm you down and sharpen you up a bit. It'll just kill you later. You ever hear the word 'Fiddleback?'"

Costapain thought hard, then shook his head. "I take it you don't mean the spider."

"Nope. Something connected to Lorica."

"Not that I can recall."

"Do you know what Loring was working on when he was ousted?"

A shrug and a cherry ember glowed brightly. "The last link in the maglev line was just about finished, so I suspect he started his post-product evaluation. He always did that sort of 'after action' report on his projects. Helped him figure out what he'd done right and wrong."

That hardly seemed the sort of thing to get him forced out of Lorica Industries, but it was possible. He could have uncovered massive price gouging and collusion that drove up costs on the project. His daughter might have been feathering her own nest. If Nero was going to blow the whistle on her, she would have wanted him stopped. Perhaps she ousted him from power before having him killed to eliminate a motive?

"Natch, if Nerys had her father killed, which security agency would handle it?"

"Scorpion. They handle the city's legal business on the east side."

"Could they be bought off?"

"You mean, would they hide evidence that linked her to the killing? Probably not. Scorpion's headed by a real cowboy who thinks of his people like the Arizona Rangers. They're fairly incorruptible, but the jails might as well have a revolving door. Here you get the finest justice you can buy."

"Something is not clicking here." I frowned and tried to figure out what Nero Loring could know that would be important enough to get him killed. The scandal of revealing price gouging would get smothered under a blanket of bribes. It might be personal between father and daughter, which would explain the ouster before execution, but I suspected there was something more there.

Rock pulled up in front of the store in a Mercedes Benz 750 SLX. The locks all clicked open, and we moved to the vehicle while Rock kept the engine running. Bat and Natch sandwiched Costapain between them in the back seat while I dropped into the passenger bucket beside Rock. The second I shut my door, he started us forward, then shivered. "You get into trouble in some of the worst places."

"I'm glad the cavalry comes when called."

"Yeah, sure." He glanced in the rearview mirror. "Natch, you wanna pitch that butt out the window? Sorry, Pops, no smoking in here."

Bat took the cigarette from Costapain and held it for him. Rock's face twisted down into a snarl, but he knew better than to bait Bat. He turned to me. "No Marit with you? I heard your evening last night turned out to be a bust because you had to leave early. You must miss her."

I shook my head. "No, we slept in late today."

Rock hit his horn and swerved around a very surprised Audi driver. Bat smiled and even Costapain looked amused. I pulled my Krait and twisted the sight elevator nob back down to zero it at 50 feet. Rock snarled at another driver, then punched a keypad and lowered the air conditioning to 72°F. He also started a DAT of "The Rolling Stones—Live at Leisure World" playing.

None of us said anything in the rest of the journey. Talking over the music was difficult, but hearing the familiar strains of "Can't get no wheelchair traction" helped take the edge off all of us. If I was going to talk, I wanted to grill Rock about the Warriors of the Aryan World Alliance, but I did not want to do it in front of Costapain. If he thought we had any ties to the people who killed Buc—and I felt certain a WAWA shooter had done the job—he'd not tell us anything.

Rock got us to the Coyote cell headquarters I'd visited previously and dropped us off. We went inside as he roared off, and I deposited my pistol on the table in the anteroom before heading into the briefing room. Hal Garrett was already there, and I could see Jytte's outline in the light of a computer terminal in the next room.

"Mr. Costapain, I'm Hal Garrett. I'm glad you're safe."

"So am I, Mr. Garrett. It's great to meet you. I'm a big fan of yours." Costapain pulled out a chair and sat, as did the rest of us.

"Thank you." Hal looked at me. "I heard what happened. What do you make of it?"

I chewed my lower lip for a second. "I think we're looking at three distinct problems. The first is figuring out where Nero Loring is. His daughter obviously wants him dead for a reason. We can find that reason out in a number of different ways, to be sure, but I think hearing it from Loring will be the easiest. Not only can he tell us what her problem is, but I suspect he has a solution already worked out and we could use that, too."

Garrett nodded. "Ever since Natch called, Jytte has being trying to locate any sort of computer information on Sedona that might tie to Loring. Unless she's found something in the last five minutes, there's nothing."

Costapain opened his hands. "Honestly, that is the best I can do. I don't know where he could be if not there. If he's moved on since he sent me that card, I can't help you."

"Oh, I think you can help us a great deal, Mr. Costapain." I patted him on the right shoulder. "You worked for Loring for 40 years. You have to know the ins and outs of the Lorica Citadel like no one else. If you'd be willing to lend us your expertise, we can start developing plans. If there is a problem in Lorica, knowing the layout could make solving it much easier for all of us."

"I can see that."

"That's the first problem, Tycho. What's the next one?" Hal asked.

"The second is 'Fiddleback.' Nerys used the term as if it were a person or corporate identity. The way she said it tied it to my background and had very heavy conspiratorial overtones. It might be another facet of the problem Nerys has with her father. I think finding out what Fiddleback is could be crucial to solving the problem with Lorica."

I leaned back in my chair. "The third problem, I think, is tied in with what you're trying to do in keeping the Blood Crips away from WAWA. A Warrior shooter did one of the Plattermen in Boxton. I may or may not have gotten him, so things could be even."

Hal's face darkened. "What's your estimate of the chances the Aryans are being paid by Lorica to incite trouble?"

"Low. I don't see the benefit in it for Lorica. Boxton is in the shadow of Genentech-Carbide. The Blood Crips are near Lorica. A race war isn't going to do either one of them any good." I held my open hands up. "I *do* think the Aryans are being financed by someone, but it would have to be someone who wants to cause trouble for all the companies in the southern half of the valley."

"Agreed, which cuts down on suspects, but not many." Hal made a note on a piece of paper, folded it, and stuck it away in his shirt pocket. "You have any solutions to these problems?"

"Sure. Let's hit them in reverse order. You need to continue to keep the Blood Crips and the other gangs in check. See if you can get them to work with Scorpion to keep an eye on the Aryans. I know they won't want to, but a war is going to get a lot of folks killed. You don't want that, and they don't want that." I sighed heavily. "If worse comes to worse, direct intervention might be necessary. I don't think the Blood Crips are any closer to being saints than the Aryans, but the Aryans have not shown they can be reasonable. Capping them might well put things on hold."

I saw in his face that Hal no more liked the idea of assassinating Heinrich now than he did before. "We will cross that bridge only if we have no other choice. I think I can keep the lid on. The Aryans do not have the manpower they need to be as overwhelmingly powerful as they would have to be to win a war, so we have some time.

"What do we do about Fiddleback?"

I smiled. "I have an idea that I want to discuss with Alejandro. Trust me, it will shake something loose, I think."

"Okay. I'll let Alejandro know you're coming to talk with him. What about finding Nero Loring."

"Barring Jytte's success, I think going up to Sedona would be a good idea."

For the first time I saw fear in Hal's eyes and shock in

Bat's. Both of them reacted as though they had been hit with an electric stunner. Bat slowly folded his arms across his chest while Hal clasped his hand together with fingers interlaced, and rested his elbows on the table. "You may want to reconsider that idea, Tycho."

"I'm not backstopping your bullet, Hal. Why?"

He drew in a deep breath and Natch fidgeted uncomfortably in her chair. "Sedona is *different*."

"Different?"

Garrett nodded solemnly. "Twenty, 30 years ago Sedona was a hotbed of 'mystical' activity. Folks used to go up there and meditate in the power nexuses referred to as 'vortices.' More and more people moved to that area and formed up into little cults following this guru or that. At first they were very peaceful, but as the government and ranchers tried to restrict their access to private or wilderness preserve land, the cults took on a positively survivalist attitude."

Natch grinned weakly. "Think Aryans who check the color of your aura instead of your skin, Caine-man."

"Exactly." Hal stared at the table about two feet in front of his hands. "The local press talks about weird things going on in Sedona, and the local talk radio stations have whole programs devoted to 'psychic phenomena' going on up there. When some shooting broke out seven years ago, both KFYI and KTAR lost news teams covering the story."

I blinked away my astonishment. "Are you telling me folks go up there and don't come back? Is there a Lectorium up there where folks get eaten or something?"

"Or something."

I looked up as Marit framed herself in the doorway. "What do you mean?"

"There are, as Hal said, cult groups up there. If you're not careful they can brainwash you pretty easily. The techniques have been around since before the Korean

War. As long as you stick close to another rational person and don't interact too directly, you can go in and come out again."

I winked at Bat. "I'm not afraid to try. Bat will go with me, won't you?"

Bat shook his head. "Bust my head, fine, but not my *mind*."

Marit walked from the door and stood behind me, resting her hands on my shoulders. "I'll go. I've been before and survived it."

Hal's head came up. "Are you crazy?"

"No, that's why I'll go. I've got a Range Rover II in a garage in City Center. It will get us there and back. I can even arrange for a local guide—I know a guy from a photo shoot done up there for the *Arizona Highways* swimsuit issue." She gave my shoulders a squeeze. "We can leave in the morning and be back tomorrow night."

Jytte came in from the other room with the cellular phone in her hand. "Coyote wants to speak to you, Tycho."

Given the tail of his message last time, I took the phone with a bit of trepidation. "Caine here."

"Ah, Mr. Caine, it is good to hear your voice. I have nothing but admiration for your ability with a gun. I trust you were not injured."

"No sir, only one of the Plattermen caught a bullet. We got Mr. Costapain out of there, and he has agreed to help us."

"Excellent, though it is too bad about the Platterman. You realize finding Nero Loring is a key to recovering your identity, don't you?"

"Yes, sir." I had a feeling Hal would not try to stop Marit and me from going to Sedona, but I wanted to ice the trip. "Toward that end, Marit and I will be going to Sedona to follow up on our only lead about Loring."

"Sedona?" The mechanically altered voice hesitated

for a moment or two. "That will be dangerous, but I believe you have the skills to handle yourself. Be careful, and do not mistake foolhardiness for courage. If you feel threatened, get out of there."

"Understood, sir."

"Excellent. Good hunting. Now, if you will, please let me speak with Hal."

I passed the phone to Hal. He listened closely, then offered two or three "Yes, sirs," before shutting the phone off. "He cleared your trip and told me to offer you any help you need."

"Great." I stood and took Marit's hand. "We'll see Alejandro right now, then head out in the morning. We will call in before we leave, at noon, four and every four hours after that until we get back. If you don't hear from us for 12 hours straight, send out the cavalry, or write us off."

Hal nodded. "You want more firepower than what your normally carry?"

I thought for a second, then shook my head. "If I have to start shooting to find Nero Loring, the problem will be one too big to handle no matter how huge the gun. With any luck at all, I won't have to fire a shot."

We took Marit's car back to City Center and beat the post-work crowds to the Mercado. We found Alejandro's gallery in an adobe-like building in the center of the Mexican pseudo-village. The exterior had been decorated with Spanish and Amerindian designs, but the colors used were bright pastels unknown to the ancients. As it was, that made it right at home with the rest of the Dizzyland village simulation—and alien to the nation and culture from which it purported to be drawn.

The interior of the gallery, on the other hand, could have been taken from any fine arts center anywhere. While the semi-circular foyer got plenty of natural sunlight, Alejandro had it set up with comfortable chairs and a small refreshment center. A couple of framed, print-quality posters hung on the walls to advertise past or coming shows, but the *real* art was kept in the upper and central viewing galleries.

Opposite the foyer, the gallery became long and narrow. The stairs doubled back on themselves, starting near the central gallery and coming out toward the foyer before twisting and climbing up to the upper gallery. On the ground floor, at the switchback, a pretty receptionist sat behind a massive mahogany desk—rather rare these days. I could see from one unfortunate chip in the corner that the desk was genuine wood—not a press or extruded plastic product.

The receptionist smiled at Marit. "Ms. Fisk, how good to see you again."

"Good afternoon, Paz. Is Alejandro in?"

The dark-haired woman nodded. "He's with a client, but they should be finishing up very soon. If you wish to wait…"

"We'll look around the gallery."

"I will tell him you're waiting."

We walked into the central viewing gallery and slowly began to stroll along, admiring the work hung there. The walls had been painted a neutral beige, which, along with the charcoal gray carpet, offered no competition for the art being displayed. Track lighting provided just the right amount of illumination to bring the colors out without bleaching them or casting inappropriate shadows on the statuary.

"Alejandro is known for obtaining new and professional work for a very discriminating clientele. Most people think he has the ability to spot excellent investments before they become astronomically priced." She pointed to a surreal fantasy piece featuring a sylvan woman in a pink cloak standing on the trail to a mystical city. Behind her sat a cloaked warrior with a sword and a small, non-human creature playing at some sort of game with painted sticks. "This is another picture by the woman who painted the piece I tried to buy last night."

"Turner something?"

"Elizabeth Turner. Alejandro tracked her down from some commercial work she'd done. He's sold a number of her paintings."

I looked a bit closer at the picture. The artist had a good technique and was able to convincingly portray the fantastic as real. "Does he ever arrange commissions?"

"I do, indeed." Alejandro greeted Marit with kisses on both cheeks, then shook my hand. "Did you want something painted? A portrait, perhaps?"

"Not exactly. Is there some place we can talk?"

"My office." He headed back out toward the foyer. "Marit, are you coming?"

She shook her head. "No, actually, I'll leave you here, Tycho, and go start things rolling for tomorrow. It will save us some time."

I gave her a quick kiss. "I'll meet you at your place in an hour?"

Marit shook her head. "No, meet me at Danny's Place about 8. Have dinner first." She smiled impishly but said no more and left the gallery. I, in turn, followed Alejandro up the stairs and back through the upper viewing gallery to a doorway in the back. He unlocked it and waved me into his office.

His workplace was as clean and open as the gallery. He had an antique standing desk that he kept clear except for a black phone, blotter and pen and pencil set. Because he worked standing, he had a conversation nook in the corner to the right of the doorway, with three comfortable, black-leather chairs surrounding a small circular coffee table. It was to these he directed me, but the pictures hung on the walls diverted my attention.

Behind his desk I saw a piece that had to be by Picasso, yet I did not recognize it. A Monet hung on the left wall, along with a Cézanne and Pollock. Back beside the door, I saw a Wyeth Helga portrait and opposite it a Van Gogh that looked to be another of the Sunflower pieces. I looked closely at the Van Gogh and knew I could not place it within any catalog of his work, yet I found it as beautiful and entrancing as any of his other work I had seen.

Alejandro closed the door. "You like Van Gogh?"

I nodded. "I do indeed, but this can't be genuine. If it were, you would have far more extensive security measures in place here. Because this isn't a copy of a known piece, it's not a forgery, but if you were to sell it as a recently 'discovered' piece, you could get a fortune for it." I glanced at him. "Did you do this?"

He shook his head. "My lot in life is to recognize talent, not possess it myself. That was done by an associate of mine who died several years ago. These other pieces were painted by others."

I smiled wryly. "I imagine it would be very tempting to offer a wealthy client a piece that he dare not have authenticated, especially after, say, a robbery of an art museum that has gotten a certain amount of publicity."

"It would, indeed." Alejandro folded his arms. "In fact, having done that was how I first became associated with Coyote."

"How so?"

"Coyote had decided, for reasons known only to him, to relieve someone of a private art collection. One of the pieces he got was Dali with a questionable pedigree." Alejandro sat down and tugged at the knee of his slacks as he crossed his legs. "I heard of the theft, then got a phone call. 'I am Coyote,' he said, 'your people do very good work, and your clients would doubtless be interested to know just *how* good it is.'"

I sat across from him, on the edge of one of the chairs. "Did he blackmail you?"

The art broker half-closed his eyes. "Not blackmail per se, but an offer of protection. He said I could get pictures into places, and that I had information that could be valuable to him. He suggested if we worked together we would both find it profitable."

"I'm unclear. What did he mean when he said you could get pictures into places?"

Alejandro smiled like a cat who'd gotten the cream. "You would be surprised by the number of people who remove their valuable paintings from a room being swept by security experts. They seem to assume that those who are in charge of security are capable of going rogue and stealing that which they hold most precious. A passive bug is very difficult to detect, and one that is not present in the room when you do the sweep is positively impossible to find."

"I see." I could easily imagine being surprised and not a little scared at getting a call from Coyote exposing my error, then offering an alliance. It was interesting to note that with Hal, Coyote had offered a warning, and with Alejandro he had used gentle coercion. I imagined with Rock he must have employed a powerful motivator.

"So, what is it you want done, Tycho?"

"What I want is a painting of Phoenix in which a giant Fiddleback spider has spun its web from the tops of the citadels and City Center. I want it grasping for or nesting at Lorica Industries."

"Interesting. What style do you want?"

I thought for a second. "As close to photo-realistic as possible, I think. It will be a surreal fantasy piece by any definition, but I don't want it that widely open to interpretation. The original should be on display, but listed as not for sale. Noting lithographs will be made might not be a bad idea."

Alejandro nodded his head. "Bait. You want me to keep track of whoever asks about it, right?"

"Dead on target." I stood. "I'll pay $5000 for the piece to be done. Who can you get?"

"You'll want it fast, I assume." I nodded, and he smiled. "Estefan Ramierez works in that style and fast. He could use the money."

I remembered seeing paint on his clothes. "Good, that will be pay back for what he did for me. How long?"

"Possibly as soon as two days from now. He works quickly."

"Great."

Alejandro stood and offered me his hand. "Very good doing business with you, sir."

"And you, sir."

"Any thought to a title?"

I nodded. "Have the spider about to chomp down on Lorica and we'll call it 'Devouring Its Mate.' If that doesn't shake something lose, nothing will."

Leaving the Higuera Gallery, I decided to get something to eat without leaving the Mercado. Rather loud and boisterous crowds filled the two Mexican eateries, so I settled on a Chinese restaurant called Sesame Inn. Why it had located a branch in the Mercado I was uncertain, but I found it a familiar and serene sanctuary in the land of plastic Aztec jaguars and gringo-ized Mexico.

I ordered a Tsingtao, still amazed at how China managed to export foodstuffs while failing to feed its masses, and settled back into the booth I had been given. The interior decor had a lot of intricate woodwork and scenes delicately drawn on rice paper graced the walls. Somewhere in the back of my mind I knew I had been here, or in a similar place before, but my amnesia frustrated my attempts to mix my present with my past.

Getting the Fiddleback solution underway made me feel pretty good. Given that Alejandro's clientele included some of the richer folks in Phoenix, word of the painting would get around quickly. If we tracked and could sweat anyone who showed an interest in the picture, we might be able to figure out who or what Fiddleback was. I felt certain the picture would draw someone out, and, as Alejandro suggested with his experience, Coyote would be more than capable of convincing them to cooperate.

In enumerating the problems we faced for Hal, I had left one out. That was the problem of the traitor within Coyote's cell of aides. I would not have minded confiding in Hal, but the presence of the others in the room at the time made me hold my tongue. Anyone there could be "it" and, while I had a front-runner, I knew better than to make any assumptions.

Hal Garrett, however, I considered worthy of trust. Coyote had told me that the traitor would do his best to kill me. While any of the people I met would be physically capable of pulling a trigger and ending my life, I did not think Hal would do that. Twice he had counseled against violence and his whole drive with the Blood Crips and other gangs was to stop them from retaliating for actions the Aryans might take. Because he balked at having me end the WAWA problem by application of a lead injection to Heinrich, I put him down as someone dedicated to breaking the cycle of violence.

My prime candidate for traitor, of course, was Rock Pell. I found him a callous and shallow individual who was too chummy with the Warriors of the Aryan World Alliance. He clearly felt a loyalty to himself first and foremost. His selling out to a higher bidder, whoever that might be, was not hard to imagine. Still, since Coyote did not direct me to him, I knew there had to be other candidates—perhaps even more than one.

Bat, obviously, was capable of violence, and I had to be certain not to let his apparent respect for my skills lull me into believing he could not betray me. Marit, too, was a candidate, though she had certainly had ample opportunity to kill me when I was defenseless. Alejandro had direct daily contact with just the sort of people who had brought me into Phoenix in the first place, which meant he could be hired to deal with whatever sort of embarrassment I might present. Natch struck me as being a low probability, but a child of the streets learns that unpleasant things may have to be done to survive. Slitting my throat could be just one such thing. Moreover, if she and Bat were in league, they would be a very difficult pair to deal with.

Jytte, in many ways, presented the greatest and the least threat. Because she functioned as the communications center for the cell, she certainly had more information than anyone else. I did not imagine she passed everything on and that she, if anyone, had the keys to figuring out who the traitor was. Extracting that information would be difficult and, if she was the traitor, I would get directed at another, totally innocent member of the group.

Coyote, on the other hand, had given her an implicit vote of confidence when he routed my communications through her. She was strange enough, with her Barbie-doll looks and computer skills, to be able to monitor our conversations. Had Coyote suspected her, he would have contacted me outside her sphere of influence, or had me work with another cell to uncover the traitor in this cell.

Still, this did not give me the freedom to tell her what was up. While her skills in navigating through computers could probably have uncovered everything I needed to know, I couldn't count on Jytte to keep secrets from whoever the traitor might be. If, for example, Marit were the mole and Jytte felt a debt to her because of their friendship, the traitor could be tipped to my inquiries and either act to end them, or skip the city altogether.

I was alone in this. Coyote knew it and, I think, wanted it that way. I got the feeling he wanted me to find the traitor, but he also wanted something else. Until I could puzzle out what that was, however, I could only continue my investigations and hope that the luck that had kept me alive so far would continue to hold.

The waiter came and I ordered both hot and sour spicy soup and tangerine beef. I took a pull on the beer and savored its sharp bite. It struck me that the only way I would uncover the traitor was to begin to parcel out information on a limited basis. When my enemies started acting on this specialized information, I would know who had gone over to the other side.

The food arrived quickly, and I forced myself to eat slowly. The soup was spicy enough to make my nose run, with not too much vinegar. It was so good, of course, that I sniffled my way right through it and on into the tangerine beef. That was another hot dish that masked its heat with a sweet, yet tart, sauce. I liked it so much that I knew, had I ever tasted it before, I would have recalled it and broken my amnesia block. I ate my way around the slivers of dried red pepper and ended up far more stuffed than I had intended.

Cheer up, I told myself, *if Sedona is as bad as Hal thinks, this might be the last good meal you manage to have.*

I paid my bill and strolled back out into the Mercado. Threading my way through the winding, cobblestone streets, I found in interactive City Center directory. Working my way through a series of touch sensitive screens, I located the listing for Danny's Place. I had to go up one level and then halfway across the center to get there. I had plenty of time before I had to meet Marit, so I decided to walk instead of descending to take one of the trains.

Walking through City Center, virtually all of which was new to me, I got a chance to really see the world in which people like Nerys Loring and Marit lived. White marbled walkways shined and bronze trim on the buildings bore no trace of fingerprints. All smudges had been painstakingly scrubbed from windows and clean, cool water bubbled up in a number of fountains. The plants all proved to be lush and green, making City Center more a rain forest than an oasis in the midst of a desert.

As I strolled along I saw one maintenance crew struggling to lever a barrel cactus, pot and all, onto a trailer hitched to an electric utility cart. Each of the three men looked sharp in his starched and pressed uniform.

Sweat appeared in circles beneath their armpits and in a dark stripe along their spines, but that hardly seemed unnatural given how hard they were working. Lifting in unison they managed to heft the plant onto the trailer, then one of them picked up a broom to sweep away the dirt that had spilled from the pot.

All around them people passed as if the men did not exist. Each of the men, in turn, had a broad smile pasted on his face. Even with sweat pouring down from their scalp and into their eyes, they maintained their idiot-grins of pleasure. I wondered for a moment if they were doped up, but the sharp quick look in their dark eyes told me this was not the case.

Hispanics all, they wore the smiles like masks. Here they were, blessed beyond all possibility, working in City Center. Probably born in the dark slums of Eclipse, somehow they had broken into the light. They were determined not to sink back into Eclipse. While they might still live there, and they would never progress beyond their station, their children or grandchildren might profit from this toehold in City Center.

Looking around I saw other invisible people working throughout City Center. Uniformed women washed windows. Young men with brooms and scoopers patrolled the mall, snatching up any litter thoughtlessly deposited by the denizens of this place. They bowed and side-stepped, smiling in the face of unkind comments and jumping to show their superiors courtesies that were never returned.

Social Darwinists, I knew, would point out that the best and most able to survive of current society were due everything that generation upon generation were able to give them. They would also note that these industrious members of the under-class were, as one would expect, rising up to fill a niche that the superior society left open. In this way they would slowly but surely evolve into the upper class themselves.

In theory, I could see, this was true. Alejandro Higuera had his own gallery, yet I suspected his parents or grandparents had come to Phoenix from below the border. Estefan Ramierez would employ his talent for art to make a bid at joining the well-to-do, but the gulf between him and Nerys Loring was more than money alone could bridge. Racial, social and economic barriers would all hamper him and frustrate him. Were Estefan to make it in this society, it would be as a curiosity, not a man accepted on equal terms. *A pet.*

The word "pet" echoed around inside my skull as I rode the escalator up toward Danny's Place. *"Pet" was what that thing in the dream called me.* I wondered if I had a keeper, a patron, that kept me much as I would expect some rich art maven might keep Estefan. *Could that person be Fiddleback? That would explain the arachnoid form in the dream.*

The most heartbreaking aspect of what I saw in City Center was this: It would take generations for people like Estefan to attain what people like Marit had now. In that time, of course, the rich would have become richer. There would always be a buffer between the new and the old, which could only irritate and frustrate the new. A lot of energy would be wasted resenting those who really should have been beneath their contempt.

Those emotions, I knew, could be positively explosive. Heinrich and his boys were a perfect example of that. Angered by what they saw as a loss of what they had a "right" to, frustrated whites lashed out at the minorities they saw taking over. Not only was their notion of racial superiority baseless, but their claim to America was purposefully blind. The Amerindians were here first and, especially in the southwest, the Spanish came before the Anglos. Using unsound logic and fabricated science designed to inspire fear and hatred, the Aryans sought to destroy that with which they could not compete.

Logic dictated that, because all humans are equal at birth, all should be treated the same throughout their lives. The realities of the world ignored logic, pigeonholing people and limiting their possible progress. Grants and welfare programs ensured that people would not starve, but they offered no incentive to try to better one's lot in life. The whole system, while it might soften the savagery of life, also doomed people to live in a twilight existence that would not kill them, but could not provide them with happiness or anything I would call life.

Working in City Center allowed the people of Eclipse to see what *could* be theirs. It also showed them how difficult it would be to attain. It guaranteed an escalating spiral of misery and bitterness on the part of the Mikes, and blissful ignorance of the building resentment by the gnomes.

When it all fell apart, it wasn't going to be pretty.

I stepped off the escalator and looked at Danny's Place. Through the big window I saw faded decorations that immediately tagged the place as a neo-retro-'60s bar. With a sinking feeling of dread in my stomach, I walked into the place and let my eyes adjust to the harsh glow of blacklight posters on the walls. Back in the corner a wide-screen projection TV showed an episode of some old sitcom about four young men in a band and The Beatles' "I Wanna Hold Your Hand" blared out over the speakers in the ceiling.

I saw Marit wave at me, and I threaded my way through the bar. In doing so I noticed two things that struck me as very odd. All of the waitresses were tall and slender, wearing long wigs with straight brown hair. Each wore a baggy-sleeved shirt, a polyester vest and bell-bottom slacks to match, though getting that much peach fabric had to have been a special order. Each wore a button that said, "Hello, have a Partridge Day."

Odder than that were the bartenders. I think they were all male, but I could only be sure of the two that had full beards. All of them were similarly attired in hot pants, knee-length boots with two-inch heels, a flowery blouse and a long, blond wig. While all of them wore their shirts open enough to see the hair on their chests, they all also wore a bra that was sufficiently stuffed to make them a very strange sight indeed. After an evening's worth of drinks I imagined it *might* be possible to mistake one of them for a woman and try to pick her up, but it would make for quite a surprise later when the truth was discovered.

" '60s-retro with transvestite bartenders." I gave Marit a kiss. "You do know some interesting places."

Marit, wearing a jeans jumper that probably had been new when people still thought Spiro Agnew was a cattle disease, kissed me back with enough passion to impress the other two people at our table. "The bartenders aren't really cross-dressers, but the owner, Danny, likes them dressing that way. They say they get good tips."

"Not my choice of careers." I offered my hand to the man seated across from me. "Tycho Caine."

"Watson Dodd, Build-more Operations." Slender to the point of looking malnourished, Dodd wore a denim vest that emphasized his lack of shoulders and accentuated his pencil neck. His John Lennon glasses, while appropriate for the setting, kept slipping down his hawk-beak nose. His Adam's apple bobbed like a harpoon barrel attached to a sounding whale and the flour-sack shirt he wore hung off him as if he were shedding his skin.

He shook hands as if he thought I had the plague and was still contagious.

Dodd put his arm around the woman with him. "This is my little baby factory, Dottie."

Dottie shook hands more firmly than had her husband. The Mama Cass Levi's tent on her did not hide the fact that she was pregnant. Her face looked puffy and judging by both her expression and size, I guessed she was about a month shy of expanding the upper class. "Pleased to meet you," she said, and meant it.

Dottie smiled at me. "Marit says you're going to Sedona tomorrow. Watson and I met there."

"I hear Sedona is quite beautiful."

"Spiritually enriching, really," offered Watson. He adjusted his glasses and did his best to look wise. "We studied under Chief Probitananda White Feather while he channeled Kesh-Hur, the 23rd Wizard-Emperor of Lemuria. In the Church of Searing Illumination we walked on fire and, had I not opted for this job, we would have learned to walk on water."

I managed to restrain my laughter. "Walk on *water*? Quite a trick, that."

Watson remained serious. "No trick, Ty, but real. With the fire walk we learned we could overcome any obstacle. We could use the power of our minds to insulate ourselves so that we would not burn when walking across a bed of glowing red coals. This is in our bare feet, mind you, and on coals that spouted little bits of flame now and again."

"But I thought I saw on the television, Wat, a show where the Phoenix Skeptics said that was all nonsense..."

His nostrils flared, stopping his glasses from a suicidal leap to the table. "Idiots. They ridicule what they don't understand. There are things that cannot be quantified by science. The mind is the key to unlocking all possibilities. With another year of studies, we would have been able to walk across an ocean."

"Quite a useful skill here in the desert," Marit offered archly.

"I wanted to learn how to fly, but Watson is afraid of heights." Dottie smiled at her husband. When he glowered at her, she stroked her swollen belly with her left hand, letting the bar's light glint from her wedding ring. Immediately the anger left his face, and he was himself again.

A waitress appeared and took drink orders. Marit opted for Ripple with a twist and Dottie requested a Virgin Daiquiri. Watson, no doubt looking to win back some macho points, ordered bourbon straight up, adding, "double, rocks," as the waitress looked at me.

"I'll have a Virgin Daiquiri as well." I gave Dottie a wink, then gave Marit's knee a squeeze under the table.

Something about Watson made it constitutionally impossible for him to carry off a look of smug superiority.

A new song started and Marit grabbed my hand. "Come on, Mr. Caine, dance with me." When I raised an eyebrow she leaned over and whispered in my ear, "There are those who think dancing is the same as having sex standing up. Care to test that theory?"

I nodded, and we joined a vast throng crowding the dance floor. Bodies mingled and jostled us until we reached a fairly stable area near the center. The song itself had a basic beat which made it easy to dance to, though if I ever hear the lyric, "I think I love you," again, it will be far too soon. Surprisingly I slipped into the repetitive and rhythmic motions of the retro-dance without much trouble.

Marit, though clad in a '60s dress and moving to '60s music, was not old-fashioned at all. She abandoned herself to the music and flowed through a series of very sensuous and fluid steps. With her hair hiding then revealing her face like veils, she kept her azure eyes on mine and a devilish grin on her lips. There, in the middle of the floor, she danced for me and were my mind on anything even remotely approximating science, I would have deemed her theory relating dancing and sex proven beyond a shadow of a doubt.

The thing about proving theories is, of course, that the experiment must be repeatable. As that first song faded into "I Woke Up In Love This Morning," she danced close and kissed me, then ran her hands down my chest and drew away. Behind her, barely registering on my consciousness, I saw Watson and Dottie cutting through the crowd to join us. I looked back toward our table and saw the waitress distributing our drinks. I also saw someone standing beside her, someone I thought I knew.

It took me a few seconds to place that pasty white face, and then I realized why I didn't recognize him immediately. Except for the blue, star-shaped scar on his cheek, he looked just like a twin of the Reaper I'd shot in the face my first night in Eclipse. As I watched him unseen, his gloved hands came up, and he made a motion over the table, but I couldn't actually see what he had done. I did notice, however, his left hand seemed smaller than his right.

Without thinking, I started wading through the crowd to get at him. He looked up and saw me, then turned and began calmly walking away. He glanced back over his shoulder at me and, when he saw I was about to clear the edge of the dance floor, he bolted and ran out the door.

I knew, instantly, I would never catch him. I made it as quickly as I could to our table, then dropped to one knee. On the ground I found half of a gelatin capsule that had a residue of white powder in it. I put that in my pocket. Straightening up, I saw a thin dusting of powder on the table in an arc that connected my drink to Dottie's.

As Marit came up, I purposely bumped the table with my stomach and tipped it over as I leaned on it to steady myself. The drinks crashed to the floor, and I managed a blush that made me feel hot enough to combust.

Marit leaned over and rubbed my back with one hand. "Are you okay?"

I nodded slowly and righted the table. Laurie, our

waitress, gave me a concerned look. I held up a hand. "Sorry, just dizzy. I get that way, some times, when I dance. Low blood sugar." I pulled a $50 note from my pocket. "Here, get us another round, and keep the change for the inconvenience."

Marit tucked a wisp of hair behind her left ear as the girl went off to get a cleaning rag. "Something wrong?"

Sure, I just saw someone who might be back from the dead try to poison us.

"Just thought I saw an old friend."

"You remembered someone?"

"Yeah, I did." I shrugged, "What I remembered is that he's dead, and has every reason to want me that way, too."

When I fully explained what had happened, Marit became more shaken up than I was. She managed to cover her discomfort as Watson and Dottie returned to our table, but she quickly made an excuse for us and got us out of there. Without speaking we went to the elevators and headed home.

When the doors closed, she hugged me, and I could feel her trembling. "Easy, Marit, it is not that bad. Nothing happened—no one was hurt."

Hiding her face in a curtain of black hair, she sniffed and wiped a tear from her right eye. "I know, Tycho, but all of a sudden it hit me that I might lose you. I'd not expected that sharp a reaction." She looked up and stroked my cheek with her tear-damp finger. "You're in my blood, Tycho Caine."

I kissed her hand. "And you are in mine." The elevator slowed, and the doors to the tranversor opened. "Early to bed and early to rise, and we'll be in Sedona before the assassins even open their eyes."

Despite Hal's reservations about Sedona and the attempt on our lives, I slept well. I had half-expected another monster dream but, to my surprise, I did not dream at all. I awakened quickly and felt excited about the trip. After a shower and a quick breakfast, I joined Marit in the tranversor, and we headed down to pick up her Range Rover.

Marit was dressed in knee-high boots, khaki jodhpurs and a khaki safari shirt with four shotgun shells in the little loops at her left shoulder. She carried a gun-case that contained a pump-action Mossberg with a pistol-grip

and a shortened barrel. On her hip rode a Colt Python
.357 Magnum and enough spare shells to win a small
war. Dark glasses and a black baseball cap completed
her outfit.

I had to rely on my boots, jeans and one of the dress
shirts Roger had provided me. As always, I wore my vest
beneath the shirt, my shoulder holster over it and the
windbreaker over that, concealing the pistol. I carried
two full spare clips and stuck a box of bullets in Marit's
gun case. While I didn't think we would have much cause
to shoot anything, being safe beats being sorry by a long
shot.

The bright red Range Rover, which still dripped water
from the washing it had been given, had been gassed up
and stocked with a cooler. Anna had filled the cooler with
soft-drinks, some sandwiches and a bag of grapes. I set
Marit's gun case on the back seat, then climbed into the
navigator's seat. Marit slid in behind the wheel, and we
set off to Sedona.

Even leaving as early as we were, I expected some sort
of a commuter rush of traffic. I mentioned this to Marit,
but she just shook her head. "You must remember,
dearest, that people working in City Center generally live
here, or commute in from Eclipse through the elevators.
Those who work in the corporate citadels likewise live
there, or commute via the maglevs. In fact, the only time
there is any sort of traffic rush around here is when,
generally in August, Phoenecians invade San Diego to
escape the worst of the monsoon season."

"Monsoons? In a desert?"

"Monsoons. They generally start a week from now,
with the beginning of July. Lightning storms like you've
never seen." She smiled to herself. "It's funny, but the
only time they crack Frozen Shade is to clean up after the
storms, and there are enough clouds left that the folks
still can't see the stars."

As she spoke, Marit guided us through a labyrinth of narrow streets running between legions and legions of parked vehicles. Most of them were covered in shrouds, and those that weren't looked as if they had been dusted—if not waxed and polished—already that morning. Aside from the utter jumble of manufacturers represented, it would have been easy to imagine we were in the hold of a cargo ship bringing in imports.

Finally Marit started us gliding down an on-ramp that brought us onto I-10 heading west. We joined the interstate just beyond the tunnel through which it passed beneath City Center and almost immediately hit the intersection with I-17. As we made the transition to the northbound road, I craned my neck to see if I could spot the Boxton cemetery where Buc had died, but I could not.

We rolled along beneath the Frozen Shade and traffic was light enough that Marit used her high beams most of the time. "We want to be able to see freesprints in time to avoid them. Poor bastards."

"What do you mean?"

"The system will take care of folks. If you can't do anything, you can sell your vote proxy to the corps or pols and they'll take care of you. That's good enough for most folks: three meals a day, enough beer to stupefy you, and all the television you can watch to finish the job. That's a hell of a lot for folks who can't hold a job."

I frowned. "I don't think the lot of a ballotman is very good."

"True, but it sets a base level one cannot sink beneath. It does not prohibit you from doing anything to improve your lot, though many folks who opt for that way of living have really surrendered. They just sort of die inside and wait for their bodies to catch up."

"So what is this about freesprints?

"They are freeway runners. They get frustrated and decide to kill themselves, yet they realize they have a responsibility to their families. Because of that, they run onto the highway and force you to run over them. When a car is traveling 100 mph, the way we are now, they do considerable damage to the vehicle and could easily kill us."

I suddenly saw what she was working toward. "They think their family will get an insurance settlement from your insurance company."

"The tale of a big payoff is an urban legend. The insurance companies, using the proxy votes from ballotmen, have gotten a law passed that states anyone engaging in freesprinting is, in fact, guilty of assault with intent to kill. The law not only absolves the insurance company from any responsibility for paying off in freesprint cases, *but* it makes the victim or his estate responsible for reparations for the damage he does to the car." She shook her head. "I've seen families ruined by that sort of thing, and I don't want to be any part of it."

Interstate 17 took us north out of Phoenix. We left Eclipse just beyond Del Webb's Near-Dead City—the remnant of what was once a thriving retirement community. Outside, where the temperature was already hitting 110°F, I saw desert that, for the most part, consisted of cracked tan earth and scrubby, leafless brush that sprouted cat-claw thorns. A bit further north the road started the long climb up the Mogollon rim toward Flagstaff. It took us through pleasantly named places like Big Bug Creek and Bloody Basin and terrain that looked like broken red pottery.

As I looked at the land I knew it was totally alien to me. Rocks, rocks and more rocks abounded, somehow balancing on the side of steep hills that had long since had all their topsoil eroded away. Cactii somehow took root in the hard-baked earth, and I had no doubt that scorpions and rattlesnakes lurked in every niche and shadow I saw.

As the vehicle made the long climb up out of the valley, the landscape began to change a bit. It went from desert to arid prairie, yet looked no more hospitable. The few trees I saw were stunted and dried out. The tan grasses looked the appropriate color for them to be ripe for harvesting, yet they lay in the fields in patchy clumps that rose no further than knee-height.

I looked for the cattle I would have expected to see grazing, but I saw no living creatures in those fields.

I didn't even see any road kill.

I looked over at Marit, but she seemed oblivious to what I saw as abnormalities. That concerned me for a second, then I recalled that my grasp on reality was not all it could have been. I took my cue from her and tried to relax.

"Marit, how did you get involved with Coyote? You explained a bit of it the other night, but not the whole tale."

She glanced over at me and looked as if she had not heard the question, but before I could repeat it, her face closed up a bit. "I had hoped this would not come up, but you have a right to know. Rock brought me into the group."

She searched my face for judgment, but found none. "I had known Rock for a long time and, well, ran into him during a time when I was *very* vulnerable. We started seeing each other, socially, then a problem came up that he thought I could help Coyote solve. He set up a meeting and that was that."

I smiled grimly. "That answers a number of questions for me. How long ago did you and Rock stop being lovers?"

She looked straight ahead at the road. "A year and a half ago. Rock has been jealous ever since, but our worlds seldom intersect, so there is nothing he can do about it." Marit smiled weakly. "I hope you're not mad. Talking about one's past lovers is not a good idea, but

Rock acts like an ass fairly often, so I feel better getting this off my chest. You aren't mad, are you?"

"I don't own you. I did not know you a week ago. How can I be angry about a situation where I did not exist?" I patted her right thigh reassuringly. "If he bothers you, on the other hand, and you are disinclined to deal with it yourself, my services are at your disposal."

"Ah, gallantry is not dead." She hit the blinker switch and turned off onto Arizona Route 179 to Sedona. "Sedona and the red rock country is very special. It's been two years since I've been there, but it was gorgeous back then. I hope it hasn't changed much."

Not having been there before, I could not gauge the amount of change, but I agreed that it was very beautiful. The red rock formations rise up from the canyon floor like mountains that have been transplanted from Mars. Aspens and other verdant vegetation thrived along the Oak Creek and contrasted beautifully with the rich bloodstone color of the land itself. Even if all the supposed power vortices did not exist, Sedona would attract a lot of visitors just because of its beauty.

Unfortunately the power nexus points did attract a large segment of the population. We rolled on into the town of Sedona and parked in front of the Guest Center. It looked like a perfectly normal geodesic dome except for the UFO mooring mast rising like a spike from it. The sign beside the door had a greeting written in French, English, German, Japanese, Korean, Chinese and Spanish. It also had three sets of bizarre symbols, most of them based on geometry, that I chose to assume were "Welcome" in extraterrestrial languages.

Marit debated it for a second, but decided to leave the shotgun in the Rover. We entered the building and were immediately assaulted by thick, cloying mesquite incense clouds. The Muzak being played in the background remained frustratingly elusive, fading in and out without any rhyme or reason as nearly as I could tell. The posters on the wall mixed retro-'60s stuff with chamber of commerce shots of the surrounding landscape and had UFOs caught in the act of hovering or air-brushed in after the fact.

The man behind the counter smiled at us and looked normal until I noticed the tinfoil lining his "See Sedona, I Did" baseball cap. "Greetings. Didn't I know you during our lives in the Court of Elizabeth the Virgin Queen?"

I returned his smile. "I don't know, friend. We were wondering, for my father, if you could give us some information about retirement communities in the area. He's in his 70s and will be retiring. We want to move him up here and get him out of Phoenix."

"The City in the Lake." The man scratched at his hat, and I saw his name tag read "Ramses."

"Is that a retirement community?"

"No, that's what we call Phoenix up here." Ramses bent down and clacked away on his computer keyboard. He glanced up at the old television he was using as a monitor, hit it once on the side, then squinted at the screen. "Does your father have any group affiliations?"

I shook my head. "Group affiliations?"

"Masons? Illuminati? Chief Probitananda White Feather's Church of Searing Illumination?"

"No, I'm afraid not."

Ramses hissed as he took a breath and typed on the keyboard again. He hit the return key, then looked up at me. "The search will take a moment, but I would not hold out much hope."

"Why not?"

The man smiled a sympathetically as he could. "Most of our group homes up here are run by the various foundations, churches, associations, networks and stellar unions who come to Sedona for the power here. Without an affiliation, I don't think we'll find anything."

The computer beeped at him and he stared, surprised, at the screen. "By the Goddess!"

His reaction caught both of our attentions. "Yes?"

"This is strange—Marie must have entered this one last week." Ramses gave me a broad grin. "You are in luck Mr....don't tell me, I am a psychic..."

"Caine," I said.

"Lane, of course. Well, Mr. Lane, it appears the Fiddleback Farm may be just what you want."

"Excuse me, the name is Caine. Now what did you call that place?"

"Fiddleback Farm. It is a retirement home for executives that opened up about two months ago, but has just gotten into contact with us. Says here, 'We welcome pets.' You drive out of town on Von Falkenberg Road about four miles, and you should see it." He circled a location on a placemat road map and handed it to me.

I nodded. "Thank you, Ramses, you have helped me a great deal."

"You are most welcome, sir. Any time you and Mrs. McLain want to come back and see us, well, we'll be happy to have you here."

Marit and I beat a hasty retreat to the Rover. As she opened her door then popped the automatic locks, she shook her head. "You get the feeling this is too easy?"

"Not if those clouds keep rolling in fast."

"That's Arizona for you. If you don't like the weather, wait a minute, and it will change."

On the horizon, but coming in fast, stampeding thunderheads slid across the sky. Yellow lightning flashed from one cloud to another. Below the clouds hung a dirty brown curtain that moved across the landscape, swallowing features of it whole.

"What is that?"

"Dust storm. This one will be nasty."

I pulled out my Serengeti Vermillions and put them on.

I knew the tinted lenses filtered light in a way that normally helped me see more detail in fog or dust storms, but not so this one. As far as my sight was concerned, it might as well have been a wall.

"Do we go, or do we wait this out in town?" Marit turned the key in the ignition, and the engine kicked over.

"You're behind the wheel. It's your call."

She glanced at the local map, then smiled wolfishly. "We go for it."

I snapped my seatbelt in place, and we took off down the main road winding its away through Sedona. On the other side of the town we saw the turn off to Von Falkenberg Road. Following the map we had been given, we turned off 197 and onto the dirt road that wound its way up through a small canyon. As we drove, a small dust cloud swelled up in our wake, obscuring our view of the town and the storm that tracked us.

We came around a particularly sharp hairpin curve and darkness descended on us as if we were back in Eclipse. The wind bellowed like a wounded ox and sand hissed as it ripped across the Rover. Gravel and stones clunked and thumped against the car as the dust storm hammered us full on forward. Marit hit the headlights instantly, punching twin light cones through the brown haze, but a sharp crack killed the passenger-side light.

A huge tumbleweed launched itself through the light and dashed itself to bits on the windshield. Marit yelped, then tugged at the wheel. "I've lost it! The road. It's gone!"

For one, sickening, agonizing second, the Rover's travel became smooth, as if we were once again on Interstate 17 racing back toward Phoenix. Then gravity pulled the Rover back down to earth, and gave us the ride of our lives.

Awakening in a dented and broken Range Rover with a raging dust storm clawing at your eyes is not a pleasant experience. Realizing that obnoxious scent you smell is leaking gasoline makes it even less so. Half hanging from my seat belts, with the deflated airbag draped over my knees, I shook my head to clear it, but I only succeeded in making it hurt more.

I raised my left hand to my forehead, and it came away bloody. I twisted the rearview mirror around and saw a nasty abrasion on my forehead over my left eye and that I was bleeding from it and my nose. The blood had actually flowed across my forehead toward the right because, with the car on its side, that direction lay toward the center of the earth.

"Lucky to be alive." I hit the release button on my seatbelt, then crashed to the ground. Both my knees ached from where they had slammed into the dashboard during the crash, and my head started pounding. I shifted around and wormed my way out the narrowed slit that was where the windscreen had been before it blew out. I knew from the condition of the vehicle that we'd rolled down an arroyo, but until I got outside the Rover and got a chance to look at it, I had an optimistic view of the accident.

Panels and pieces of the vehicle littered the landscape for as far as the dust storm let me see. The hood, some of which still remained in place, had been torn in half like a piece of tissue paper. The aft end of the Rover bent down where the frame had snapped. The passenger compartment had not completely collapsed, but only by the grace of God as the roof showed some deep dents and a couple of jagged puncture wounds.

Standing there, with the storm winds battering my back, I dimly recalled someone else having been in the vehicle with me. "Marit! MARIT!" I shouted in competition with the wind. *No driver door!* I started scrambling up the hillside we had tumbled down, calling her name and trying to find her amid the dust-milked tears in my eyes.

As the howling dust storm died, I found her. She had been thrown clear of the wreck and, by some miracle, appeared largely uninjured. She lay on her left side, her face shrouded by her black hair. Kneeling beside her, I rolled her onto her back and brushed the hair from her face. Pressing my fingers to her throat I found a strong pulse and saw she was breathing normally.

Her left forearm, however, had been seriously broken. Her hand lay flat against the ground while the top of her arm had twisted more toward the sky. The jagged end of a bone poked through her skin and blood formed a bracelet around her arm. It had to be painful, and would be even more so were I to attempt to set it. *Shelter. She needs shelter, then I need to get help.*

Even in my state of shock I realized enough to know that I could not carry her to safety. I'd suffered a concussion, as had she. I might be able to walk back to Sedona and get Ramses to send some folks out here to get Marit, but I could never bring her with me. I had to hope she would be all right while I went off, and I took the dust storm's death as a good omen for my chances of success.

Then the thunderstorm began.

Even suffering from amnesia, I knew I had never seen a storm like that one before. Black clouds appeared, that from my vantage point were darker and more substantial than Frozen Shade. Multi-tined lightning forks blasted down, their brilliant light momentarily revealing the depth of the cloud cover. Thunder exploded like concussion grenades and ripped through me like bullets.

The first raindrops hit big and fat and hard. Their warmth surprised me. They felt more like blood than they did water. Like an invasion force, the heavy drops pounded down into the desert, their frequency building swiftly until I felt the blackness had been given the substance necessary to finish the job the crash had started.

The landscape remained dark and invisible until a dazzling lightning bolt drenched it in silver fire. In that second, with the sensation of blood being poured over me, I saw in the red rocks visual confirmation of what I felt. Wind-whipped rain scourged me as I used my body to shield Marit from the storm's violence.

All around the ravine in which we crouched, lightning assaulted the ground with no mercy. Bolt after bolt fell in lockstep, their thunder becoming one nearly constant roar in my ears. The light froze sheets of rain in midflight, stopping them for a second, then freeing them to pummel me.

Almost as quickly and savagely as the front hit us, it pushed on, leaving a light drizzle in its wake. For a moment or two I remained braced for a renewal of the onslaught; I knew the storm was tricking me. I knew the second I tried to stand, it would chop me back down to my knees. We had dared defy it, we had tried to outrun it, and it had taken us down, like a falcon trained for the hunt.

As the thunder trailed off, and the ringing in my ears began to die, I stood and looked around me. I realized at the fastest rate possible for my befuddled thinking, that I could see things. The tallest rocks standing sentinel around the canyon glowed with a purplish fire. I reached out toward the nearest one and felt no heat from it.

I pulled my hand back and discovered on each finger a cone of the purple fire. It traveled down my hand and to the elastic wristband of my windbreaker. It circled my arm with a nimbus of fire, yet the only thing I felt was a gentle, playful tickling sort of tingle. It was almost as if the storm, after having abused me, now wanted to make amends.

A golden glow from behind me cast my shadow long over Marit. I turned and raised my hand to ward off the brightness. A shimmering gold ball with a coppery corona floated six feet from me at the height of my head. It slowly began to circle me, as if watching me and trying to decide exactly what this dripping creature could possibly be.

Somewhere from the back of my brain came labels for all I was seeing. The purple fire on the rocks and my body was St. Elmo's fire. The sphere was ball lightning, and I knew the atmospheric conditions were perfect for both of them to exist. Intellectually, I understood these things to be naturalistic phenomena, but standing in that arroyo, the lone survivor of the thunderstorm's blitzkrieg, I felt fear in my heart. Whatever these things were, whatever explanations dispassionate scientists might have given them, I knew they were not natural at all.

The gold ball completed its circuit, then shot straight up into the air to a height of 20 or so feet. As I watched it began a strange metamorphosis. The gold shifted to green as the sphere began to lengthen into an egg-shape. It continued to grow beyond that, into a bluish rod that crackled as it hovered. In the midst of the shift from egg to rod, it shed a number of tiny green spheres that reminded me, in both size and color, of peas.

These little balls, in numbers too great for me to count, spilled down toward the ground. Before I could move to stop them, they blanketed Marit, sealing her in a glowing green cocoon. As I reached my right hand out to scrape them away, the blue rod swooped in on me, hissing and sparking as it came. I leaped back and smelled the stink of melting plastic as it lanced through the edge of my windbreaker.

It shot on past me and impaled the Rover's leaking gas tank. The blue light died amid a roiling ball of red-gold fire that sent the flaming wreckage cartwheeling across the canyon floor. It made a run halfway up the far side, then lazily tumbled back down to wallow in a pool of fire.

The shockwave hit me hard and knocked me down over Marit. My knees hammered into the ground, renewing the pain caused by their impact with the dashboard in the Rover. I managed to get my hand under me, so I didn't fall full on her, and I felt pressure as a rock punctured the palm of my left hand. As I pulled my hand back I saw the cut in it, but the stigmata gave me no pain.

Focusing beyond my hand, I saw the green light had vanished. In the flickering light from the burning Rover, Marit's eyes opened, and she turned her head toward me. "Take it easy, Marit. We had an accident. You've been hurt. I'll get you help."

She frowned and rolled up onto her right elbow. She reached out and grabbed my left wrist with her left hand. "Looks to me, love, like you're the one who is hurt."

I stared down at her left arm. The compound fracture had been healed. The blood had been washed away. I looked more closely at her arm and couldn't even see a scar from where the wound had been. "Your arm. It was broken."

Her left hand rose past my eyes and gently probed my forehead wound. "Are you sure? How do you feel?"

Did I imagine that? "I'm not crazy, Marit. I know what I saw. Your arm was broken, then the gold ball became...." My voice trailed off as I realized how truly mad my story would sound. "We have to get out of here."

"I agree." She scrambled to her feet and helped me up. A wave of dizziness passed over me, and I started to fall, but she held me up.

"Thanks."

"No problem. That knock on your head looks nasty." She guided me around to a rock and eased me down. "You sit here. I can go back into Sedona to get help."

"No, I'll make it. I will!" I felt weak and confused. My clothes suddenly felt heavy and cold and I started to shiver. In the background I heard the rumble of thunder, but it slowly faded—as did my confidence in the reality of anything I had seen.

My head jerked up as a bright lightning flash silhouetted two creatures on the edge of the canyon. Their outlines looked all spiky and cruel, like people sculpted from barbed wire. I had a sudden urge to draw my gun and empty the magazine into them, but I couldn't be certain they even existed, much less were as evil as something inside me was telling me they were.

The question of their reality solved itself quickly enough as they started their horses down a narrow trail. In the firelight I saw they were clad in big, black slickers and wearing cowboy hats. As they came closer I heard the clop of hooves on the ground, the jingle of spurs and the creak of leather. They reached the canyon floor and skirted the fire, backlighting themselves against it as they approached.

"Howdy, folks," the lead rider greeted us. "'fraid we don't have triple-A out in these parts."

Marit, despite being rain-soaked and bedraggled, turned on the charm. "Storm took us by surprise."

"That happens." The man spit to his left, causing me to recognize the bulge in his cheek as a chaw. "We were checking some head when the storm rolled in. We were heading back home when we saw the fire. We decided to check it out."

The second rider came forward, and I realized she was a woman when she tipped her head back and presented me a soft profile. "We can take you back to the house, get you fixed up, then drive you into town in the truck." She laughed gently, but it sounded unspontaneous enough to put me on my guard. "'Lessin you're of a mind to stay here while we ride back and call this in to the police."

The man looked at her. "*If* the storm didn't take the phone lines down again."

"True, this was a nasty one." She smiled at Marit. "I reckon I have some dry clothes that would fit you, if you won't mind cinching them up a might tight."

The man cleared his foot from his stirrup and offered his left hand to Marit. She put her foot in the stirrup and swung up behind him. He looked at me and shrugged. "Gotta even the load for the horses." To her, over his shoulder, he said, "Now you hang on tight to me, darlin', so you don't go and fall off."

The woman brought her horse forward and reached down to me. Because Marit had so willingly gotten on to the man's horse, I resisted my immediate urge to pull her from her horse and pump five or six rounds into her. I put my left foot into the free stirrup and was amazed at the strength with which she helped me up.

She reached back and grabbed my left buttock. "Snuggle up close here. I don't want you to slip out of the saddle when we go up the hill. Just put your arms around my waist and hang on." She pulled me forward, then settled my arms around her more to her satisfaction and comfort than mine. "Don't be afraid," she whispered, "I won't break."

We left the burning Rover behind quickly enough, and I actually did have to tighten my grip to remain in the saddle as we went up over the lip of the canyon. Up top I could see a dim, distant horizon line where the clouds were thin enough to let sunlight lay down a gold layer between the mountains and the sky. Over the vast, flat plain across which we rode, I could see lightning strike from time to time. In the backlight I made out the squat, angular shape that marked the house toward which we rode.

As we got closer the house appeared to be old and well-weathered. "Looks like the power is out."

The woman nodded at the man's comment. "Looks like we'll have to use candles, again."

The man half-turned toward Marit. "Know anything about horses?"

"I have ridden quite a bit, actually."

"Good." He dismounted in front of the house, then turned and caught Marit around the waist. He lifted her clear of the saddle and set her down gently. His hands lingered on her waist a bit longer than I thought necessary, but neither Marit or the woman seemed to notice it. "You can help me put the horses up while your friend and my wife rustle up something to eat."

"Don't mind working for a meal," Marit smiled.

"Good."

The woman eased me down from the saddle, then dismounted quickly, turned around and accidently bumped belly to belly with me. She steadied herself by grabbing my waist, then smiled. "Sorry, didn't think you'd still be standing there." As her husband took the reins to her horse, she grabbed my right hand and pulled me toward the porch steps.

Marit, lost in a whispered and giggled conversation with the man, didn't notice.

A wood-burned sign tacked to a porch pillar read "The Donners."

The woman opened the door without benefit of keys. "Out here we don't have much cause to go locking doors. We might get a coyote in the yard from time to time, or some New Agers looking for a vortex, but they're never any trouble."

Inside and out of the rain, she doffed the slicker and hat. She struck a match and set it to a candle on a table just inside the door. Once the scent of burning sulfur cleared my nostrils, I caught the musty smell of an old house with older furnishings. The air seemed a bit stagnant, as if the house had not been lived in for a while.

This made me suspicious, but I put it down to the paranoia I'd been suffering since the Rover's explosion. It could have been that they had been away from the main house for a while, living in another building on their property while they tended their herd. Even more plausibly, the contrast of the clean smell of a rain-washed desert and this house accounted for my misgivings.

The woman moved away from me like some fey creature. She touched the candle to a half-dozen others, literally blazing a trail toward the kitchen. In the candle-light I saw what my hands had confirmed during the ride. Though an average-sized woman, she had a very narrow waist and full hips. The damp jeans she wore looked more like a second skin than a garment, and this woman compared quite favorably to Marit in all ways.

The candlelight burnished gold highlights into her long, blond hair. As she turned and caught me staring at her back, she smiled as if she welcomed the attention, then laughed throatily. "Let's see if we can find something in here to quench your hunger."

As if in a trance I followed her into the kitchen. She drew a long bread knife from a block near the stove, then pointed with it toward a huge, rectangular spectral hulk in the corner of the room. Light from several small flames played along the blade's sharp edge. "In the icebox you'll find some meat. We can take slices off the rump roast for sandwiches."

I looked away from her, albeit very reluctantly, and crossed to the refrigerator. I felt so confused that I didn't attach any significance to her having called it an icebox. Nor did the true meaning of a light going on when I opened the door hit me. I knew lights came on when refrigerator doors were opened. My brain was unable to connect the supposed lack of power to the house with this being a problem. It did not sound an alarm in my brain.

Seeing an old man's head on the top shelf did. Lidless eyes stared at me, instantly transplanting the terror of his last moments to me. Below his head, on the different levels, various body parts had been stacked quite carefully. A charred hunk of meat sat in congealed juices on a plate, right next to two-thirds of a liver wrapped in plastic-wrap.

Adrenaline jolted through me like lightning. I whirled, my right hand going for the Krait. As I moved out of the light, it washed full over the mad woman rushing at my back with her knife upraised. She slashed down through where I had stood, then snarled at me like some feral monster in human form.

I snapped the Krait's safety lever down and stroked the trigger. The first bullet caught her in her flat belly and tossed her back against the kitchen counter. She rebounded from it, the knife flying from her fingers, and I shot her again. That bullet slammed into her left shoulder and spun her to the ground.

I leaped over her, but as I did so, she clawed at and caught my ankle. I stumbled and went down, landing hard on my left arm. As I rolled onto my back, she rose up like a malevolent shadow in the refrigerator's light. Without conscious thought, I stabbed the gun at her and tightened my finger down on the trigger.

The first shot sent her flying back into the fridge. The old man's head bounced up and over her body. My second shot hit solidly and sprayed crimson over the refrigerator's interior. The light shifted to a lurid red as my last shot blew a chunk from her head and destroyed a bottle of wine on the top shelf.

Blood mixed with wine ran down and flooded out onto

the floor. I kicked the old man's head away from my feet and stood. I glanced back at the woman again and was prepared, at the least little twitch, to shoot her yet again. Then I heard a scream from outside. Seeing an image of Marit's head replacing that of the old man, I sprinted down the hallway to the door, outside and along the porch. I vaulted the railing and started running toward the small stable.

The man, pulling Marit along behind him by the wrist, ran out the door and around the corner. I hit top speed crossing the open ground, then flattened with my back against the stable. I took a quick peek around the corner and saw the man standing there, weaponless, with Marit's right wrist held tightly in his left hand. I pulled my head back, took a deep breath, then cut around the corner and dropped my gun on him.

They were gone!

I darted forward, to where they had stood, right there, out in the open, and could see no trace of them. Then, one step beyond that, I caught sight of them again, but they appear far further distant than they could have gotten in just a second. "Let her go!"

The man stopped and his slicker melted back into a cape. The red-checked shirt and jeans I imagined him wearing became a scarlet tunic and blue pantaloons. His cowboy boots shifted into the floppy-top boots I associated with ancient corsairs. His hat even shifted into a black velvet beret and sprouted a long, green feather. His ears, I noticed for the first time, were pointed.

Marit clawed at his wrist, and he released her. Then, striking faster than a cobra, he backhanded her and knocked her flying. She hit the ground and lay still. His eyes glowed with blacklight intensity as he brought his right hand forward. "Now you are in my realm, man-child! Here you will die."

St. Elmo's fire sprouted from his fingertips and condensed into a large ball of fire. It arced toward me, but I triggered two shots, and it imploded when my bullets pierced its shell. I shifted my aim point and pulled the trigger twice more. Both those shots hit him in the chest and toppled him backward.

Wary because of his wife, I ran up and pumped the rest of the clip into him. I saved the last bullet for his head, then slapped another clip into the Krait and watched him for a while to make sure he was dead. Slowly, still keeping my eye on him, I backed toward where Marit had fallen and found her amid some yellowish ground fog.

She had a bruise on the side of her face and blood dribbled from a split lip, but otherwise she looked fine. Though she remained unconscious, I smiled and stroked the uninjured side of her face. "Don't worry, kid, I'll get you home."

As I listened to the regular whisper of her breathing, I realized I didn't hear any more thunder. I stood and turned back toward the house, but no gravel crunched under my feet. The ground fog was possible in Arizona, especially after a thunderstorm, but why *yellow*? Completing my turn I saw no house, no stable, nothing. As far as I could see, the landscape was gray on purple with yellow-mist trim.

I looked up expecting to see stars, but I saw nothing. My paranoia roared back with a vengeance, and I instantly regretting being so generous with the bullets I'd used on the man, if, in fact, that was what he was.

Kneeling beside Marit again, I waved the mist away from her face. "I'll get you home again, Marit. I promise." *Just as soon as I figure out where the hell we actually are.*

"You might try tapping your heels together and repeating 'There's no place like home,' but I doubt its efficacy in this case."

I looked up and saw a man or, more accurately, the cameo of a man. It seemed, to me, to have all the dimensions of a normal body, but it was black on black. Still, I did not get the feeling he was black in a racial sense. In fact, doubtlessly projecting from myself, he could have been me except for the outline of a full goatee and his ring.

While his entire body was made of shadow, the fourth finger on his right hand had a bright gold band on it. As his hand moved, I saw the same curious design on it that I had seen in my dream and drawn for Hal. It was the symbol that Juanita said belonged to El Espectro.

"The first time I saw you I was dreaming. Am I dreaming now?"

The shadow laughed politely. "No, you are not dreaming, and if you were, this would certainly be a nightmare."

"According to Marit's cleaning woman, you are El Espectro."

The man laughed again, but more heartily this time. "I supposed that is, indeed, possible. I have lost track of how many different names I have worn." He opened his arms to indicate the area surrounding us. "I also think we had best leave this place."

I looked around the smoothly featureless plain. "Where are we?"

El Espectro moved over to the dead body and prodded it with his toe. "I believe this is the protodimensional haven he has used for centuries to gain access to our world. This is not good because it bleeds into his home dimension, and that could cause us some trouble."

"Dimension? Who is this Donner guy, anyway, and what do you mean by dimension?" My mouth began to get dry, and I detected a sulphurous tinge to the yellow fog. "What is that smell?"

He turned back to me. "I will answer your questions, perhaps not to your satisfaction, then we must move if you want to leave this place. You will have to do everything I tell you to do, without questions. Do you understand?"

"Yes."

"Good. This was a Draoling—consider it a sociopathic human for all intents and purposes. This one has been around a long time. He took the place of Lewis Keseberg at Truckee Lake in 1846, inspiring the acts of cannibal-ism surrounding the Donner Party legend. When the crimes were discovered, he returned here and left the real Lewis Keseberg to face the music. This one, or another of his vile race, was responsible for the Jack the Ripper murder spree and, 40 years ago, may have signed the name 'Zodiac' to a series of murders in California. This one had a sense of humor, hence his use of the Donner name."

He pointed off in a direction I sensed was south. "Tell me what you see."

"Gray landscape, patches of purple." As I spoke I found myself focusing more clearly on things. "The purple is textured. It might be rock formations or vegeta-tion. I also see the yellow mist in hollows like this one."

"Good. What do you smell?"

"Rotten eggs, sulphur."

"Excellent." He walked over to me and probed my forehead with his right hand. The shadow touch felt not unlike the St. Elmo's fire in that it didn't hurt and actually tickled a bit. "The blow to your head is clearing up. You will continue to have increasing sensory acuity in this place. Someday you may even learn to come here again."

"I don't think I would like that."

"I understand your reticence, but you might find this place useful to you at some point." El Espectro held out his left hand, with the palm skyward, and lifted. Marit's unconscious body floated up in the air and hovered at waist height. "Being here makes this *much* easier for me. If you are ready, we can begin traveling. We should have you home in under two hours."

"On foot? Fat chance." I glanced at my watch and saw something very odd. The analog portion of it seemed to be functioning perfectly. The second hand swept on as if the whole watch were brand new. The little LCD window, by way of contrast, flickered and flashed with lines and dots. The patterns, when they looked anything but random, seemed to be playing out an infinite sequence of numbers determined by a formula that was well beyond me.

I decided, at that point, that if I gave too much thought to what I was seeing, my head would begin to hurt a lot more than it did now, and the situation would *not* get any better. "Home, did you say?"

"Yes, back to Eclipse, I think. You will find nothing in Sedona that will aid your mission." El Espectro began walking south, and Marit drifted smoothly behind him. In a few steps he got far distant, it seemed, but when I ran to catch up with him, I reached his side in only a few strides.

"How do you know what we were doing in Sedona?"

"I know because I know." He gave me a sidelong glance that, despite being totally blank to me, had to have contained some amusement in it. "In this case I know you came to Sedona searching for Nero Loring. You came to Sedona because a friend of his received a postcard from Loring that was postmarked Sedona."

"Okay, that's right. How do you know?" *Could the traitor be selling me out to him?*

"No, your traitor and I have no connection. And I know about the postcard because I am the one who sent it, at Loring's request."

I stared at the shadow man. "You read my mind. That, or you are Coyote."

"Me, Coyote? Please, no. I have met him, and he is a most interesting individual, but I am not him." He led me up and around a grayish standing stone topped with a thorny, purple-leafed bush. "I am able, in certain places, at certain times, to pick off surface thoughts. Right now, because of your injury, you are confused enough not to be exerting as much control over your mind as you might otherwise. Even in a dream state your control is admirable. And if you really do want to bet a million dolmarks that I am insane, I can find you plenty of takers for that wager."

I blushed. "Forgive me, but my memory goes back less than a week. All this dimension stuff is confusing and, quite frankly, unbelievable." I followed him down a hill and through a cloud of the yellow fog. "I assume, if you sent the card for Loring, you know where he is now?"

"I do."

"Tell me. It is imperative I find him."

El Espectro shook his head as we cleared the mist. "I will not do that without Nero's permission. I will not violate his confidence or security."

I knew, just in hearing the words and a sense I got from him, that El Espectro would brook no argument and would not waver. "You will tell me if gives you permission to do so?"

"Death itself could not keep me from giving you the news."

He made that declaration with enough confidence that

I found myself believing him. *Sure, I believe a man made of shadow in a dimension that apparently lies parallel to Earth will come back from the dead to share information with me. Hell, he's called 'the Ghost' by some of the city's Hispanics. Maybe he's already dead.*

"Who in God's name are you?"

"Names will mean nothing to you, and I sincerely doubt that, 'in God's name,' I am not much of anyone at all. I am someone who, years ago, while the world was still rational, learned secrets I should not have learned. I walked places men were not meant to go, and I saw things that were meant to torture the soul. I discovered, in myself, powers and abilities the normal world would not recognize. They told me things upon which I was compelled to act, but ultimately proved unable to stop.

"In many ways I am like your Coyote. I chose to battle things I see as evil, to help people beset by troubles. The difference between us is that Coyote acts in the material world because he lacks even the nascent empathic skills that allow one to discern *anything* in this place. I act here or in the realm of dreams to delay and defeat abominations."

I shook my head. "I'm not even going to pretend I understand any of this."

"At this point, a wise choice." He held up a hand and crouched. Marit floated back down to the ground, and I crouched next to him. "I had not expected this."

I looked off in the distance but could only make out a dull gold ring lying on the ground in the distance. "What had you not expected?"

He reached out and laid his left hand over my eyes. For a half-second I saw darkness, then I saw the distant ring through eyes much sharper than mine. Around it I saw a dozen or so individuals wearing clothing reminiscent of that on the Draoling I had killed. "Keseberg's friends?"

"I doubt it, but I don't think they will be granting you a

reward for killing him." He took his hand away from my face, and my own vision returned. "How many bullets do you have."

"Twenty-eight, but they're split into two clips."

I saw his brow furrow in profile. "And that is a 10mm Colt Krait?"

"Yes."

"A bit small. Figure three bullets per Draoling, provided you don't miss."

"I don't miss." I conjured up my memory of shooting the sniper in Boxton.

"Fascinating." He stood and brushed unseen dirt from his knees. "We will be there in a very short time. That ring is a dimensional gate that will take you back to Phoenix. It is important, therefore, that we gain control of it. If we have the time, you can account for nine of them. You will only need to get six, I think. Speed will be of the essence, however, because the amount of power we release in killing them will attract all sorts of attention."

"I understand."

"Good. I will leave Ms. Fisk here, then bring her along when it is safe."

I took the Krait off safety and eased the hammer back. "Ready when you are."

"Let us proceed."

In the back of my mind I knew my head injury had to have affected me more than I could tell. As we rushed forward, the distance between us and this dimensional gate melted away. The Draolings standing around it did not notice us until we were at optimal range. El Espectro pointed at them, clenched his hand into a fist, then flung his hand open as he twisted it palm up.

One of the Draolings in the center of the group spontaneously combusted. He screamed in a language I've only heard whispered in nightmares. His companions turned toward him, then recoiled and started to run away. The flaming Draoling flailed about, catching on to one of them, but the others escaped and those who ran in our direction made a nasty discovery.

I knew El Espectro assumed it would take three bullets to kill a Draoling, and my experience with the Donners suggested he was very right in his assumption. By the same token I knew it would only take one to attract some attention. In rapid succession I pumped one round into each of three humanoids, then let the nearest have two more before I blew the head off a fourth with a lucky shot. I started cutting to the left, drawing the Draolings off as El Espectro went right.

The four of them closest to me closed like sharks smelling blood. One had already been hit, and he went down when a shot hit him in the shoulder and all but tore off his right arm. Two bullets in the stomach jackknifed one Draoling forward, and the Draoling running behind him vaulted over his dying body. I met his long, clawing dive with a left foot in the face. That snapped his neck but the impact still knocked me down, and his dead body fell on top of me.

The last one kept coming in. I twisted to the right, turning toward him. My first shot missed, but the second broke his right thigh and dropped him face first to the ground. He tore at the ground to crawl forward, but the next two bullets disrupted his higher brain functions and put an end to his desire to kill me.

I tossed the dead Draoling from me and stood. Across the circle, near an obsidian obelisk trimmed in gold, I saw El Espectro. Around him burned a number of Drao-fires. I waved, and he returned the gesture, then slumped against the obelisk. Holstering my pistol I ran to him and helped support him.

"Do not concern yourself with me. I will survive." He pointed back in the direction we had come and Marit floated toward us, but not as high as she had before. "Get her before I drop her."

I ran over to Marit and accepted her in my arms. Only when my left hand smeared blood on her sleeve did I realized El Espectro had been bleeding. "You're hurt."

"A scratch. Nothing." He urgently pointed to the circle. "Get in the middle. I will send you to Eclipse. I do not know exactly where this will come out, but wherever it is, get out of there quickly."

"Why?"

"Because I was careless. There are things out here that sensed the power we have used. They also sense our vulnerability. I must send you through, then destroy this portal or they will find you—and you would not like that."

I leaped over the gold and obsidian ring and ran to the middle. The black stone inlays looked like decoration, but ran along the gold ring and looked almost identical to the pathways on printed circuits. Every so often they ended at cloudy quartz lozenges that had a pulsating gray-pink light in the middle of them.

The gold began to glow with a bright light that cycled around and became more intense. "What about you?" I shouted over the keening shriek rising from the circle.

Worry not about me, Tycho Caine. Fiddleback and I have played this game many times.

The light and sound reached an inaudible and invisible climax at the same time, and suddenly I found myself in the dark basement of a tenement building. Across from me I saw a set of stairs leading up and the weak light of a sodium lamp bleeding down it. I stepped over what looked like a yellow circle painted on the floor, then carried Marit up the stairs. We raced through the building as fast as possible. I shifted her to an over-the-shoulder carry as I shot down a hallway and out through the opening to the outside.

True to his word, El Espectro had delivered us to Eclipse again. Across an open killing ground I saw a barricade. As I ran toward it I recognized the area. Off to my right, I saw the clutter of trailers comprising Boxton. Without a second thought I scrambled up the barricade, then slid down off a car on the far side.

Behind me something flashed white-gold. For all of a second Eclipse saw the sun at its heart and knew what it was to be out from under Frozen Shade. I set Marit down and turned around as a rumbling sound started. The middle of the tenement began to crumble. Dust filled all the windows, then gusted out as the building caved in on itself. In a handful of heartbeats the building went from six stories to memories.

I looked at the fallen building, then stooped and lifted Marit up again. *He said he and Fiddleback had played together many times. I hope he made it.* Then I remembered his promise. "I know he won," I laughed aloud. "Fiddleback didn't stand a ghost of a chance against him."

And yet, even laughing, I looked at my left hand and still saw wet blood.

Once I got Marit back to her apartment, Juanita called a doctor and we put Marit to bed. The doctor checked her over and said she looked fine to him, if a little dehydrated. He questioned me closely to determine if I had hit her, but he accepted my story that we had been slumming in Eclipse and had been involved in an unsuccessful mugging.

He left a prescription for some heavy-duty ibuprofen tablets, and Anna ventured out to fill it. The doctor insisted Marit rest in bed and get plenty of fluids. He also took a look at me, cleaned up my head wound and taped a bandage into place. "You may want to take one or two of her pills if you start having headaches. If you have any serious neurological symptoms, call me and get to the Phoenix General Tower."

"Thanks, Doc." I showed him to the tranversor, but he had wait as the box was in use. When the door opened, a messenger stepped out, and the doctor vanished behind the closing doors. "Can I help you?"

"I have a message here for Mr. Caine. Would that be you, sir?" The fresh-faced kid held a clipboard out. "Sign at number 33."

I scrawled my name, and he handed me a small ivory envelope with no return address. My name had been carefully calligraphed across the front. I flipped it over and opened it. I found another smaller envelope inside the first, again with my name carefully written across it. From that second envelope I pulled a square piece of very expensive printed cardstock. It read, "Ms. Nerys Loring requests the pleasure of Mr. Tycho Caine's presence for a private dinner this evening at 8 p.m. Dress will be formal, with cocktails at 7 p.m. RSVP by return messenger."

I tapped the card against the fingers of my left hand. Despite the drive to Sedona and the bizarre adventures so early in the day, El Espectro had returned us to Eclipse before 2 in the afternoon—or so the digital part of my watch reported. The analog portion, before I reset it, said 10 p.m. Glancing at my watch, I saw that I had three and a half hours before Nerys expected me, and I knew I could not refuse the invitation. *This should be* fascinating.

I looked up. "You're waiting for the reply?"

The messenger nodded.

"I accept."

"Very good, sir. I was told to tell you that a VIP pass for the maglev to the Lorica tower will be waiting for you at the Madison Street station. You can use the upper lounge. You will be met when you arrive."

I punched the button to summon the tranversor again, then handed him a 10 dolmark bill. I left Juanita watching him until he departed, then retreated to Marit's private office. In her Rolodex I found a number for the Sunburst Foundation and dialed it. I was not surprised to hear Hal answer the phone.

"Hal, it's Caine. We're back." I filled him in on the outing, but left the bizarre parts out. As I told it to him, we got a lead, got caught in a strange storm and arranged for alternate transport back to Phoenix. I let him know Marit had been hurt but not seriously, then I dropped the bombshell of Nerys' invitation.

"My, my, you do travel in, ah, fast circles. Eight o'clock dinner? You should be through and free by midnight, unless you're planning to spend more time with Nerys."

"Thanks, but I don't think so." I remembered the picture she had purchased during the auction. "I don't think her idea of fun and mine overlap."

"Good. I have a meeting scheduled for here, at my home, at 1 a.m. I'd like you to be here, if possible." He hesitated, and I heard some ambivalence enter his voice. "I'm meeting with the leadership of the Blood Crips, Jade Dragons and Diablos here at my house. They are getting harder to calm down. I'd like you to be here to show them I have the tools necessary, if it comes to that, to restrain the Aryans."

"You're the velvet glove, and I'm the steel fist?"

"Something like that. I don't need you shooting anyone, but you have the stone killer act down as well as anyone. A new face will make them think I am making moves that will keep things on the level for them."

"I understand. I'll be there."

"Thanks. I'll see you later."

"Later."

I quickly made one more call. None of the clothes I had were formal, so I dialed up Roger's number at The Gentleman's Wardrobe. "I'm afraid I have to impose on your services, Roger."

"Not to worry, Mr. Caine," he said soothingly, "We have already begun work on your tuxedo. It will be styled similarly to the other suit we made for you. Ms. Loring will be impressed."

"Do you read minds, Roger?"

"Would that I did, Mr. Caine. It would save me oodles of money that I now pay catering services to furnish me with guest lists for parties." He tried to sound world-weary, but I heard plenty of self-pleasure in his voice. "Your name came by this morning, and we started work immediately."

I frowned. "Why would a catering company need a guest list?"

"My dear Mr. Caine, you would not expect the social doyens of our glittering metropolis to give substandard soirées, would you? The caterers in this city have a massive database with information about everything from dietary restrictions to social feuds. They toss the guest list into this vast program, and it sets menus, provides seating charts, settles questions of protocol and even sets distances between guests depending upon how torrid their affairs are or how amicable their divorces were. You are guaranteed that you will never taste the same entree in a calender year and, if you own a winery or distillery, your table will be supplied with the best you have to offer. It is quite impressive."

"So I see." I thought for a second, then asked, "So, if you have a guest list, perhaps you can tell me who else will be there."

"Well, Mr. Caine, only because you are such a good customer. The party will be quite intimate this evening. You are the only guest and, from what I see of the menu, Ms. Loring may even be intending to have you for dessert."

"I consider myself duly warned. Thank you, Roger."

"Thank you, Mr. Caine. We will have your tuxedo for you by six o'clock."

Roger was as good as his word. When the tuxedo arrived, Juanita awakened me from a dreamless nap. I showered, taped a new bandage over my forehead, then dressed. The tux fit perfectly. I opted not to bring my Krait, but I did still wear my bulletproof vest beneath my shirt. While I hardly expected anything weird to happen, the encounter with the man at Danny's Place made me cautious enough to want body armor.

Juanita was kind enough to give me instructions on how to get to the Madison Street maglev station. I noted amusingly that she referred to it as the "mangle train," but I gathered the term came more from the hopes and wishes of the folks in Eclipse than any actual historical incident. Armed with her directions, I took the elevator down to Level 20, then took a people mover from Goddard Tower #1 to the Southern Pacific Tower and down to Level 10. There I found the maglev station, and after identifying myself, was given a pass and admitted to the VIP lounge.

A poster on the wall gave me an overview of the whole system. "Local" trains ran from City Center to the various corporate citadels. "Circuit" trains ran counterclockwise around the corporate citadel circuit. The bullet train, which ran on the ground, left from the Madison Street/Southern Pacific terminal annex in Eclipse to go to the regional airport southeast of the city. It ran through a tunnel for the entire length of the trip through Eclipse, so no one would be subjected to having to see how the majority of people in the city lived. Moreover, each of the windows had been fitted with a flat, LCD screen that could be tuned to the local TV stations or, if a passenger so desired, a "scenery" channel that, no matter time of the year, presented simulated real-time views of the desert outside.

To complete my journey, I had to take the local train from the Madison Street station to the Honeywell & Koch local station. From there I would only have to walk across the VIP lounge to the circuit side and catch the next train out, which would deliver me directly to Lorica Industries. Taking a local train to Lorica would have forced me to travel across City Center to the Randolf Road station. Given the relative speeds of the maglevs with the local trains in City Center, the less direct route would save me a minimum of 15 minutes.

The maglev train that rolled slowly into the station had a triangular shape to it. The lower, wider section serviced the workers from City Center heading out to catch the circuit train and the people who were coming into City Center for the evening. The smaller, upper deck on the train car was reserved for VIPs who, from the look of the other people waiting in the lounge, were corporate officers or visitors from foreign nations.

I waited for a handful of people to disembark, then I got onto the train. The upper deck's luxurious appointments rivaled the beauty and comfort of Marit's apartment. Instead of the tightly packed, lightly padded fiberglass benches down below, we had plush, velvet upholstered couches and a ring of televisions up along the sloped roof. A uniformed stewardess greeted us and helped us fasten seat belts. She pointed out how to tune the little earpiece she handed me, then she tended to the others and signaled the engineer we were read to depart.

We rocketed out of the station at 6:30 p.m. The dying sun cast long shadows from City Center over the eastern half of the city. As we rode high above Frozen Shade, I could easily see how and why the world views of those who lived in Eclipse and the corporate executives never meshed. From this vantage point the people of the corporate power set saw a city of unparalleled beauty. Frozen Shade, except where the sunlight glinted up from panel joints, appeared a flat black, pacific ocean. The corporate citadels rose from the black waves like mighty island nations. The protrusions of natural rocks like Camelback Mountain and Squaw Peak to the north or South Mountain to the south turned the whole valley into a Zen garden maintained by giants.

From here there was no clue to the grimy, grim conditions in Eclipse. Like angels in heaven, or gods living high in mountain strongholds, the privileged of the world did not have to dirty their feet with the affairs of mortals. Frozen Shade gave them the power they needed to make their world function, and it also shielded them from having to even acknowledge the people living outside their domains.

The local train took me into the heart of the Honeywell & Koch citadel. I made the transfer easily to the circuit train and arrived at Lorica with 10 minutes to spare before I was supposed to arrive. I wondered very briefly how I would recognize my escort or I would be recognized, but I dismissed my concern as I knew Nerys was a clever woman.

Only when I stepped from the maglev train did I realize exactly how clever she was. I saw three men waiting for me. Two were improbably large and wore suits big enough to have been tailored for cement sewer piping. The third man was not dressed as well as I was, but certainly better than when I had seen him last. His eyes shaded behind dark glasses, he extended his hand to me. "Welcome to Lorica, Mr. Caine. I am Radu Leich. Ms. Loring sent me to get you."

Close up the man did, in fact, have a star-shaped scar on his right cheek and a limited amount of left-right facial asymmetry. It looked as if the cheekbone on the right side of his face had been pared down. Still, the scar did not seem nearly as pronounced as it had only yesterday in Danny's Place. His left hand, which was not gloved, did not look that much different than his right, though the bluish veins did not show through the pale flesh quite as well.

Coincidence I told myself. Yes, Leich looked remarkably like the Reaper I had shot in the face, and the star scar could have been a reminder of that injury. That was assuming, of course, that having forced a bullet through his head and out the back of his skull had not killed him. That, I knew, was patently impossible.

Then again, returning from Sedona by strolling through a land of gray and purple was impossible as well.

"Please, Mr. Leich, take me to your leader."

He nodded and preceded me from the VIP lounge. From the narrow walkway we used to get from the lounge to a central elevator cylinder, I was able to get a good look at the entire Lorica Citadel. The cylinder formed the hub of the complex with walkways going off in six directions like spokes. Unlike City Center, which had been done in white marble and bright colors, the Lorica Citadel boasted mostly dark colors and mirrored trim. The whole of the complex, from there in the middle, looked like a tunnel created to connect heaven and hell.

The two apes dropped in behind me and said nothing. I sensed from them a high degree of boredom tinged with anticipation of possible excitement. That anticipation grew as we stopped at an elevator, and Mr. Leich inserted a card into the slot. A car descended through the clear elevator tube and stopped before us. The door opened to an empty car, but Leich shook his head. "You two will wait here."

I entered the capsule behind Leich, and he inserted another card into the panel there. The elevator did not speak to him, but silently whisked us up into the rarified reaches of the Citadel. I watched floor after floor race pased through the smoky glass walls, then we passed through a section that surrounded us with blank cement walls. We stopped after 20 feet of cinderblock, and the door opened.

Initially the similarity in color and design between the foyer and the dimensional gate nearly overwhelmed me. The elevator opened onto a small room with black marble on the walls and floor. Gold joints joined the blocks. The ceiling, done in a burnished gold, reflected light down from panels hidden at the tops of the walls. Off to my left, two black satyr statues held up a block of black marble as a table and above it, on the wall, hung a gold mirror so guests could make last minute adjustments to their dress.

Across from the elevator stood two doors plated with beaten gold. As I approached them, they slowly opened and a white, foglike mist rolled out and over me. I caught the faint scent of pine as I walked through it, then felt the light breeze as the doors swung shut behind me. Standing still, I waited for the mist to settle down, which it did quickly, leaving me with the impressions that I had some how ascended into heaven.

In complete and stark contrast with the foyer and the whole of the Lorica Citadel, Nerys' domain had been done every possible shade of color save black. The over all impression of the place was that she had chosen white as her color, and doubtlessly that would linger in the minds of casual visitors, but it painted a woefully inaccurate picture of her lair.

As the last of the mist dissipated, I found myself on a white marble walkway between two gurgling streams. The streams looked as if they had been lined with mother-of-pearl and, though the water doubtlessly made my task impossible, I could see no joints between sections of inlay throughout the 12-foot lengths I saw. As nearly as I could tell, Nerys had located some unknown species of gigantic tube-oyster and had fashioned the streambeds from the halves of its shell.

Above them, strung between two Doric columns of white marble, white silk sheeting formed softly billowing walls. Where they parted I saw other columns and sheets that formed, as nearly as I could determine, a ghostly labyrinth that could change in an instant. Still, there were times when I could see a fair distance through the area, and it seemed to me that Nerys' home might well fill the entire top of the Lorica Citadel, giving me roughly 1.5 square miles in which to search for my hostess.

The impression that Nerys had found talented oyster

artisans continued as I walked forward toward a pulsing fountain. As the water rose and fell from the central spiral, I decided it reminded me most of a spiral horn of some sort. I would have guessed it had come from some mutant narwhal, but I knew the last of that species had died four years before. Moreover, the spire had the same opalescent, mother-of-pearl look as the streambeds. That coloration extended to the basin surrounding the fountain and the trough that caught the excess water and channeled it into the streams.

I crossed a small, crystalline bridge over the stream to my right and walked down the white corridor before me. My steps sounded hollow, but the silk walls absorbed any echo they might have made. At the end of the corridor I turned right again and smiled at the beautiful young woman standing there. I kept my smile polite even though, aside from the strip of dark blue silk tying her black hair back and the matching loincloth, she wore nothing at all.

"Please, Mr. Caine, follow me."

"As you wish." Following her was not difficult, but the addition of other women similarly clad did provide a certain number of distractions. The apes' anticipation and disappointment were now clear to me. More importantly, Mr. Leich never even made a move to look in through the doors, as if the potential glimpse of such beauty meant nothing to him. Oddly, though, I had not gained the impression he was a homosexual. Instead, I thought, he might have just seen me and them as a source of revenue for the Reapers or, worse yet, had the same use for us as the Draolings.

My guide led me to an island inside the stark white world. It necessitated my crossing another stream on a crystal bridge, and I noticed how the pulsing, soothing sound of the water enhanced the beauty of the surroundings. Off to my left I saw a gold and glass cart with a dozen decanters of various liquors, a clear ice bucket and a number of cut crystal glasses. Standing beside it a blond woman in an emerald green loincloth waited to take my order.

Not desiring to drink when Hal wanted me to attend his meeting later, I smiled and ordered a club soda with a twist of lime. She set about making the drink while I looked around the island. Aside from her, me and the cart, the circular room described by the white curtain walls was featureless. I had the annoying feeling that I was being watched, but I could not determine a focus for that sensation.

The woman crossed to me and handed me my drink. I thanked her but she said nothing to me. I noticed her green eyes matched the color of her garment and she, too, had her hair bound back with a green strip of silk. She seemed happy and quite at ease with being half-naked while I was fully and formally clothed. While she was certainly attractive enough to interest me, her casual attitude toward her nakedness stole carnality from our encounter while still making it exotic and erotic.

"A pretty child, is she not?"

I turned around at the sound of Nerys' voice, a bit disturbed that she managed to have made it over the bridge I had crossed without my seeing or hearing her. My irritation quickly faded as I looked at her, and a smile spread across my face. She wore a black gown with a mandarin collar and sweetheart neckline that showed her throat and bosom to great advantage. The bodice hugged her tightly, then flowed gently from her hips to end at ankle height. The long sleeves even had a bit of a triangular tab that covered the back of her hands. She wore a cinnabar necklace in which parallel strips of the stone formed a crescent at her throat and which was matched by two cinnabar earrings that

were carved like cameos. The earrings showed a
spider design on each, though the arachnids depicted
looked to be black widows, not fiddlebacks.

"Her beauty evaporates in your presence." Unaware
if her servants constantly worked in this state of undress,
I saw the wisdom of her having them do that. Surrounded
by such beauty, yet clad in a garment that revealed little
and promised much, Nerys Loring became much more
mysterious and seductive. Her mature beauty and strength
of character made her the equal of her quiet servants
while her charm and intelligence pushed her well beyond
them in desirability..

Nerys walked over to me and brushed her hand along
the front of my coat. "Roger does superior work. This suit
flatters you."

Her perfume smelled of orchids and conjured up a
momentary, fleeting memory of heat and darkness. I
tried to capture it, but it faded in a flash. "Thank you. You,
of course, look absolutely lethal in that gown."

"You have an amusing way with words, Mr. Caine."
Nerys nodded to the woman, and she brought her what
I assumed to be straight vodka with a twist of lemon.
Nerys accepted the drink with her right hand, then
gently caught the woman's chin in her left hand. With
its long, curved incarnadine nail lightly brushing tanned
flesh, Nerys' thumb stroked the bartender's cheek,
then she released her. The girl retreated as she had
after serving me, but I detected a certain joy in her step
at having passed muster with her mistress.

"You doubtlessly noticed, Tycho, that I have a number
of beautiful women here to serve me. Do you know
why?"

I shook my head and sipped my drink.

"You will agree they are all spectacular. I find their soft,
gentle lines pleasing to the eye. They move with a fluid
grace that fits with all this." She pointed at the silk

curtains and the moat surrounding us, then caressed my shoulder with her left hand. "They are not, like men, angular and hard and bellicose. They are the yin of my world, while the outside is the yang. They serve me in my sanctuary from all that would distress me."

I smiled appreciatively. "You are fortunate that you can isolate your world so easily."

"My goal is *insulation*, not isolation. I find running a multinational corporation very draining. When I have been vampirized by business demands, I am able to retreat here and recover amid this paradise." Keeping her hand on my shoulder, she slipped behind me and whispered in my ear. "If I thought you wanted her, I would give her to you. And, at my request, she would give herself to you. She would doubtlessly enjoy it, as would you, I am certain. You could live here forever with her or others, but I sense in you aspirations for something more than being kept as a…pet."

I drank a bit more to cover my discomfort at her use of the word 'pet,' "What would lead you to believe that?"

She completed her circle around me, having spiraled in closer so we stood as close as I had with the female Draoling that morning. "I had understood it was your custom, once you had completed a task, to return home to await your next assignment. I also know that in preparing for your visit here, you would have studied Lorica and its situation quite thoroughly. I know you would have seen the possibilities here. You know, very soon, I will be able to offer you limitless power."

I looked into the depths of her black eyes. "And for this power, what would you have me do?"

"I'd not ask you to be my consort. Your talents, while they might be considerable in that area, are too valuable to squander on sexual excess. There are others who can sate my hungers, but you have skills I need. Poor Radu

is the best I have in that area and, as you know, he is
barely competent." She reached up and caressed the
side of my face. "Now, you should tell me what it is you're
doing by remaining in Phoenix."

I needed time to think because a number of things
were beginning to cascade together. "As you suspected,
I decided to remain to study the situation. I wanted to get
the lay of the land, as it were."

"Oh, you did—you're living with her," Nerys laughed
aloud. "Were dear Marit half as pretty as she is vain, I
might have even offered her a place, here in my sanctuary. And yet, here is how much I wish you to work for me.
If you so desire, I will accept her here and even tell Mr.
Leich to refrain from killing her—not that he accomplished anything with his pathetic attempt yesterday."

"I would appreciate that."

Nerys' eyes narrowed as she turned away from me.
"You went with her to Sedona today. Why?"

I decided to see if I could make her jump. "I heard a
rumor about your father."

She did stiffen for all of a second, then she dipped a
finger in her drink and let the liquor drip from her nail onto
her tongue before she curled it back into her mouth. "I
thought that situation had been handled."

"As had I, which is why I decided to follow up this lead."

"How did it turn out?"

"A dead end, or so it seems." I shrugged lightly. "I will
continue to pursue it."

Nerys swung back around and her face had hardened.
"And you will report to me when you hear anything?"

"I will."

She nodded once, curtly. "You will have to forgive me,
Mr. Caine. I have suddenly developed a headache." She
looked over at the bartender. "Lilith, dear child, you will
entertain Mr. Caine in my stead. You will see that he is,
in every way he desires, satisfied."

The woman nodded solemnly.

"Remember this, Mr. Caine," Nerys hissed in a whisper, "Whatever pleasure she gives you, I can extend beyond infinity. This I will do when you tell me this rumor business is ended. But also realize that my ire with failure similarly knows no limits and cannot be escaped."

Nerys' sudden and very sharp twist of mood put a severe damper on what could have otherwise been a very pleasant evening. Lilith excused herself while another of her compatriots led me to the dining alcove. As with the rest of this place, silken curtains described the boundary of the room, but it had been left open on one side to supply us with a full and glorious view of City Center in the darkness.

I sat in a chair at the end of the rectangular table, with the window to my right. At the other end of the short table, beyond two candelabra and an orchid centerpiece, the dinner setting originally meant for Nerys remained in place. Lilith, when she returned, sat at my left hand and was provided another table setting. Despite her lack of physical presence, I very much sensed Nerys was still with us.

Lilith, when she returned, had put on an emerald green gown that was, in terms of design, identical to the one Nerys had been wearing. Lilith also turned out to be intelligent and quite entertaining. She had a quick sense of humor and was polite enough to laugh at my jokes. This made the meal survivable because, if not for the laughter, I would have thought myself at some bizarre sort of wake.

Each dish, from salad and soup through entrees to dessert were served first at Nerys' empty place and to me. After a minute or two, Nerys' place would be cleared, then a plate with smaller portions would appear for Lilith. I had no doubt that the food she ate had been taken from Nerys' plate, though the exact symbolism behind that reality escaped me. Lilith, for her part, seemed not to notice and, in any case, finished all she had been given.

I regretted Nerys' departure because she, more than anyone else I had met, knew enough to help me rediscover my true identity. As solving that mystery was the only thing that would have satisfied me in all I desired, Lilith could never do what her mistress had demanded of her. She did, however, make for a charming dinner companion and, in the face of Nerys mercurial mood shift, let me relax more than I would have otherwise.

Had Nerys still been there, a phone call would never have interrupted dinner. A woman in blue brought me a small radio-phone. "Excuse me, Mr. Caine, but it is for you, and it is urgent."

"Thank you." I took the phone and pressed it to my ear. "Caine."

"Mr. Caine, you must leave there immediately. A car is waiting for you in Eclipse. Go, now!" The caller hung up with a click, but I had no trouble in recognizing the faintly mechanical voice. *Why does Coyote want me out of here?*

I snapped the phone shut and handed it back to the woman. "Lilith, I have to leave, there's been an emergency."

Lilith reached for the phone. "I will call a car for you."

"I have one waiting, thanks." I smiled at her and kissed her right hand. "I'm afraid all I need is for you to show me the door."

She took my hand, then gave the phone back to the serving woman. "Call and make certain the elevator is waiting for us. Have them lock it out for express service." She glanced at me, then added, "To Eclipse."

Navigating by some system I could not puzzle out, she took me through a direct route to the elevator lobby. The door stood open, waiting, and the car was empty. "Get in and hit any button. It will take you to Eclipse."

"Thank you." I frowned. "My leaving like this will not

cause a problem for you, will it? Nerys won't be angry, will she?"

Lilith kissed me lightly on the cheek. "Do not concern yourself. She is very understanding. You desire transport, and I have provided it. She will understand. Go."

I stepped into the elevator and pressed the "Close Door" button. The second the doors slid shut, the cage began a near freefall. Floors blurred as they rushed past, and I stumbled back to grab onto the railing. For a moment I imagined the bloody heap I'd be if the elevator never stopped, but by that time the mechanisms had begun to slow my descent. With nothing more than an elevated pulse to mark the ride, I emerged in Eclipse.

A horn honked, and I saw Alejandro waving from the driver's side of a green Mazda Dragonfly convertible. I sprinted over to him and vaulted into the passenger seat. I snapped the seatbelt shut and we started off, accelerating almost as quickly as had the elevator. "What's happened?"

"Hal's been shot. The Warriors of the Aryan World Alliance tried to assassinate him."

I glanced at the dash clock—11:30—an hour and a half before Hal's planned meeting with the southside gangs. "Details?"

Alejandro punched the gas and popped ahead of a smoky truck. "Three kids, not yet part of WAWA, came to Hal's house and said they wanted to help him. He let them in, and they opened up on him. His kids are okay but his wife didn't make it. He was hit. Looks like she tried to shield him. Two ran away. One panicked, ran into a closet, and it shut behind him. Bat's watching him now."

Alejandro swung the Dragonfly wide to pass a Cadillac and sped out onto McDowell Road at the 46th street exit from the Lorica Citadel. We fish-tailed wide, bumped the curb, then straightened out and shot down the road. In the distance I could see a set of flashing lights reflecting from Frozen Shade.

"Who knew about the meet?"

"Everyone. It was not a secret."

"Heinrich sends in some kids so he can deny having had anything to do with this."

"Looks like it." The art broker shot through a red light at 44th, squealing brakes and angry horns in our wake. "Glove compartment."

I opened it and found a .38 snubnose in a clip-on holster. "Thanks. Is it that dicy?"

"The Blood Crips, Jade Dragons and Diablos have surrounded Hal's place. The already nailed one of the kids who escaped, and they're waiting for the one we have in the house."

The red light at the intersection of 36th and McDowell threatened to stop us, but Alejandro needed to make the turn, so he cut across the corner of the lot and bumped over the curb on 36th. He cranked the wheel to the right, getting us back into our lane, then cut through a driveway opening to park the car on the sidewalk next to a school yard. We ran across 36th and forced our way through the crowd lining the street near Hal's condo.

"No cops?"

Alejandro shook his head. "Scorpion stays away from this area."

I ran past the ambulance and into the living room. There I stopped. Blood covered the carpet and soaked the couch. Bullet holes lined the walls, starting low and tracking on up into the ceiling. A bloody handprint on the wall to my right and a trail of blood led to a back bedroom. I followed it, passing by Bat as he stood guard beside a closed closet door.

"Alejandro, who's got the kids?"

"Natch has them. She's taking them to stay with their grandparents over on the west side. Diablos granted passage and the Blood Crips are running as outriders."

"Good."

Two EMTs worked feverishly in the back bedroom with their equipment boxes and monitors spread all over the place. They had Hal on a stretcher with an oxygen mask over his face. His shirt had been torn open, and they had two compression bandages on him. Both were already soaked with blood. One had been a high hit on the left and the other was stomach. He already had an IV drip punched into his right arm and that wrist had been fastened to the stretcher by a restraining strap.

When Hal saw me he started to stir. One of the emergency medical technicians turned toward me, saying, "You wanna tell him he can't wait no more? He's gonna die if..." The man paled.

"Hi, Jack!" I greeted him enthusiastically. "Long time no see. Played pool lately?"

Ignoring anything he said, I knelt beside Hal's head. "Hang on, Hal."

Hal grabbed my sleeve with his left hand. "My kids?"

"Safe."

"Candy?"

"She's gonna be fine, Hal," I lied. "You gotta let these guys get you to the hospital. Your job is to recover. We'll take care of things here."

A painful grimace contorted his features. "Take care of my kids, Caine. No war."

I nodded. "No war."

"Caine, no killing. Not while you have another choice."

"No killing, Hal. Let them get you out of here."

His grip tightened on my arm. "Promise me, no killing."

"No killing, Hal. I promise, as long as you promise not to die."

"Deal."

"Deal." I freed his hand from my arm and stood. "Get him out of here." I grabbed Jack's shoulder as his partner wheeled Hal outside earshot. "If he dies on the way to the hospital, or I find his wife didn't make it to the morgue, you'll take a long time to die. You understand me?"

"Y-yess."

"Good. Leave me that green trauma box. You can get it later."

"S-sure. Just let me out of here."

I followed him out into the front room, but stopped beside Bat. "The kid in the closet?"

The big man nodded. "No bullets. No blades."

"Take him out, blindfold him and bind him." I pointed to the wide pool of blood on the floor. "I want him kneeling there."

I stepped outside as the ambulance slowly started to make its way through the crowd. I saw a large number of people, black, brown yellow and white, staring at the house and talking to each other. They managed to segregate three other groups of individuals who, I imagined, were the three gangs Hal had planned to meet.

Off to my right I saw a knot of Hispanic men, all wearing sleeveless black T-shirts with an inverted star screened on the shirts in bright red ink. It had been stylized to look like blood dripping down from the design. As had WAWA people, the Diablos had also chosen to undergo some cosmetic alteration which, as nearly as I could see, constituted the addition of little horns on their foreheads and a peaking of their ears. They wore black fingernail polish and the older male gang members had grown very devilish Van Dykes.

The Jade Dragons had also engaged in body augmentation. Most notable, of course, was the scaly flesh covering their faces, throats, chests, backs and hands. Unlike the Diablos, who apparently ranked each other by the length of their horns, the oriental gang differentiated themselves by scale color. The younger members had pale blue scales while the older Dragons had graduated to a deep green hue edged with gold. The eldest members also had modified their ears to lengthen and flatten them, making them look like bat wings covered in lizard flesh. The Dragon I thought to be the leader also had a sagittal sail that rose and fell like a fish's fin as he breathed in and out.

The Blood Crips, by comparison, looked positively normal in their red and blue leather jackets. Once arch-enemy gangs, they had consolidated their forces around the turn of the millennium because of the pressure from other gangs. Their augmentation looked, to me, to be fairly utilitarian. Their brows and cheekbones had been enlarged to sink their eyes back to less vulnerable depths. Likewise the backs of their hands looked improbably smooth, as if each had inserted a weighty prosthesis to increase hitting power and help control the recoil on automatic weapons. They had also adopted the tradition of their Afro-American ancestors in employing ritual scarring on their faces.

I pointed at the two Diablos members with the longest horns. "You two, in here." I picked out the leader of the Dragons and the person who looked most like his lieutenant. "Inside, now." Lastly I turned to the Blood Crips and knew their leadership had to be embodied in one of the surliest individuals I'd ever seen. "You and your second, let's go."

The leader just let his body slump half sideways as he made a big show of crossing his arms. "Fancy man don't order me."

The other gang leaders stopped, waiting to see how I'd handle this revolt. "Seeing as how you have nothing better to do with your time, and Mr. Garrett asked me to act in his stead, I request the pleasure of your company inside, *now*."

"Or else what?"

My voice dropped to a low growl. "I didn't give you an

'or else' because I don't make idle threats. I'll tell you this: It's obvious that the possible alliance Hal was engineering has some people scared. If you're together, no one can hurt you. If you want the Blood Crips to be outside the fold, fine. You walk away now." I turned and walked back into the house, with the two Diablos and the two Dragons following me. The Blood Crips came a bit later, moving at their own pace.

Keeping a decent space between each other, the gang members stood there and silently regarded the Aryan kneeling in the blood. It had already begun to soak into his faded jeans and white socks. Bat had bound him hand and foot, then used a torn strip of material from the boy's thick white T-shirt to blindfold him. The kid shivered and swayed a bit.

"This, gentlemen, is one of the three assassins who tried to kill Hal Garrett. Though Heinrich will deny it, he sent these three boys out to do a job with no training. You can see by the bullet tracks in the walls that the guns recoiled unchecked and tracked right out of the killing zone."

I dropped down on my haunches in front of the kid. "What's your name?"

"Screw yourself, nigger-lover!"

The Blood Crip leader took a half-step forward and aimed a kick that would have crushed the kid's skull except that Bat grabbed the ganger by the collar and jerked him back. "What chu do that for, man? I'll do the murdering piece of shit."

I shook my head. "No. No killing. Hal made me promise no killing."

The Blood Crip leader jerked his thumbs back at himself. "Hey, Rafe didn't promise Hal jack!"

"And I didn't promise Hal I wouldn't kill you, so we're even, aren't we?" I grabbed the white kid's jaw. "What's your name?" Fear radiated off the kid like heat from a bonfire. He wanted to defy me, but his last outburst had seriously depleted his nervous courage. Blind, kneeling in a sticky liquid that was chilling his knees and toes, he knew his situation couldn't get any worse.

He held his head up. "*Ich heiße Willem.*"

"Good. Now listen, Willem, I know it's probably futile to get you to say anything against Heinrich. There is very little I could do to scare you into that, especially since I've already said I'm not going to kill you. Therefore I've decided to do something else that might, oddly enough, save your life. You won't like it, but it's for the best, really." I looked over at Alejandro. "Get me the *green* box from the bedroom, please."

Emphasis on the word green made Willem uneasy. I took advantage of that. "I'm sure, Willem, that Heinrich, your fearless leader, has told you all sorts of things about the 'mud people.' He's told you how they're savages, and Rafe here would love to dance a little tattoo on your head to reinforce that message." I quickly read the name embroidered on the breast of Rafe's lieutenant's jacket. "Jalal, on the other hand, is rather quiet and civilized. You've been twisted by stereotypes, and I mean to let you correct those lousy impressions."

Alejandro set the box down beside me, and I flipped it open. I quickly located and tore open the biggest syringe I could find. I gently slid it under Willem's nose as I might have done with a fine cigar. "This, my friend, this syringe, will be the instrument of your enlightenment. You know, of course, how whites are the superior race because our blood is pure. Well, Willem, I'm afraid your name is about to become *Mud.*"

Rafe looked hard at me. "What chu doing man? You want answers from him, not to edjukate his sorry ass. Leave him to me, I show him who's the deffest race. Then we go and kill us some lilywhite priss-boys."

"Shut up, asshole, or I'll tell Bat to twist your head off

and use it as a bowling ball." Willem started laughing, but I cut that short with one hard slap. "Moron, your arms and legs will be the pins, and there won't be picking up any spares for you. What I'm going to do here is I'm going to fill this syringe with blood, and I'm going to pump it into you, Willem. Your blood will become tainted. Then we're going to take you out in the desert and leave you in the sun so you darken up nice and good."

"Oh, man...," wailed Rafe. "I'll get you whitey blood by the buckets."

"That's it!" I pulled a needle from the trauma box, broke it out of the paper and fixed it to the end of the syringe. "Rafe, since you seem to have a single function-ing brain cell, I think I draw from you first. Bat, bare his arm."

Rafe tried to move out of the way, but Bat jerked his jacket down to pinion the black man's arms at his elbows. A nice, fat vein pulsed across the top of Rafe's bicep. "Stay away from me, man. I ain't givin' no blood to that trash."

I shook my head and laughed. "That trash? By what warped sense of equality do you see yourself as superior to him? You're the bonehead who's all hot to go out and start a war, and over what? Over the shooting of man who wanted anything *but* a war! Lying on a stretcher with a hole in his chest and one in his gut, he made me promise, dammit, *promise* I'd not let a war get started. Hal Garrett apparently saw a lot more in you than I do, because he figured you had enough brains to see that dying doesn't help anyone. Hal, on the other hand, was offering you a way out of the hellhole."

I turned and looked at the other gangers. "You can all walk out of here and pick up guns if you want to, and go off to shoot the hell out of the Aryans. I'll make sure that any of you who survive that stupidity get slabs in the morgue together. Hell, maybe I'll just see to it you get pieced out by the Reapers, with the money going to the Sunburst Foundation, because that's the only way a war is going to benefit anyone."

I grinned at Rafe. "Maybe after I take some blood from you, I'll pump some of his back into your veins. Make you blood brothers because you're both of a like mind."

"Don't you go touchin' me with that thing." Rafe's eyes grew wide, and he struggled helplessly against Bat.

I popped the plastic cap off the needle. Rafe saw it, and his eyes rolled up in his head as he fainted dead away. Bat looked positively surprised as the ganger went limp. I motioned to Bat to lay Rafe down, then I pantomimed drawing blood. "Oh, yeah, Rafe, that's great. Dark, steaming, this stuff will do the trick."

As I moved back in front of Willem, I saw Jalal edging toward the door. "Where do you think you're going?"

The Blood Crip smiled at me. "I brained out as how if you pump that much black bride into Willem there, he's going to change fast. I was going to send some of the posse to get him some fried chicken and watermelon." He exaggerated his words, turning a racial slur into a statement dripping with sarcastic sincerity.

"That's very considerate of you."

Jalal grinned broadly. "Anything for a *brother*."

Reaching back into the trauma box, I pulled out a small vial of epinephrine. I drew enough of the synthetic adrenaline into the syringe to give Willem a real jolt, then swabbed his arm down with alcohol soaked cotton. "Won't hurt a bit, son." I looked over at the Dragons. "After this takes, I'll want a donation from you so we can give him almond eyes and make him better at math. Then from you Diablos I want enough blood so he can speak Spanish and eat jalapeños without a problem."

"Anything to save him from Aryanism."

I plunged the needle into his deltoid muscle. "There you go. Boy, look at that. It's starting already."

Willem, helped along by the epinephrine, started to shake. Jalal nodded his head, "Color of weak tea, but it's building."

"Si, soon he looks the color of beans."

"Mahogany, really," commented the Dragon leader.

I ran my hand through his hair and mussed it up nicely. "And look at the hair darken. Rafe, you've got *great* blood."

"Billy," Jalal taunted, "you got a woman? My sister needs a squeeze."

The lead Diablo shook his head. "No, my sister will want him."

Willem broke a sweat that started to soak the blindfold. "No, you can't be doing this to me. You can't."

"We have, Willem, and it'll stick once we get you out into the sun. Once we do that, you're going to be one of the mud people forever! Have you ever read the book, *Black Like Me*? No? You should have tried it while you had the chance. It's old, now, but I'm sure Jalal and the others will give you the pointers you'll need to survive. Anyone got a watch? What time is it?"

"Midnight."

I let air hiss through my teeth as I breathed in. "Damn, he changed quick, but we've got six hours 'til sunlight. He may revert unless we can *fix* the change. Anyone know of a tanning salon near here?"

"Yeah, there's one at 30th and Thomas, about a mile and a half from here." Alejandro slapped Willem on the back. "I can have Bill over there in no time."

"No, you can't."

"Got to, Willem, otherwise you'll change back to your old, stupid self." I laid a heavy hand on his shoulder and squeezed it sympathetically. "My hands are tied, son."

"No, please! No." He began to cry and shake uncontrollably. I knew a chunk of it came from the drug, but he was scared down to his soul and then some. "No, please."

"Willem," I began in a slow voice, "you're asking me for a favor here, but you helped shoot a friend of mine. You have to show me you're sorry and you're willing to make amends for what you've done. You nearly killed a man who invited you into his home because you came asking him to help you. If I hadn't promised him, you'd be dead right now."

"What do you want from me?" His cry echoed with desperation. He slumped to the side against Alejandro.

"You have to answer me a question."

"If I know it, yes, anything."

"Hang on, Willem, you're almost home."

I stood and drew the gangers with me into a knot near the door. "You know Garrett wants you at peace, right?"

I got shakes and nods in response. "Good. The answer he's going to give me would probably prompt all of you to do something less than prudent. Garrett trusted me to deal with you, now you have to trust me to handle this. You have to leave and take your people with you. Okay? Leave this to me."

The Dragon leader's ears spread then retracted once. "Done." He looked at the other two gangs' members. "Continue the truce at least until Garrett's back on his feet?"

Jalal and the Diablos agreed to that. Jalal nodded at me. "I'll keep Rafe in line."

"Thanks."

Jalal hauled Rafe out of the house, and the crowd outside began to disperse. I dropped back down in front of Willem. "Willem, the question is this: Heinrich is getting a lot of backing to buy weapons to start a war here in the southside of Phoenix. Someone is financing him. They are good. They have supplied H&K weapons, which makes the culprit look like Honeywell & Koch, but their citadel is in a prime war zone. So, tell me, who's playing Fatherland to Heinrich's Fuhrer?"

The boy hung his head. "Build-more."

"Do you have a name there?"

"No, but he's in security and he has lots of dolmarks."

"Good boy. Alejandro here will take you to a place where you can sleep until morning. You should be okay by then. We'll keep the blindfold on because the trans-formation makes eyes rather sensitive."

Alejandro helped the kid up, and I slit the ropes on his ankles with a knife from the trauma box. Standing, I looked over at Bat. "Did you hear all that?"

He nodded.

"Good, relay it to Jytte and see if she can get us some likely candidates for our mystery man. Have her run a check that shows areas of conflict between Build-more, Lorica, H&K, Sumitomo-Dial and Genentech Carbide. I want to know what the target is. Oh, and have her compile a dossier for me on Nerys Loring."

Bat nodded slowly. "You did good work here. I would have started breaking bones."

"I was tempted, but I promised."

"I don't make promises I don't want to keep."

"Well, I only make promises I think I *can* keep." I looked out the window at the gangs melting away in the darkness. "I only hope circumstances don't force me to break this one."

I returned to Marit's home by 1 a.m. I looked in on her and found she was sleeping peacefully, so I undressed in the guest room and crashed on the bed there instead of disturbing her. While I knew I would find it both comforting and soothing to have her lying next to me, I was not certain I wanted to be soothed or comforted at that moment.

There was no question in my mind that Coyote's traitor had leaked word of the meeting to Heinrich and his Aryans. Knowing that the Aryans were working for Buildmore meant I had a possible employer for the traitor, but that was a grand leap in logic that I wanted to avoid. The last thing I needed to be doing was looking for evidence that confirmed my theory, instead of finding the theory that fit the facts.

So, what were my facts? From Nerys' reactions to me, I was outside talent brought in, apparently, to take her father out of the picture. Her mood shifted abruptly and radically when I hinted her father still was alive. Clearly he still knew something that could cause her problems, but what it was I could not tell.

I also had the fact of Nerys' animosity toward Marit to deal with. That appeared to explain Leich's attack on us at Danny's place. His tie to Nerys had been firmly established by his being my escort to her home. I still wondered if he was in some way related to the Reaper I had shot. I knew it was impossible for anyone to have survived the damage I did to him in my escape, but after visiting an alternate reality and seeing how hard Draolings were to kill, my resolve on that point was beginning to erode.

The fact of a traitor in our midst was one of the toughest to deal with. Because everyone in the cell knew about the meet Hal had arranged, anyone could have played Judas. Handing out restricted information was the only way to determine who the spy was, and, despite the odd stuff that had happened in Sedona, Rock Pell looked like a good candidate on that count. We had not been ambushed by any predetermined setup, and he had not known we were going.

Still, that was negative evidence and provided a direction for further inquiry, not proof of guilt.

Somewhere in the middle of trying to organize different tasks for different people I drifted off to sleep. My subconscious mind kept gnawing on that difficulty, which manifested itself as a strange dream. It was set at a posh cocktail party, and in it everyone I had met appeared to be animated, but, as I moved around, they turned out to be paper-thin cutouts. On one side I saw them as they appeared to be on the surface, but from the other I saw them at their worst. Rock, for example, counted 30 silver coins over and over again while wearing a Nazi uniform.

Weirdest of all, Coyote appeared as a white silhouette that always kept his back to a wall. I could not get anything from him except an occasional nod of approval. While I found that chilling, the one time I stepped in front of a mirror I saw a blank image staring back at me. In my mind, then, Coyote and I were one and I found that idea unsettling for reasons I could not figure out.

A black shadow entered my dream. I looked for and found the familiar gold ring. "El Espectro. Are you really here, or are you part of my dream?"

The shadow turned a circle, showing itself to be more substantial than the other denizens of my dream. "Here, in the, ah, flesh."

"You've spoken with Loring?"

The shadow man nodded. "I have communicated with him, and I found it disturbingly easy. I am afraid he has ventured into realms where he is not equipped to go."

"Meaning?"

El Espectro motioned with his right hand as if he were wiping the fog from a mirror. As he did so the background of my dream went away. I saw through the opening he had wiped and found myself staring out at a reddish plain with a dark bowl of sky and twinkling stars. He stepped through the streak he had created, and I followed him. As I looked back I saw my dreamworld contract down to a pinprick of light, then soar up to become the third star in the belt of Orion the Hunter.

"What you and I have just done is shift from one frame of reality to another. One mark of this ability, for example, is being able to dream in color instead of black and white. That is your conscious mind being able to accept and deal with a vast array of input. Some people are blind to that input, others cannot process it—without help, that is."

"I'm not certain I understand what you're telling me." I shrugged my shoulders. "For as long as I can remember, which is not long at all, I have been able to dream in color."

"You and I are among the gifted few of humanity. We are what charlatans and psychics have called sensitive. We have a natural ability to pull in and deal with more sensory input than others. It is a form of empathy, really, and is roughly akin to being able to see in the ultraviolet or infrared ranges of electromagnetic radiation. We know insects can do the former and some snakes the latter. For us, until we are educated and equipped with skills, our empathy may be little more than feeling uneasy in a bad situation, or getting uncomfortable feelings from another."

I smiled. "Whereas you, who have studied and refined

your skill, can read minds and perform other miracles."

El Espectro inclined his head in a concession to my point. "True, though my miracles are really little more than parlor tricks. Telekinesis, pyrokinesis, telepathy, psychometry, clairvoyance—all of these are branches of this thing that makes us different. We are still human, but we are adept where others are blind."

"And Nero Loring is one of the blind."

"Exactly. And unfortunately. He is, as a creative person, one of the most brilliant I have ever had the pleasure of meeting. His mind works so quickly and in such a complex manner that I can do no more than pick off stray surface thoughts. I could more easily read *War and Peace* in Inuit than I could fathom his mind. Yet, for all that, had he been with us in the proto-dimension yesterday, he would have found himself in a world of gray-flannel Jell-O. He would have seen nothing but us, and would have been helpless if we chose to abandon him."

A comet of ill-omens streaked across the heavens. "I sense danger in your use of the word 'unfortunately.'"

"Quite a bit of it, in fact. About four years ago, as I piece it together now, he started to see clues of some very disturbing things. At the very least he began to suspect the existence of dimensions other than the one in which Earth exists. He began to toy with a device that would allow him to detect signs of that universe. He thought of it as a radio-telescope for looking through dimensions. It was something that was akin to the dimensional gateway I used to send you and Ms. Fisk back to Eclipse.

"This he did on his own time. Apparently, about four months ago, he discovered something that deeply shocked him. His daughter ousted him from the company two months later and tried to have him put away. Company loyalists managed to hide him."

"And I was brought in to kill him."

El Espectro's head came up. "Conjecture, or you know this for a fact?"

"Solid conjecture. The signs are there." I folded my arms. "I have since suffered from amnesia, so I am not certain about anything. Nerys acts as if that was my mission, and she was quite disturbed when I told her I had gone to Sedona on the track of a rumor about her father."

"This could complicate things." The shadow man thought for a moment, the shook his head. "You will have to proceed very carefully."

"I intend to. Now, bring me up to speed on Nero."

"Ah, yes. When Loring was ousted, he lost access to his machine. He spent much of his time on the run studying certain mystical texts which describe other dimensions, other creatures and the like. I do not think he ascribed to any one in particular, but was looking for something that matched what he had discovered by using his dimensionscope. He found it in a work of fiction—a collection of short stories by Edgar Allan Poe.

"Nero chose to believe the pernicious slander about Poe promulgated by Rufus W. Griswold."

"Namely that Poe was an opium addict?" inquired Tycho.

"Correct, or, rather, incorrect. Poe may have been, as are you and I, a very creative empath who was able to peer into other dimensions. Nero, starting from that point, has secluded himself in a place where he can obtain and use psychotropic drugs to free his mind to roam where he was able to go using his dimensionscope."

"And it won't work?"

"This is the rough equivalent of a man who has studied an atlas jumping on a raft and waiting for Brownian motion to carry him from New York to Europe. He may get there, but he has no control over his travel. He is destroying his mind with these things—and for nothing." Anxiety filled El Espectro's words. "Whatever he thinks is so urgent he is unable to handle in any event."

"What do you need from me?"

"The wound I suffered was a bit more debilitating than I had imagined. I cannot fetch him and dry him out. I need you to do that for me. Once you get him, I want you to leave him with friends of mine in Eclipse."

"A cutout?"

"More for your protection than mine, Mr. Caine." El Espectro reached out and pressed his left hand to my forehead. I felt a tingle run over my scalp and instantly I knew the route I was to drive both to find Loring and to bring him to El Espectro's people. "There, that should help you. I wish you Godspeed and suggest, unless you know who your traitor is, you travel alone."

El Espectro's image faded with his voice. Through where he had been, the sun began to rise over the edge of the planet, and I shielded my eyes against the light. As I turned away from it, I felt sheets twist around my legs, and I opened my eyes. Letting my arm fall, I saw the sun dawning from the reflective face of the Sumitomo-Dial citadel.

I smelled coffee and looked over at the doorway. Marit stood there in a loosely belted silk robe, the color of blue in a housefly's body. As she leaned against the door-jamb, the gap in the robe ran from her throat, down between her breasts, across her flat belly and down to trace the line of her hip and right leg. She clutched the steaming mug right below her face and seemed more intent on inhaling it than actually drinking it.

I smiled. "If coffee tasted half as good as it smells, it would be a winner."

She took in a deep sniff, then smiled. "I needed it to wake up. I had a nightmare."

"Oh?"

"Yes, I dreamed I woke up and you weren't in bed beside me."

"Sorry, I didn't want to disturb your sleep last night."

"I know, but with the news about Hal, I was worried."

I sat up in bed and held my arms out to her. She set her cup on the nightstand, then crawled into bed beside me and I held her. "I didn't know you knew about Hal."

"Jytte called last night with the news. She said Candy didn't make it."

I felt a shiver run through her. "No, she didn't. We do, however, have a lead that Jytte and Bat should be following up."

"Really? Can I help?"

I shook my head. "Not with that, but you *can* help by spending one more day in bed."

She snuggled in more tightly to my chest. "With you here too?"

"Don't I wish." I tipped her chin up with my left hand and kissed her on the lips. "I have to head out and do something on the reservation. If you can call down and have your Ariel ready for me to use, I would be very appreciative."

"I can call for you. How soon do you want it?"

"An hour?"

"An *hour*?" With the pout on her face and the tortured tone in her voice, she made it sound like a nanosecond. She rolled over onto my chest, pinning me to the bed. "Make it two hours, Mr. Caine, and give me a down payment on the appreciation, and you have a deal."

"My pleasure, Ms. Fisk."

"I'm counting on that, Mr. Caine."

Having left bed well after I was awake, I showered quickly and dressed in very casual clothes. Marit offered to wash my back for me, but I reminded her she had to call about the car. She went to do that, but she noted that she expected the other 90% of my appreciation to be paid when I returned. I offered to sign a note, but she agreed to take me at my word.

Feeling a bit paranoid, I not only packed my Colt Krait, but I also brought the one I had taken from the Reapers and my sniper rifle—though I did leave it in the case. Given that I was headed out into the trackless wastes of the Salt River Indian Reservation, I assumed having a long-distance weapon would be a good idea.

Marit concurred in this thinking. "If you are right in thinking that the Witch hired you to kill her father, taking along as much artillery as you can carry to retrieve him is not a bad idea at all. I can still ride backup."

I shook my head. "No. I want you to take one more day to recover. I want you ready in case anything we learn from Loring demands action."

She reluctantly agreed to stay home and had Juanita pack me a lunch. I accepted the brown bag from the Hispanic woman, then Marit gave me a kiss as if she were a housewife sending her husband off to the office. "Be careful."

"As always." I winked at her. "Oh, look, don't tell anyone else about this, okay? Hal doesn't need the burden, and it might not pan out."

"Right."

I took the elevator down to Level Five and picked the Ariel up near the McDowell car transport area. The attendant directed me toward the "hellavator," which is resident slang for the car elevator that takes vehicles straight down to ground level if that is quicker than picking up one of the freeways out of City Center. Because I wanted to head directly out McDowell toward the reservation, I decided that was the best way to work things.

I guess, in the back of my mind, I had expected to pick up a tail, but I never expected it to be so blatantly obvious. I spotted it first at 16th and McDowell and confirmed it by the time I shot under the Squaw Peak Parkway. Streetlights strobed across the hood of the car as I hit the accelerator and started to run. My tail, knowing they had been made, picked up speed as well.

I eased the Krait from my shoulder holster and laid it on the seat beside me. Hitting the switch to roll down my driver's-side window, I kept an eye on my rearview mirror and the pickup truck with two Aryans in the cockpit and one in the back. The man in the back raised a rifle, and I saw a muzzle flash a second before the back window shattered and blew back out in a jagged ice storm.

So intent was I on making my car a tough target to hit that I almost didn't notice the new danger. All traps require bait and a sting. I had mistaken the pickup for the sting, but it fulfilled all the requirements of bait: It caught my attention. It didn't allow me to notice the hammer until almost too late.

The Harley came out of a side street, crossed traffic and pulled up along side me with a blond-haired, bare-chested Aryan riding it. He wore mirrored sunglasses, but beneath the left lens I saw the hint of a star scar. On his chest, as he twisted to smile at me, I saw two other roundish scars that looked so old they couldn't have been from the shooting a week ago. In his gloved left hand he held the pistol grip of a double-barreled, sawed-off shotgun.

I tapped the brakes and he shot ahead of me. As he shifted the gun from his left hand to right to shoot out my front tire, I jerked the wheel to the left and bumped his bike. As he fought to control it, the shotgun clattering to the ground, I pulled parallel, filled my hand with the Krait and pumped two rounds into him. One hit his hip, the other hit his chest, and his bike swerved into the left-turn lane.

In one respect he was lucky. The Ford-Revlon Elan was not moving very fast when he hit it square on the nose. Leich vaulted from the bike, slammed into the windscreen, then flew over the top of the car. He landed on his feet, but continued in a somersault that ended with him skidding on his back through the glass, dirt and bits of chrome detailing left behind in the turn lane by other cars.

His bike, which had completed a cartwheel over the Elan, wobbled along and flopped over on top of him.

The pickup stopped near the wreckage, and I continued on. My ears rang from the sound of the gun going off in such a confined space, and the cordite left a bitter, dry taste in my mouth. *Maybe Marit was right. Perhaps I should have just stayed in bed with her.*

I stopped behind a GDM Trotter for a red light at 36th Street. This was a mistake. Off on my left I saw the lower reaches of the Lorica Citadel, which prompted me to try to match up Mr. Leich with both the rider I'd just killed and the Reaper I shot in the first night of my new life. I desperately wanted the job to be difficult, but the three images slid together more easily than bullets slide into a clip. *He didn't look like a Draoling...*

I realized the light had lasted longer than it should have just about the same time I saw the pickup truck in the rearview mirror. I cranked the steering wheel to the right and gunned the engined, vaulting me up onto the sidewalk. Sparks shot as the passenger side of the car scraped along the Lorica Citadel wall. Pedestrians leaped out into the street, and I bull's-eyed a metal cart full of groceries. Cans of soup and veggies bumped up and over the Ariel, then I cut back into the street and hit the gas.

Behind me, having swung wide to get through the intersection, came the pickup. The driver hunched over the wheel and his passenger stuck a pistol out the passenger window. I swerved right in front of the truck, which threw off the passenger's aim, then I cut back as the driver tried to ram me from behind.

The truck tried to pull parallel as we shot through the intersection at 40th and on to 44th, but I hogged the whole road and kept them back. Then, just on the other side of 44th, the sniper stood up in the back of the truck and shouldered his rifle again. With deliberate care he wrapped his left forearm in the sling to sharpen his aim. I jerked the wheel to the left and a string of shells ripped through the passenger half of the car.

I looked in the rearview and shifted into overdrive. The first sniper had not been wearing gloves, I suddenly realized. The wind blew parallel triangles of blood back across the sniper's face from the corners of his mouth. Torn flesh flapped in the wind and one patch on his shoulder showed his deltoid muscle. Worse yet, at hip and flank, I saw bullet wounds.

That's Leich. That's impossible!

Two more bullets punched through the passenger seat headrest, then I saw Leich furiously working the rifle's bolt. As we streaked across 52nd Street and started up between the Papago Buttes, I pulled my foot off the accelerator and pulled into the right lane. The pickup driver shot ahead, then made to drop in right in front of me so Leich could blaze away to his heart's content.

As the driver tried to pull the truck in front of me, I punched the accelerator again, catching the pickup exactly behind the right rear passenger wheel. With all of the truck's weight up front, I started it into a skid. I hit it again, then pulled back as it shot off at a 45-degree angle to our previous direction of travel.

Flying along at roughly 60 miles per hour, the pickup hit the curb and jumped up all of three feet before it hit the low restraining wall on the other side of the bike path. That started it rolling which, in turn, catapulted Mr. Leich and the body of the original sniper from the bed of the truck. The sniper flopped around like a dead thing, but Leich made an attempt to control his flight. He landed on his right leg, with his momentum continuing his backward somersault, and tried to steady himself with the Armalite assault rifle. He went down, of course, leaving patches of flesh on the tarmac, but managed to roll to his feet 10 yards from the crash site.

I tagged his left leg with the Ariel. He spun around and slammed into the side of my car, then flew off and into the median. I heard him scream as he landed in the arms of a big saguaro and hung there like a grim, southwestern Easter spectacle. On the other side of the road the pickup rolled down an embankment and came to a rest with all four spinning wheels in the air.

As I sped away from that tableau, two questions came to mind: What the hell is Leich? I'd shot him six times, all total. I'd forced his bike into a car at 60+ miles per hour and watched him give himself an asphalt massage. After that he quenched his thirst with the blood of an ally and was still steady enough to shoot very well from the back of a moving truck. Finally, after he's knocked out of pickup truck, he rolls and stands. I hit him with the Ariel, and he still manages to be alive enough to scream when he gets impaled on a cactus.

I knew things were strange, and I didn't mind that while sharing a hallucination with El Espectro, but unkillable creatures on the streets of Eclipse were not something I'd bargained for. "The logical explanation is that Leich really is, ah, one of a set of identical quadruplets that all share the infirmities of the others through this empathy thing El Espectro talks about."

It sounded no better spoken aloud than it did echoing around in my head. The alternate explanation was that Leich, like the Draolings, was a native of another dimension. How he got here, how he got hooked up with Lorica and Nerys, and how he knew to go after me this morning were all open to conjecture. Of all of them, the last bothered me the most, but I tabled consideration of it until I successfully completed Nero Loring's recovery.

The other question, of course, was how I would explain to Marit what had happened to her car. "I'll just have to be *very* appreciative, I guess."

Frozen Shade covers the eastern half of what used to be known as the Valley of the Sun right up to the Salt River Indian reservation. I'd seen the break on the map I'd reviewed, but I hardly expected it to be so abrupt. Frozen Shade panels actually covered the eastern edge of Scottsdale to catch the morning sun, with only 20 feet of clearance along the major roads.

Fortunately McDowell Road was a major road, so I shot out into the reservation, passing beneath the 101L, without a hitch. Out there, in the gloriously warm sunlight, I took the car up to 70 mph and let the through-current of air sweep glass and seat stuffing out through the back window. I reveled in the heat and, somehow, the bright light nibbled away at the dread Leich had inspired in me.

I picked up Route 87 heading northeast and took it through some of the driest, most inhospitable land I'd ever seen. In the distance I could see small, ramshackle houses the ruddy color of the dirt. It took me a moment to realize they were actually made of adobe bricks, and that astounded me. In this day and age, in the shadow of one of the largest cities in North America, there were people living in homes made of mud.

Somewhere beyond where the Beeline Highway cut across the Arizona Canal, I turned north onto a dirt track. I followed it as faithfully as possible, leaving a huge cloud of dust in my wake. Twice I flushed jackrabbits and three times drove past the rusting skeletons of cars. Always, though, I kept the Ariel's nose pointed at Sawik Mountain.

A rounded red hunk of rock, Sawik Mountain sat on the surrounding flat plain as if it had been formed from clay and squashed into a lump there by the potter. I followed the track as it cut east and stopped on the far side of the formation. Re-holstering the blue Krait, I pulled the gun case and sandwich bag from the car. The case showed a dent where it had deflected one bullet and one of the two sandwiches had a rather big hole in it.

Trekking around through the small gullies was not particularly difficult. As I had seen when El Espectro mindfed me the location, I found the footpath leading in toward a small split between the mountain itself and a large hunk of rock as soon as I entered the mountain's shadow. At the base of it I saw two men, both Indians, one young and one ancient.

"Howdy, gentlemen." I did my best to approach easily and openly because the younger man had a lever-action Winchester .30-06 rifle hanging from the end of his right arm. "Nice day for a hike."

The old man started laughing in a wheezy voice. The younger man brought the rifle up and laid it in the crook of his left elbow. "Mister, if you came all this way for a hike, you're bound for disappointment. This is reservation land, and it's not open to the public. You might as well turn around and head back out of here."

A phrase El Espectro had implanted in my brain

floated up to my conscious mind. "I'm just seeking visions, friends. The Witch's father needs my help."

The young man made ready to wave me off, but the old man said something to him. The rifle slipped down so the forward handgrip rested in his left hand, and he motioned down with it. "Get rid of the bag and case. Take off your windbreaker."

I did as commanded, leaving me with a sleeveless T-shirt and shoulder holster covering my chest. "Now what?"

The old man tossed a waterskin out into the crescent of sunlight to my right. "Get the bag my grandfather has thrown there," the young man commanded. "Pour water out onto your arms and wash them off. Wash them good."

Given the way my morning had gone so far, this request even sounded reasonable. I picked up the skin and poured some water into my hand. I sniffed it and smelled nothing. I washed my arms off, then capped the skin and tossed it back into the shade. "If you ask me to put on surgical greens and perform an operation, I'll just leave now."

The younger man winced at my joke, but his grandfather wheezed out another laugh. We waited for five minutes, with the old man constantly checking the sun and then me. Finally he spoke to the younger man, and the rifle swung up and away from me. "Come on in. You're clean."

I frowned as I recovered my gear. "I'm clean?"

The old man spoke in a voice that was at once quiet and impish, yet commanding. "In the old days, evil creatures could not stand the touch of sunlight. Now they have sunblock." He rested a palsied hand on his grandson's strong shoulder. "You will wait here, Will. You must stand guard while we go to the Cave of Dreams."

"Yes, Grandfather."

The old man, whose long gray hair was restrained by a leather thong encircling his head, led me up the narrow path. "You have been sent by Ghost Who Lives. Did he tell you what you would find?"

"No."

The old man looked back at me over his shoulder with sharp gray eyes. "Here we are far from the world you know in Phoenix. Nero Loring is as far from us as you are from Phoenix. Loring entrusted himself to me, and I agreed to help him on his quest, but I can help him no more. This will be up to you."

"I'm Tycho Caine, by the way."

The ancient one just laughed lightly. "My given name is, in your tongue, He Whose Antics Are the Light in the Eye of the Raven. It is not a compliment. You may call me George."

"George?"

He shrugged. "In my youth I learned to write English by copying the words on money. In signing up for service during the Korean War, my name choices were either George or Novus and the first seemed easier for my sergeant to learn."

While we talked, we worked our way up a steep, twisty trail that hugged the mountain. The years had weathered the volcanic rock, but they had not made it smooth. One misstep and I'd end up looking like the road pizza Leich should have been.

George stopped me at a wide ledge. To the left a series of hand- and footholds had been carved into the rock generations ago. Up at the top I could see, over the lip of another ledge, the top of what I took to be a hole in the mountain. He pointed toward the opening.

"This is a sacred mountain, and the Cave of Dreams is a magical place. Nero Loring has been in there for three weeks. Will and I have brought him food and water each day. We also stand guard to prevent those who would come to hurt him from disturbing him. When you go up there, do not say anything to him until he speaks to you. You do not want to break him from communion with the gods until they are done with him."

The old man sat down in the mountain's shadow. "I do not know what you will find up there. I have not been in the cave since I first took him up there. Whatever you find, do not disturb it, for it will be a symbol of power for him. It may be all that is keeping him alive. Listen to him, and when he speaks to you as you, then it is that you may take him from this place."

"In the meantime," he pointed at my luggage, "I will watch your things."

I sat the case down and tossed him the sandwich bag. "Help yourself, but watch out for lead poisoning."

He nodded solemnly. "It is a crime to waste food."

I started to climb up, straining to hear any sounds from above. The climb proved easy and every time I looked back down at George, he saluted me with smaller and smaller pieces of sandwich. At the top of the climb I saw a jug of water and an empty plastic plate resting on a ledge that seemed just smaller than a twin bed.

The hole in the mountain had obviously been carved by human hands. Three feet in diameter, it led into a tunnel of similar dimensions that slanted up at a 70-degree angle for 10 feet. I kept my head down as I crawled through it, devoutly wishing to avoid having my scalp scraped off by the rocks, then stood slowly as I entered the Cave of Dreams.

The only light in the whole place came through a hole in the domed roof, and it came down in a brilliant shaft that washed over Nero Loring's seated body. Lacking an accurate frame of reference, it took me a moment or two to realize that Loring was physically a rather small man. Seated there in a lotus position, and with the sunlight making his bald head, bare shoulders, arms and legs bright patches of white, and with his eyes rolled up into his head, he looked like a creature wrapped in a light-cocoon in preparation for a spiritual chrysalis.

Keeping one hand on the cavern wall, I carefully picked my way around the outer edge of the spherical room to a small alcove. I did not have much room in which to work because Loring had filled the cavern floor with an intricate sandpainting. It looked familiar because of the medium. I had seen many sandpaintings on sale in Phoenix—Eclipse and City Center both. What struck me as odd was that while the technique used was traditional, the images were not.

Loring seated himself at the hub of the circular painting. Seven lines came out from the middle, splitting the drawing into seven even parts. Each slice contaned a bizarre creature of some symbolic import, I had no doubt, but I could not puzzle them out. One, for example, had a cracked egg from which was emerging an insectoid monster. Another appeared to be a big-mouthed, rapacious creature shoveling earth into its mouth with arms that ended in steam-shovel buckets. They made no overt sense to me, but I felt I had the key to their meaning inside me somewhere. I just needed one more piece of the puzzle.

That piece was the outer circle itself. It had been done almost entirely in black sand except where golden sand had been layered in. The gold bits were all angular, beginning and ending in dots. I knew I had seen that design before, but it took me a second or two to remember where.

The dimensional gate! Loring has built himself one out of sand. I swallowed hard. *Whew, must be some serious pharmaceuticals at work here.*

At seven spots around the room, in small pots placed at points beyond where the spokes ended at the outer circle, incense burned. Thick ropes of it filled the air and drifted like clouds of cosmic dust through the universe. I caught some of the spicy scent but couldn't place it. It burned my nose and eyes enough to start the one running and the others watering. As tears filled my eyes and blurred the scene, things shifted.

Suddenly I found myself out where I had been with El Espectro. I floated above the red planet. Surrounding me I saw all sorts of humanized creatures in traditional Amerindian garb. They regarded me closely, then shifted in shape to become stained-glass saints, and then again into the myriad gods of the world's pantheons. None of them said anything to me, yet I sensed from them an insistence that I act. And about the same time as I began to wonder if they truly existed, they began to vanish, and I wondered if what I had seen was nothing more than an externalization of things lurking within my own mind.

Below me, seated in the dust of the red world, I saw Nero Loring. Pointing my toes, I forced myself to drift down to him. As I did, behind him, on a sheer mountain face, I saw images begin to take form as if a movie were being projected on the mountainside. On the mountain I saw Nero Loring's head and shoulders as they were now, but the crosshairs of a rifle scope slid down over them. I saw the purple dot the Allard Technologies Espion UV laser sight used to mark its victims. It clung to Loring's forehead like the biblical mark of Cain, then I felt my right index finger spasm.

In agonizingly precise slow motion I saw a hollow-nosed, 180-grain bullet that had been drilled and patched core through the sighting dot. Upon impact, the droplet of mercury inside the bullet shot forward, bursting free of the front of the bullet. Its microfine beads ripped through the tissue like shotgun pellets. The rest of the bullet fragmented, expanding to create an exit hole five times the size of the entry wound as it went out just above his neck.

As the head snapped forward, it dropped from the camera frame, and the movie ended. I knew without question that what I had just seen was a memory conjured up from before I woke up in the body bag. Whatever it was that was in the incense had freed that vision when I saw Loring. I had shot and killed him, I knew it. I felt it right down to my soul. I had killed Nero Loring, yet here he sat before me.

The man's eyes rolled down and skewered me with a feverish stare. In a voice I heard as being as mechanical as Coyote's phone voice, he spoke to me. "He told me you would come. Once the destroyer, once my salvation." He lifted his hands to me as if transferring an invisible burden. "You must find her and bring her to me. He cannot have her."

I concentrated, frowning, to pierce the mystery of his words. "Who is he and who is she?"

"He is Fiddleback." Loring's eyes blazed with madness. "She is Nerys. Into your hands I commend the spirit of my daughter. If you cannot save her, we all will die!"

The real world came crashing back as Loring collapsed in the middle of his sandpainting. I shivered all the way down my spine, then called out to George. He arrived a minute later and gingerly stepped over the lines Loring had drawn. Following his lead, I made my way to the center of the picture and lifted Loring's emaciated body. A man his size should have weighed at least 130 pounds, but he was easily below 100.

George and I wormed the comatose man through the tunnel and with Will's help managed to get him into the car. I belted him into the shot-up passenger seat and put my rifle case in the seat behind him. Straightening up, I slammed the door shut. Turning to George I started to thank him, but he stalked his away around the car with his arms held wide like a bird facing off against a snake.

Will and I backed away, watching him carefully. He made a circuit from the radiator all the way back to the rear bumper, then dropped to the ground. As we came around that end of the car, we saw him wiggling his way back from under the vehicle. In his left hand he held a sticky cocoon covered with grayish silk. Without hesitation he set the cocoon down on a flat rock and smashed it with another stone.

"When you came out here, you were followed."

I glanced between the black liquid dripping down the stone and the nearly destroyed car. "Yes."

George nodded proudly. "That was why. It was evil. I suggest you do not return the way you came because they will have forces arrayed to stop you."

I decided not to point out that his thesis was, in fact, unprovable unless I *did* return by the route that had brought me to the mountain. As that had never been my intention in the first place, I had no trouble agreeing to his plan. "Thank you, for everything."

Will frowned. "I deeply love and respect my grandfather, but you, a white man, you cannot believe all this mumbo-jumbo that he has been teaching me. The old ways and the old monsters have no power in the real world."

In Will's words I sensed he had reached a decision point in his life. One half of him, the modern half, dreamed of living in City Center just like everyone else. That world had no room for superstitions and bogeymen. That was a world of superficiality where being seen in the right place far outweighed actually doing anything real. In many ways, though difficult to attain and maintain, it was an easy way of life because it required only a willful dedication to work mixed with an equal dedication to hedonism and social climbing.

The other part of him, the part that had listened to stories of the old ways from the day of his birth, had seen just enough to question things. He'd doubtlessly been involved with his grandfather in ancient rituals. If Will had what El Espectro described as latent empathic abilities, his grandfather could be using ancient rituals to teach him to harness those abilities. Will knew enough to make him wonder if his grandfather might not be right and, if he was, Will knew his whole world view became one leaf on a tree instead of the whole tree itself.

"I don't know how to answer that, Will. I've seen things that make me question what is real and what isn't." I nodded at George as I opened the driver's door. "If I had the opportunity to learn what he could teach, I would. If he is wrong, at the very least you are rescuing from extinction traditions that predate recorded history. If he is right, you will be infinitely more able to deal with the world than you would be if you remained willfully ignorant."

I climbed into the car and started it. As I drove away I saw the two Indians walking back toward the Cave of Dreams. George offered Will half of one of my sandwiches, and the younger man draped his arm over his grandfather's shoulder.

On another two-tire track I drove from the mountain into Fountain Hills and picked up Shea Boulevard. I took that back into Scottsdale, passing into the darkness of Frozen Shade at 120th Street. I picked up the 101L and headed south to Thomas. There I exited, having skirted the heart of Drac City, and dropped Loring with El Espectro's friends at a little house set back from the road between Hayden and Pima. At no time during the journey did he wake up, and when I left him his eyes were still fairly dilated from whatever drugs he had used.

I drove a bit away from there, checking for unwanted tails, then stopped at a convenience store with a pay phone. I shoved a copper Columbus into the slot and called Marit. Juanita answered and got her for me quickly.

"Hi, Tycho. What's up?"

"Did anyone else know I was going out to the reservation?"

"No, didn't tell anyone, just as you asked." Her voice lost its cheery tone. "What happened?"

"Aryans picked me up soon after I left City Center. I managed to elude them, but your car got chewed up." I frowned. "Maybe they just had a lookout for your car. No one else knew?"

"No...wait. When we went to Sedona yesterday, Rock took the Ariel off to have it serviced. He does that for all of us. Before I called down to get the car ready for you, I called him to find out if it was in the garage or still being fixed. I didn't tell him where you were going, but I did say you were using the car." As she spoke she realized what she was saying. "Rock may be tight with the Aryans, but he'd never set them on you."

No, my dear, but he'd sell me out to Lorica as per Nerys' orders. "You're right. Heinrich probably has connections all over the place and was angry for what I did to that kid of his yesterday. I'll have to let everyone else know to be careful."

"True." She hesitated for a second, then a little more life returned to her voice. "Listen, Jytte called and said she'd done the computer work you asked for. She's at the meeting place, if you want to go down there and start sorting through it."

"Will do. I'll see you later?"

"I'll be here, keeping the sheets warm for you." I heard the sound of a pillow being plumped in the background. "So, how badly is my car damaged?"

"Oh, gotta go, someone here wants to use the phone. Later."

I hung up and returned to the Ariel. I kept looking for Aryans or others as I drove down to the headquarters and ended up doing a full circuit around the area before I felt confident that I'd not been followed. I parked in the back and checked my weapons, as per usual.

In the conference room I found Bat sitting in front of a daunting pile of reports.

"Anything good, Bat?"

He grunted and flipped one report toward me. I snapped it out of the air and decided, based on the title, that it was surprisingly thin. "Nerys Loring. Fascinating reading?"

"Gossip, some transcripts, medical records. Like other corporators—all skin, no bone." Bat glanced back over his shoulder toward the parking lot. "Nice body work on the Ariel."

I smiled. "Hope to start a fad. It'll give the gangs something to do other than shoot each other. I had a lead to follow up on Nero Loring and someone thought that was a bad idea. Loring's safe and, if we're lucky, some people will be able to get something useful out of him."

Bat nodded and went back to the report he had been reading. I sat down and started in on the report about Nerys. It took me about 10 of the 70 pages in the report to decide Bat had been correct.

Nerys' life, as chronicled in this report, was almost straight normal for a woman in her early 40s. Born in 1968, she was the daughter of a successful engineer and inventor. She did all the normal things kids did in those days, including Brownies and Girl Scouts. Her school transcripts showed her to be a bright student with her language skills slightly outstripping her mathematical skills in testing and grades. At the age of 12 she even won an Arizona state poetry contest.

Things changed at 14. She had been given a puppy for her birthday and named it "Buttons." As nearly as anyone could make out, she opened the gate around the pool and the puppy shot through less than a week after her birthday. Buttons jumped onto the floating pool liner which began to wrap around it as the dog sank. Nerys dove in to save the dog, became entangled in the pool liner herself and was under for at least six minutes. Her father found her and pulled her out, but she was clinically dead.

The Rural-Metro Rescue Team managed to get her heartbeat back and start her breathing again. She was air-evacced to Phoenix Children's Hospital and ended up in a coma for three months. She had no brainwaves to speak of and she required a respirator to keep her lungs working. Her parents reluctantly agreed to turn the respirator off.

They did, but she kept breathing. The EEG monitor showed renewing brain activity. She awakened within a day and left the hospital after a week. She continued intensive physical therapy for another six months to get her body back into shape—the doctors agreed that the brain damage she had suffered made learning how to use her body again normal. After that, she was given a clean bill of health and even worked hard to make up the half year she'd missed at Gerard High School.

After graduation from high school, she went to Arizona State University, taking a double major of business and engineering. She joined Lorica at the bottom and started working her way up until, at the time the maglev project started, she was assisting her father in design work. After the initial design phase was completed, she shifted her attention to the business side of Lorica and started its expansion into a host of projects that diversified the company and actually helped it survive the recession in '05.

Her time spent strengthening the business also consolidated her power within the company so, two months ago, she was able to oust her father easily. Once he was out she purged his loyalists and the data flow used to compile the report all but dried up. End of story.

I double-checked something in the school transcripts section. Before the accident Nerys had been very literate and had above average language skills. After the accident these skills did not diminish much, but her mathematical skills shot past them by all the measures listed in the charts. SAT scores showed a hundred point gap between the two, with her math score being as close to perfect as most folks ever get.

Jytte came into the room as I finished reading the Nerys report. "Satisfactory?"

I nodded. "Excellent work, especially on such short notice. You saw the score shifts after the accident?"

The woman nodded woodenly. "I did some checking of contemporary medical literature regarding personality and intelligence shifts after brain trauma caused by oxygen deprivation. What happened in her case is atypical and manages to push well beyond the mean improvements in those few cases where the accident appears to have proved beneficial as opposed to neutral or detrimental, which it is in the vast majority of cases. I would also note that her case is the only case in which such a beneficial result was noted in a case where brain trauma was not secondary to cold water-induced hypothermia."

"Wow, I'm impressed."

Jytte handed me another piece of paper. "This is a ballistics report from Scorpion about the gun that killed Buc in the graveyard. They think it was a Steyr SSG-PIV Marksman .308. Bolt action, five- or 10-round cartridge clips, it comes fitted with mounts for NATO-type scopes. It is a very good gun, but inferior to the PVI model."

"I know. Thanks." She started to turn away but I stopped her. "Back to Nerys for a second. Have we got any writing samples from before the accident to compare with what she's written since then?"

She shook her head. "I made the attempt to obtain samples, but I have found nothing. I am in the process of trying to get current addresses for all her schoolmates, but Gerard closed in 1988, so obtaining that data is difficult. Once I have it, I will communicate with them to find out if they have anything."

"Good luck."

Jytte regarded me curiously for a second, then turned away. Coldly efficient, it would have been easy to think of her as no more than a mobile extension of the computers with which she worked. I knew that was not true. She was a person who had been grossly traumatized physically, emotionally and mentally by a monster. Her amnesia about the whole incident was a blessing for her, but cutting herself off from her past meant she defined herself through her computer work and her altered body.

Reflecting on her situation, I wondered if I truly wanted to find out who I had been. Apparently I had gladly murdered people for money. Having met Hal, and having seen his concern for a stranger like me, let me know that people were much more than just walking targets. I fervently believed some of them, like Heinrich and Leich, deserved killing, but not for money and not because they managed to offend some bureaucrat's sense of decorum.

I realized I could not be content with not knowing who I had been. Certainly the skills I had learned in my previous life had served me well here. They made it possible for me to recover my identity. To find out who and what I truly was I just had to continue the tricky job of navigating between megacorporations in this world and whatever other things might be arrayed against me outside it.

The best way to do that, I figured, was to start in on the reports Bat had been reading. I took half the pile from him and started going through them. Most were short pieces that detailed areas of competition between the corporations in the southside of Phoenix and Build-more. It appeared, from what I read, Build-more was trying expand and diversify, much as Lorica had done under Nerys in the last four years. The expansion had Build-more in competition with all the companies in the southside, so we ended up cataloging points of conflict to see who won the race.

Alejandro arrived late in the afternoon and avoided death by not laughing when he saw us up to our ears in paper. "Tycho, I wanted to show you the color sketch of the painting Estefan delivered to me today."

He handed me a small piece of bristolboard roughly 6×8 inches. Estefan had produced in miniature a three-quarters view of Phoenix, as if the viewer were in a helicopter heading in toward City Center. In the picture a giant brown recluse sat perched amid a huge web that covered the maglev line and connected all the towers. The spider itself had a dark tunnel near the Lorica Citadel and Estefan had even included the web-bound body of an insect dangling from one of the towers.

"I love it."

Alejandro nodded proudly. "He says it will be three feet by four feet, and he expects to have it finished in a couple of days. I'll call when it comes in, and you can come down and see it." He chuckled lightly and tapped the color sketch. "I've shown this to a couple of people already and one made a photocopy of it to fax around. It should be all over by this point."

"Great! When you call, I'll get the money and come right down there."

"Good." Alejandro took back the sketch and headed for the door. "Oh, by the way, if Marit wants to get rid of her car, I'll buy it. I've got a client into retro-Guevarista-realist pieces."

Alejandro's offer mollified Marit a bit when I told her about the car. She seemed less upset about its destruction than she was about my almost having gotten killed. This I appreciated very much, and was very appreciative in return. We spent the next two nights out seeing shows and dining at Avanti City Center and Vincent's in the Macayo Tower.

The days I spent in the conference room going through lots of reports. Marit helped out when she could and between the three of us, we actually caught up with the flood of material Jytte managed to coax from the computer network tying the city together. At the end of it all, we came to two conclusions.

The first thing we agreed upon was that the Build-more sponsorship of the Aryans was not directed at any one of the other corporations—it was aimed at *all* of them. The Build-more strategy appeared to be designed to cause trouble to see what the other corporations would sacrifice to beef up security. If any of their subsidiaries became neglected, Build-more would stage an executive raid, or would offer to buy that corporation and fit it into their empire.

Jytte pointed out that this strategy was a modification of 20th-century Yakuza tactics employed against megacorporations in Japan. There it only had to go so far as disrupting stockholder meetings. Because the Japanese could not stand open conflict, they would pay the Yakuza off to keep them out. In the United States, causing a disruption of business was necessary to shake anything loose, and the tactic had been applied by other companies in Chicago, New York and Miami with apparent effectiveness.

It did not take her long to cross-correlate employment records of Build-more's staff with places where this tactic had been used to come up with a candidate for employing it here. Barney Kourvik had worked with all the companies who had employed the tactic and had, most recently, been employed as a consultant by Build-more to school them in how to defeat that sort of thing. Build-more officials apparently feared that Lorica would start using strong-arm tactics to increase their power in Phoenix.

His star pupil and liaison with the company was Sinclair MacNeal, one of four sons of Build-more's tyrannical founder Darius MacNeal. Sinclair had managed to be disowned once already and had spent time in Japan working for a corporation whose interests clearly conflicted with those of his father's company. He rejoined the company three years ago as a security specialist and had finally risen to the number two spot in that department. It seemed very apparent that Sinclair was our man.

"We'll have to have a talk with Mr. MacNeal, I think,"
I commented as the phone rang.

Jytte answered, listened for a moment, said, "I will
inform him," and hung up again. She turned to me and
said, "Alejandro says Estefan Ramierez has delivered the
painting. He has a few people coming over for a private
viewing tonight, but thought you might like to see it this
afternoon before anyone else gets a chance to look at it."

"I would. Marit? Bat? Jytte?"

Marit shook her head. "I'm going shopping with Dottie
in a half hour, so I'll pass. I'll see what she can tell me
about Sinclair MacNeal since her husband works at
Build-more."

Bat nodded.

Jytte looked from Marit to Bat and then to me. "I
cannot leave here." She headed back into her dark
sanctuary, then stopped halfway through the door and
turned back. "Thank you for asking."

The three of us piled into the new Ariel Marit had rented
and drove to City Center. The valet who accepted
custody of the car looked a bit askance at Bat, but held
his tongue and drove away without squealing the tires.
Marit and I waved to Dottie up on the Level Nine, then I
kissed Marit and left her at the elevator while Bat and I
trekked across the mezzanine. On the other side we
found the escalator that went up one level and deposited
us near the Mercado.

I noticed Bat looked around a great deal and seemed
to study everything with intensity. "Have you not been
here before?"

He shook his head. "Not in public."

"But you have been in City Center before?"

"Once, the Bookbinder Building. Rich fan of pit fights
offered me $10,000 dolmarks to fight a Thai fighter he'd
flown in. Had a ring in his penthouse suite."

"What happened?" I smiled. "I know you won."

"Fight left the ring. I tossed the Thai through a window. Broke some other stuff, too."

"What?"

"Ming vase. Revere silver service. Rodin bronze." Bat furrowed his brow. "Oh, and an all-pro linebacker for the Cardinals."

Bat cracked a bit of a smile, and I laughed openly. "So they never asked you back?"

"You got the picture." He pointed to a cantina that was part of the Mercado. "Fought in that place down in Acapulco."

As we followed the nearly deserted, winding street around the restaurant, Alejandro's Gallery came into view. "There it is." I gave Bat a wry grin. "You'd best try not to break anything."

Suddenly fire blossomed in the windows and doorway of the gallery. Flames and black shot through the bars on the windows, spitting shards of glass and chunks of wooden window framing into the air. The ground shook with the thunderous detonation and one of the two doors danced madly across the cobblestone street. It smashed against the restaurant's wall as the force of the blast knocked the both of us down and shattered windows throughout the Mercado.

Because Bat and I had been in the street and a bit back from the explosion, the only damage done to us came when we fell down. Behind us people ran from the bar in a blind panic. Clothing hung tattered on those who had been closest to the windows, with blood quickly soaking it.

Bat got up first and pulled me to my feet. We both ran toward the gallery, but the fire raging inside burned so hot we could not approach closer than five feet from the door. Roaring flames licked up and out of the windows and doors, blackening pastel colors and making the

window bars glow red hot. I tried to look inside, but I could
see nothing in the smoke and flames.

Bat pulled me back as firefighters arrived and started
spraying chemical foam in through the door. I sat down
on a bench, and he stood beside me. "God in heaven,
Bat, I never thought..."

"They'll rule it accidental, electrical, and blame it on
paint stored in the back." I saw muscles twitch at his jaw.
"It was the Witch."

"How do you know?"

"It was you who said she had no taste in art. This gets
the spider painting and gets Alejandro for bringing the
other one to auction. It was her."

I pursed my lips and nodded slowly. "Okay, you know
it, and I know it. We can't prove it."

"Don't need proof, I *know* it. Proof is for your friend
and Nero Loring."

"Okay, what now?"

"I want you to meet a friend of mine." Bat grinned.
"You'll like him. He sells guns."

Bat took me to what looked like a small pawnshop nestled in the shadow of City Center. The thick coat of dust over the whole place made me feel I was walking into a museum more than any sort of viable commercial establishment. Old and tarnished musical instruments lined the left wall and a plethora of rifles the right, like soldiers preparing to battle over the battered televisions, radios and toaster ovens huddled in the middle. The glass cases ringing the walls had some pistols and a number of interesting jewelry items, but nothing like what we would require to bust Lorica open and take the Witch.

Bat walked through the dimly lit shop like it did not exist. The teenager sitting in the cashier's cage glanced at him and buzzed him through the gateway into the back, then returned to reading an old science-fiction paperback. He paid me no attention at all.

A left turn, then a right put us in front of a thick steel door. A periscope built above the door surveyed us, then a buzz sounded. The door unlocked with a click and Bat ushered me into a narrow spiral stairwell that led down. He had to duck his head to avoid scraping it against the low ceiling, and his broad shoulders brushed against the hole's edge as he went down.

"Bat, I thought the ground in Phoenix was too hard to make underground construction common."

"It is. These are *old* tunnels. This was once in Phoenix's Chinatown district. Opium dens."

Bat remained half-hunched as we came out into a place that appeared, to me, to be a bunker more than any sort of shop. The walls had been covered with pegboard so they could hold up the inventory of weapons but, other than that, they were as unfinished as the ceiling. Old boards covered the floor and plywood sheets had been laid down where the original flooring had rotted away. The flooring had completely collapsed beneath a Chrysler Combat Exoskeleton in the corner. I had no idea how they'd gotten it into this hole. The former opium den had electricity and phones, but all the wiring remained exposed on thick wooden beams.

A dwarf came waddling out from behind a counter. "*Dzien dobry*, Chwalibog."

"*Dzien dobry*, Bronislaw." Bat's huge hand swallowed the smaller man's normally sized one, then Bat looked over at me. "Tycho Caine, this is Bronislaw Joniak."

I offered the dwarf my hand, and he shook it. I found his grip strong and his hand rough with calluses. "Pleased to meet you, Mr. Joniak. Bat thinks you can meet our needs for some weaponry."

The little man smoothed back brown hair and folded his arms. "I deal in quality weapons, Mr. Caine. If you're looking to take down a Circle K or a 7-Eleven, I have what you need upstairs."

I shook my head. "I am a bit more ambitious than that. I need to outfit an expeditionary force of eight individuals. We will be looking at a substantial purchase—fully automatic weapons, personal side arms, ammunition, communications devices and sundry explosives. I can pay cash or gold, your choice."

A smile slowly crept across the man's face and had taken up residence there before I mentioned money. "I like seeing someone who knows what he wants." He walked back around the counter and clambered up onto a high stool. Pulling a steno pad into his lap, he flipped to a new page and picked up a pencil. "Shall we start at the beginning?"

I nodded. "I will need eight portable radio units with

earpiece microphones, complete with batteries."

Bronislaw scribbled. "Possible, though I may have to buy Japanese."

"Whatever. I will need two kilos of Semitek or C-4 with 12 radio detonators, 24 unburned PROMs and the equipment needed to burn them with a voice command for detonation. I'll return any chips I don't use, as well as the burner."

The little man looked up at me with dark eyes. "Next?"

"Assault rifles, eight." I looked at the section of pegboard to which he pointed. On it he had mounted two dozens different models. "Bat, does Natch shoot?"

The big man nodded. "We all do."

"Good, let's make it easy, then. Give me eight Colt AR-15 A2 carbines. I want six full 20-shot clips loaded with duplex shells. I'll want another 2000 rounds of loose ammo for the guns, duplex as well. Possible?"

The dwarf shrugged. "Duplex rounds are a bit difficult, but I can do it. You'll want them full-auto, correct?"

"I'd prefer a selector that allows for single, trey-burst and full auto."

"Done. Next?"

"Personal side arms." I pointed to Bat. "You probably know our compatriots' tastes."

Bat turned to study a pegboard section of the wall when the phone started to ring. Bronislaw and Bat both ignored it, which struck me as odd. What struck me as odder still was that I had an overwhelming desire to answer it. Without thinking, I snatched up the heavy receiver and held it to my ear. "Caine here."

"It's me, El Espectro. I need to see you immediately." I recognized his voice, then a mental picture of where he was blasted into my brain, just as I had seen Loring's location in my dream. "Hurry."

"Give me a half hour."

"This is important."

"So is this."

"Very well. Hurry."

"Later." I returned the receiver to the blocky black base. I looked up and saw both men staring at me strangely. "Well, neither of you made a move toward it."

Bronislaw slowly shook his head. "It didn't ring."

"Sure it did." I looked over at Bat. "It was for me."

Bat narrowed his eyes. "Never should have gone to Sedona."

I frowned at the phone. "Maybe I got it before it rang."

Bat grunted. Bronislaw consulted his list. "That's two Colt .45s, four Beretta 9s and a Desert Eagle .44 Magnum for you, Bat." The dwarf turned to me. "What would you like?"

I started to tell him that I thought my Kraits would be enough, but the image of Leich having survived as much as he had stopped me. "I want a gun that shoots a heavy cartridge that will bore a big hole. What I really want is an automatic pistol that can handle a rifle cartridge. The .44 Mag is probably the best I can do, right?"

Bronislaw slid off the stool wearing a grin that meant the phone incident had all but been forgotten. He wandered deeper into the armory, dug around behind the Chrysler Exoskeleton, then returned bearing a rosewood box like it was a gift of the Magi. He set it up on the counter, resumed his seat, then opened it reverently.

"This, my friend, is the answer to your desire. It is a Wildey Wolf with a 10-inch barrel. It shoots a .475 Wildey Magnum shell which is a wildcat round mating a 250-grain bullet to a rebated-rim .284 Winchester cartridge. You get seven in a magazine. The pistol, because it's gas operated and weighs just over four pounds, has less recoil than Bat's Desert Eagle. Muzzle velocity is 1750 feet per second with foot-pounds of energy coming in at 1725. If it can die, this will kill it."

"And if it can't?"

"One of these rounds through it, and it'll hurt enough that it will *wish* it could."

I picked up the Wolf and smiled. The grip and weight felt good in my hand. Double action, ribbed barrel in a brushed steel finish, it felt and looked like a rifle in pistol-clothing. "Sold." I returned it to the box and closed the lid.

"Anything else?"

"Only if you can supply close air support."

The dwarf smiled. "Not in Eclipse." He ran down the list, checking items off as he went. "I have everything you need in stock or available for immediate delivery. You can have the complete kit tomorrow."

"Good, I'll arrange payment…"

The little man held his hand up, cutting me off. "You pay Bat. He brought you, he trusts you and, more importantly, I owe him."

"I will do that, Mr. Joniak." I shook his hand again. "A pleasure doing business with you." I slapped Bat on the shoulder. "See you back in the conference room this evening—two hours. See if Jytte can get everyone there. We have some planning to do."

The building on the northeast corner of 12th Street and Roosevelt looked very out of place for a number of reasons. It sat nestled in a little box canyon carved out of City Center. Unlike the area near it, this building had somehow avoided decoration by graffiti artists. Likewise the urban decay in evidence all around it had somehow passed it by. Dirt and grime and litter stained the neighborhood and even the walls of City Center, but left this place inviolate.

The two-story building had been constructed of brick, with a plantation-style front including a double-deck porch with thick pillars. The pitched roof looked unusual amid a bed of squat, mushroom colored houses with flat roofs, and the building very much gave the impression of having been transplanted here from another place and another time.

I opened the gate in the wrought-iron fence and traversed the circular walkway to the front steps. I mounted them and crossed the porch, but before I could knock on the glass-paneled door, it opened for me. I stepped into a small foyer, and the door closed behind me, leaving me alone with two animals that looked like Doberman pinschers but possessed the bulk and height of Irish wolfhounds. Their sheer size combined with their low growls and an ugly red glow in their eyes to make me wish I'd not left the Wildey Wolf behind.

"Kara, Amhas," I heard El Espectro's voice call from elsewhere, "Bring Mr. Caine to me."

One of the dogs approached and took my left hand gently in its mouth while the other circled around behind me and leaned against the back of my legs. Given a choice between moving forward or becoming kibble and bits, I went with the animals. The lead dog, Kara, let go of my hand and mounted the stairs on the right side of a narrow hallway leading back into the house. I followed up the steep stairs and found the dog waiting in the doorway of a darkened room.

An antique four-poster bed dominated the slant-ceilinged room. A man I took for El Espectro lay on the bed in a dressing gown with his left arm in a sling. He had been propped up on a whole stack of pillows, and the light on the nightstand beside his bed sank half his face into impenetrable shadow. A thick book with yellowed pages lay open on his lap and reading glasses sat perched on the end of his nose.

I noticed two peculiar things about him that surprised me very much. The first was that he wore pearl-gray gloves. That was odd, but I'd heard of people who had an obsession with cleanliness—which, combined with the dogs, went a long way toward explaining the immaculate conditions outside his house. That was a personal quirk and nothing I couldn't live with.

The second and far more startling thing, to me, was his age. When I had seen El Espectro in my dreams and in the Draoling dimension, he had only been a black silhouette, but it was a silhouette of a much younger man. The El Espectro lying on the bed had white hair on his head and in his goatee and moustache. His green eyes still had plenty of fire in them, but his body had thickened, and dark bags underscored his eyes.

He gestured toward a chair at a small writing desk in the corner, and it slid across the hardwood floor toward the foot of the bed. "Please, be seated."

I accepted his offer, and the two dogs flanked me. They laid down, but I had no doubt that at a single command they would rise up and tear me to pieces. "I'm here."

"So you are." He smiled at me in a most curious manner, then removed his glasses and set them on the night table. "Permit me to introduce myself."

From the nightstand a small white rectangle floated toward me. I accepted the card and read the name aloud. "Damon Crowley."

The man smiled weakly. "Actually, the last name rhymes with 'unholy,' but that is a tired and old joke begun by my grandfather. Forgive my rudeness in not having mentioned my name earlier to you, but we seldom had the time for polite chatter."

I shrugged and slipped the card into my jacket pocket. "How are you doing?"

"The Draoling's blade was clean, which was a miracle in and of itself. More annoying than the cut is the rib another of them cracked. I'm getting too old for this."

I leaned back in the wooden chair, and it creaked. "What, exactly, is 'this'?"

"I do what your Coyote does, but, as I said before, I do

it in realms he cannot access. In this particular case, I have managed to unravel what Nero Loring has been seeking. To solve his problem, however, I will need your aid, and the aid of others as well."

"What's going on?"

He eased himself up a little taller in bed and winced with some pain. "We need to backtrack a bit. When Nerys Loring was born her father was deathly concerned that she might suffer from Sudden Infant Death Syndrome. Like any concerned parent, he took precautions. In his case, being an engineer and inventor, he hitched up an EEG machine to his daughter and recorded her brainwave patterns. He did this again at age four when it was believed she might have a rare form of epilepsy. She did, and it made her EEG rather distinctive, but she controlled the condition with medicine. Nero's actions might seem a bit obsessive perhaps, but he was merely doing what he could with the means he had at hand."

My mind raced ahead of Crowley. "So he had a baseline EEG reading for when his daughter came out of the coma. He mentions it to the doctors and even notes the discrepancies. The doctors tell him not to worry about it, that it's a miracle and he should be happy, right?"

"Exactly. And he was, especially when Nerys began to follow in his footsteps. He found her help on Frozen Shade and the maglev system most useful, but her quick distancing of herself from him during the implementation phase of the maglev project allowed old anxieties to resurface." Crowley's head came up. "Do you know what a changeling is?"

I shook my head.

"In the old faery tales there are stories of elves and other fey folk stealing human newborns and substituting their own offspring for them. It is akin to the cowbird or European mockingbird laying its eggs in another bird's nest. The old stories concentrate on what happened to the purloined child and often chronicle attempts to return those children to their human parents. The old storytellers did not dwell upon what benefit the faery folk would get from placing one of their own as a human.

"Nero came to believe that his daughter went under the water of the family pool, but she was not the one who resurfaced. He decided that in an alternate dimension where time flows far more swiftly than it does here, creatures monitoring our world could have the time to create and substitute a changeling for his daughter within the time it took for her to go down."

I chewed on my lower lip. "Had I not seen the Draoling dimension I would think of this as paranoid ravings, you know."

"Quite so. Nero thought the same thing, so he began to work on his dimensionscope. He linked it in with the equipment on which he had recorded his daughter's EEG. He used her brainwave patterns to search the dimensions for a match. Just before he was ousted from Lorica, he found it."

"What?"

Crowley slowly nodded. "He found a match for his daughter's brainwave pattern. Chances of a match like that are millions to one."

"Where is she?"

El Espectro smiled slightly and closed his book. "In 1924 Valdimir Obrutcev published a book titled *Plutonia* that detailed the journey of a Russian expedition to what they believed was the center of the earth. They found a land they named Plutonia. At its center they found a giant volcano surrounded by black rocks and sand. They called it the Black Desert and in it, in a vast forest, they reported finding giant ants building vast, skyscraperlike nests. From what I have been told, Nerys is there."

"You aren't saying this expedition actually took place

over a century ago, are you?"

Crowley shrugged. "Whether it did or did not is immaterial, really. Obrutcev's description jibes with what Nero has described to me. I believe, as I do with Poe or King or Donaldson, that there are individuals empathic enough to pick up impressions of other dimensions that they fully describe or embellish as best they can. Obrutcev's only failing was in not ascribing more than rudimentary intelligence to the creatures he called 'ants.'"

"What is important is that we get into Plutonia, get Nerys and get her back out again."

I frowned. "Why?"

"Because, if you don't save my daughter, this world will be opened to the greatest invasion it has ever seen."

I turned in my chair and saw Nero Loring leaning heavily on the door jamb, only barely able to keep himself upright. I quickly vacated my chair and offered it to him. He staggered over to it and sat down. He looked feverish and defeated, yet the energy in his eyes told me sheer willpower was driving him. He covered his hands with his face, then wiped them off on the striped pajamas he was wearing.

"I realized, belatedly, that I had unconsciously incorporated pieces of the maglev system design into my dimensionscope. That is what allowed it to see outside this dimension and into other places. When I began my reevaluation of the maglev project, I realized that those bits of design had been things Nerys had insisted upon including. She always had good reasons for her changes, with many of them being that such things would facilitate expansion in the future. I took this as a sign she would continue our work and that Lorica would live on forever. I did what she told me to do, gladly, because I saw her as my gateway to immortality."

The little man trembled as he spoke. If not for the even

tone of his voice I would have thought him a madman. Everything he said was insane, but I weighed the words carefully and, allowing for the existence of other dimensions, everything he said remained consistent.

"I decided my daughter had been taken, and I wanted her back. I put in a software patch that uses her brainwaves to key the energizing of the dimensional gateway. I knew they would have to bring her here to operate the device, and I had thought, while still controlling Lorica, I could wrest her away from them. Now I know I can't, not without help."

I shook my head. "I'm missing something here. They need your daughter's brainwave pattern to allow them to stabilize a dimensional gate's energy pattern?"

"Yes. Maintaining a viable gate is simple, but opening it very difficult. The power has to cycle properly or the thing can be thrown off. This gate needs an incredible amount of power and only by drawing off the energy of Phoenix and combining it with the power of a lightning storm can they hope to do what they need to do."

"Okay." Something still wasn't adding up in my head. "Where's this gate, why can't we destroy it now and who is 'they'?"

Loring turned and clutched at my arm. "The gate is not a 'where.' It's too big to blow."

"Nothing is too big to blow, Mr. Loring."

"Haven't you heard anything I've said?" Loring tore at his hair. "The dimensional gate is surrounding us. It is part and parcel of the maglev line!"

My jaw dropped open, and I looked at Crowley. "They?"

Crowley nodded. "Fiddleback."

The image of Estefan's giant spider perching over Phoenix in the middle of a lightning storm exploded in my brain like a bomb. I could see gigantic arachnoid creatures invading Phoenix through the hole created by the dimensional gateway. They would descend on Frozen Shade from above, using silken parachutes they themselves extruded. They would punch through the solar panels like fishermen chopping ice in the dead of winter. They would descend and attack or perhaps just sit up top and dangle sticky lines of silk to catch passersby.

"Why, Crowley, why?"

The old man simply shook his head. "I don't know. Perhaps they want us for food or they feed on our mental energy. Maybe it has nothing to do with *us*, but that our planet appears to be a dimensional nexus. Fiddleback may just be using us as a stepping-off point for a war with the Draolings or he may be fleeing an invasion of his own homeland. The reasons are endless."

Had I never been in the Draoling dimension, I would have assumed these two old men were drunk or senile or both. Having been there, having seen Leich survive clearly fatal wounds, I could believe what they had told me. "So you want a team of people to go in and pull Nerys out of this Plutonia?"

Crowley nodded solemnly. "I can get you in very close to where she is being held. Nero had some things his daughter had treasured before the accident, so I have a feel for her nature. I can bring you within 100 meters."

"A hundred meters inside an arachnoid nest, right?" I thought for a moment. "Are you two going?"

They both nodded yes emphatically. "I know I told you

Nero Loring would be unable to see outside our dimension, but, as I did with you, I can share my sight with others. This should help the rest of your team as well."

"After we get her, we'll have to go to Lorica and kill the Witch. We'll also need to destroy the controlling mechanism for the dimensional gate. How close inside Lorica can you get us?"

"Close. If you have a map you can pick your spot."

I smiled, remembering the work Costapain had done with Marit to create a map of the facility. "Done. I'll have to round up Coyote's people, but we can do it. I trust you want it done soon?"

"Tomorrow afternoon is the latest we dare wait." Crowley tapped a newspaper lying on the bed beside him. "The monsoons start tomorrow and the biggest lightning storm in the last hundred years is expected."

I left Crowley's home and returned to Marit's apartment to pick up some things before heading out again. Roughly two hours later I arrived at Coyote's headquarters. I placed my aluminum case on the table, pulled out $20,000 in cash, then relocked the case. To that I added another $5000 in winnings from the dog track. I left my Krait beside it and noted with a smile that our purchases had been stacked on shelves in the antechamber.

I walked into the conference room and slid the money across the table to Bat. I expected a reaction out of him, but I got none. Natch stood behind him massaging his shoulders while Marit and Costapain half-heartedly went over details on one of the maps. She looked up at me with red-rimmed eyes. "Thank God you're alive. Where have you been?"

I frowned and pointed at the money. "I went to Greyhound Park and did some betting. I needed time to relax and think. What's happened?"

"I was afraid they got you." Marit brushed a tear away

from her cheek. "Rock's been hit."

"What? When, where, how?"

As if summoned by my questions, Jytte appeared in the doorway leading to her haven. "I have just recovered the phone company's records for Rock's mobile phone and the pay phone bank where he died. At 7 p.m. Rock got a call on his car phone. It lasted 30 seconds. From there he proceeded to the Circle K on the corner of 16th and Thomas. A phone call from another pay phone—one located in Wong Plaza across the street—came to that bank of phones. This new phone stands next to the one used to call Rock's car phone. It lasted for two minutes. Apparently, Rock immediately placed a call from there to a number I have listed as a front number for the Warriors of the Aryan World Alliance. That call lasted five minutes and was terminated when a single bullet punched through the handset and exploded in Rock's head."

"Dammit! We needed him." I frowned and sat down. "Wait a minute, what was Rock doing calling Heinrich?"

"It doesn't matter. He's dead." Marit looked at the empty chairs in the room. "Hal's in the hospital, his wife's dead, Alejandro is dead and now Rock. They've tried to kill you and me. Recovering your memory is suddenly a lot more dangerous than solving little problems for Coyote."

"It's a lot more dangerous than that, but it's something *I* have to do. I have no choice and I need your help." I placed my hands flat against the tabletop. "More specifically, Marit, I need you to call Dottie. I need to find out where Sinclair MacNeal is right now. Bat, you and I will have to visit him to get him to pull back the reins on the Warriors. Jytte, I need you, Marit and Natch to find all of us some body armor—including helmets, if you an get them." I pointed at the money in front of Bat. "There should be enough left over from that to cover it. We need seven sets—one for each of us, a second roughly Marit's size and a second my size."

Jytte's face froze as she shook her head. "I cannot leave."

"I'm afraid you're going to have to. Without Rock, I need another gun, and I know from Bat that you can shoot. Moreover, what we have going down is going to need someone with the touch to handle a computer. You're elected." I stood and gently squeezed her shoulders. "I know you don't want to go, but you must. I have no other choice but to draft you. You can call Coyote, if you wish, but I don't think he will gainsay me."

Jytte remained standing stock-still for 10 seconds and the tension in the room grew with each one of them. Here I was, the newcomer, the one they were helping, and I dared give orders to the group's coordinator. I'd even gone so far to tell her to call her boss and that he would support me in this decision. If she chose to oppose me, I'd have to operate alone in the future. If she went along with me, on the other hand, I'd be given free reign to structure what we were to do in the manner I felt would best allow us to accomplish it.

Jytte nodded. "I will need an hour to set everything to handle itself in my absence. Is this satisfactory?"

"More than. Thanks." I clapped my hands together. "Once Bat and I return from dealing with Mr. MacNeal, I'll burn the chips for the detonators, so I'll need to take a voice sample from everyone on the trigger words. If we have the body armor by midnight, we can get everyone outfitted, and I will brief you on what is happening."

Phil Costapain looked over at me. "What do you want me to do, son?"

"Just what you have been doing, sir. That map you've made of the Lorica tower is very valuable to us." I tapped it in the center of the elevators running up to Nerys' penthouse. "This is the key to our getting in and stopping the Witch."

Marit came in from Jytte's sanctum with a phone in her hand and put it down on the conference table. "Dottie says Sinclair is hosting a very formal stag dinner party for some Japanese businessmen at his home. I called Roger—everyone on the guest list is Phoenix Forty material. You might rethink trying to see him tonight."

I shot Bat a grin. "Wanna bet your old City Center friend is there?"

He smiled and cracked his knuckles.

"Don't worry, Marit, we'll be very careful." I sat back on the edge of the table. "If Bat stabs anyone I'll make sure he uses the correct fork."

The phone on the table rang. Jytte picked up the handset, listened, nodded and handed it to me. "Caine, it's Coyote, for you."

"I understand, Mr. Caine, the traitor problem no longer exists."

I nodded. "I believe that is correct, sir."

"Good. This gives you one less thing to worry about. I have been briefed on what you and Crowley discussed. It seems like the thing to do." Coyote's voice sounded distant, as if he were speaking from another dimension himself. "You can trust him."

"I do, as much as anyone. This is likely to get bloody."

"Take precautions, but do what you must. It is in your hands."

I hesitated for a moment. "Do you mean you won't be with us?"

"As difficult as it may seem to you, I am involved in something that precludes my participation in your operation. I am confident with it being in your hands, however. And don't worry. You and I have actually met before, and we will meet again after all this is over."

The phone went dead before I could demand he explain his remark. It suddenly occurred to me that if we *had* met before, Coyote could have told me much more about myself than I had already pieced together. *Was he lying, or has he been manipulating me all along?* He needed me to separate the wheat from the chaff in his cell, and my skills were going to be useful here. *Did he plan to tell me who I was after I took out Rock, but then decided to delay rewarding me because this thing with Nero Loring cropped up?*

Crowley had noted that he did what Coyote did, but in places Coyote could not go. The Loring problem was one that Coyote might not be able to handle. In return for the secret of my identity, he would have me act in his stead in a place he could not go. As with Alejandro, I was being coerced into acting for Coyote. Coyote would use whatever tools he had at his disposal to actually get done what he wanted accomplished.

The bargain Coyote offered me was one I would have willingly accepted. The fact that he did not offer it to me up front however, reminded me that I was, in his eyes, a tool. I could be used and disposed of, much as I had set up and killed Rock with my phone calls to him. My announcing that Bat and I had procured the arms needed for a quick strike at Heinrich prompted Rock to warn the Aryans.

A bullet in the head was kind.

Coyote is good, I told myself, *and has to be to play this way and survive.* I smiled and motioned for Bat to follow me out. *I wonder if I am that good?*

I had a sinking feeling I'd find out far sooner than I wished.

Marit had said the dinner was formal, so I dressed for the occasion: I wore the silvery Krait. Aside from that, Bat and I dressed alike in boots, blue-jeans, T-shirts and black leather jackets. I bought the coat at the place across the City Center walkway from where Bat purchased his black "Hell's Belles" shirt.

When we met outside I looked at the image of the blond female thrash guitarist in black leather with spiked boots stomping on someone who looked a lot like Watson Dodd and shook my head. "I'm not sure, Bat. Marit *did* say 'formal.'"

"I know, that's why I bought this one." He started walking toward the Randolf Street maglev station."

I caught up with him. "Ah, Bat, 'formal' means a bit more than 'clean.'"

"I know. That's why Heidi Stiletto isn't naked." He bared his teeth in a fierce grin.

"You're enjoying this, aren't you?"

"People stomp on ants all day, every day. Is it any wonder ants *love* picnics?"

"Good point."

We boarded the more crowded common-carrier section of the maglev train. We found enough room to get seats, but Bat seemed to enjoy roaming up and down the car we were in. He didn't say anything, but he glared at corporators who wore clothes similar to ours. Those poor individuals may once have thought themselves chic in dressing like folks from Eclipse, or brave for actually having ventured down below Frozen Shade, but their encounter with Bat doubtlessly gave them reason to question either idea.

The Build-more citadel could have been dubbed "the Lobby Archipelago" because of the vast amounts of area given over to the intersection of corridors. Each lobby had at least one scale model of some building the company had produced somewhere in the world. I gathered, from a quick sampling, that the whole citadel had been laid out over a virtual map of the world and, as projects were completed, a scale model went up in the lobby that most closely corresponded to the construction site on the map.

A model of the Sears Megalith in Rio dominated the lobby we wanted. The elevator went up to the floor just beneath the one on which MacNeal lived. Bat boosted me up through the ceiling hatchway, then pulled himself up onto the top of the cage. We climbed up the interior girder lattice, and Bat pried the elevator doors open.

We found ourselves in another lobby, of course, but this level of the tower only had four apartments on it. We found MacNeal's, and Bat threw his shoulder against the double doors. They snapped open, and we sauntered in like guests who were mildly miffed at having been shut out. A butler tried his best to stop us in the hallway, but Bat just picked him up and carried him back into the room he had just left.

Marit had not been wrong when she said everyone on the guest list was Phoenix Forty material. That informal group of business heavyweights had run the city since the 1960s, passing their positions in it from father to son or CEO to CEO. It had long since expanded beyond the original 40 members, but alliteration kept the name alive. Of the dozen men in the walnut-paneled room, I recognized seven from ads I'd seen on Marit's television. Four of the remaining men were Japanese and only the last person, an Anglo, was young enough to be the evening's host.

Marit had mentioned the meeting was stag. The charming dozen young ladies seated beside some of the city's most powerful men probably had something to do with that decision. Their presence at the long mahogany table made me smile, and not just because they were very pretty to look at. Because they were there, no one would want to arouse official or media scrutiny of this gathering unless absolutely necessary.

It was my job to make them think it wasn't. "Excuse the intrusion, ladies and gentlemen, but I need to speak with Mr. MacNeal." I motioned toward the door to

Sinclair. "If you please, sir, I think privacy would be preferred."

Sinclair started to get up, moving slowly and deliberately to show me he wasn't afraid, but his father clapped an iron fist over his wrist and pulled him back down in his chair. The white-haired MacNeal patriarch looked at me with fire in his blue eyes. "I remember you from the party the other night. If you have business with my corporation, you come see me during business hours. I can fit you in, say, in a month?"

His little joke brought polite laughter from the other diners. Sinclair, on the other hand, was doing a slow burn. He played with a silver fork in his free hand, his blue eyes burning with the same fire as in his father's, but not directed at me. His left hand knotted into a fist and twisted slightly, but he could not pull it away from the old man without making a scene. Knowing the Japanese set great store by a son's respect for his father, I could see Sinclair restrain himself, and I admired the dark-haired man for that.

I glanced at my associate. "Bat, clear the room."

I had half expected him to throw the struggling butler at the table, scattering candelabra and shattering china soup bowls and plates. I didn't really want to see anyone get hurt, but I had no time to fool around, and there did have to be some sort of payback for Hal's injuries. Bat, I knew, liked to hurt people and was quite good at it, but never did I dream he had style as well.

He dropped the waiter. "There's a bar down in Eclipse called the Lost Dutchman. In the corner it's got a spitoon that's been there since the days when the sun used to shine through the window and heat it up every day. Everything went into it—chaw, dribble, beer—everything, and no one ever cleaned it out."

He slowly started to walk around the table and stopped at a big silver tureen of New England clam chowder.

"Yeah, it was about this size. Anyway, last week, a guy came in. He said he was a prospector and he'd lived in the desert for the past 20 years and wanted a drink. He also said he didn't have a red Columbus on him. The bartender told him to get out, but the prospector said he'd do anything for a drink."

Bat smiled in a way that I finally figured out his true nature: He didn't just like hurting folks, he liked being cruel. "The bartender pointed at the spitoon. He said, 'I'll give you all the beer you can drink if you take one swig from that spitoon.'"

Bat was good at cruel.

The women already started shifting uneasily in their seats. The men began to wince. The Japanese huddled together as one of their number translated the monologue. My palms began to sweat, and my mouth got dry.

Bat slowly lifted the tureen in his hands and stared down into the creamy soup as if it were a long-fermented vat of saliva and used chewing tobacco. "The prospector picked the spitoon up. He looked at it, then looked at the bartender. Then he did it!"

Bat lifted the big silver bowl to his lips and drank. He tipped it back, swallowing again and again, very loudly. Soup spilled out from around his mouth and splashed off his shoulders. Chunks of potatoes and cream-covered pieces of corn flew like shrapnel, flecking the diners, yet they watched him as if hypnotized. Finally he tipped the tureen all the way up and captured the last drop on the tip of his tongue. His dark eyes filled with joy, Bat curled his tongue back into his mouth.

His chin white from the liquid, his shirt dripping soup, he let the tureen crash to the floor. The bartender looked at the prospector unbelievingly. "You only had to take one swallow, old man!" He let the words bubble up through more soup as it spilled from his mouth.

"'I know, I tried,'" Bat said in the prospector's voice,

"but it was all...*one piece.*'"

My stomach convulsed at the punchline, but unlike the other folks in the room, I was working on an empty stomach. MacNeal's American guests retched first, followed quickly by the Japanese when the translation was finished. Darius MacNeal pushed his chair back and hunched over, which allowed Sinclair to recover his arm and stand. He dabbed at the corner of his mouth with a napkin, then said nothing as his guests bolted from the room.

Sinclair looked slender and quite dignified in his tuxedo. A good five inches shorter than me, he had an athletic build and enough control over himself to have sublimated any visceral reaction to the joke Bat had told. In fact, as everyone but his father filed out, he arched an eyebrow and looked at Bat. "I trust you found the soup to your liking?"

Bat belched loudly.

"I'll pass your compliments to the chef." He glanced at his father's pale face, then looked at me. "You have my undivided attention."

"You're paying the Warriors of the Aryan World Alliance to start a gang war that will put pressure on your competitors in this city. I want you to stop."

"No."

I frowned at him. "You won't stop?"

Sinclair picked up a glass of white wine and sipped it. "No, you're wrong in your assumption that I'm paying Heinrich and his boys to start a war. I know the technique, and I know how to stop it. I put them on retainer so they won't let themselves be used against us. That's all, nothing more."

I listened carefully to him and while I half expected him to lie to me, I knew he was telling the truth. Even so, I couldn't believe it because Willem had been positive, and Sinclair was the only man who fit the profile. "You admit giving them money?"

"'Admit'? You make it sound like a crime." He set his glass down. "I initiated the contact, I arranged for a monthly stipend to be paid, and I've even paid them bonuses when they've driven off thieves trying to rip us off. However, I'm not financing a war. Not only does that cause more trouble than it's worth, it's expensive. I'm giving them enough to keep them drunk and happy, nothing more. Only a fool would arm them and point them at a target."

"If you're not doing it, who is?"

Darius MacNeal sat back in his chair and laughed quietly. "I am."

"What?!" Sinclair turned on his father. "We discussed this. You said you wouldn't do it!"

The older man slammed a fist onto the table, splashing chowder all over and making wineglasses jump. "Build-more is *my* corporation! I make the decisions, and I don't have to answer to you. Why pay for an asset if you aren't going to use it? So what if those little fascist bastards go and shoot Lorica up? Who cares?"

"I care, Mr. MacNeal." I leaned forward on one of the abandoned chairs. "I care because one of my friends got caught in the crossfire. His wife was killed, and he's in the hospital."

Sinclair shook his head. "Hal Garrett..."

"Right," I nodded.

"Who?"

Sinclair stared at his father disbelieving. "Hal Garrett, the basketball player. You met him last year when you threw a benefit banquet for his Sunburst Foundation. You gave a speech in his honor, then gave him $10,000 in corporate funds."

The old man shook his head. "Huh. Really? I can't remember."

"Let me tell you something you can remember, Mr.

MacNeal." I met his defiant stare with one that was pure holocaust. "If Heinrich and his people do anything, absolutely *anything*, I will personally make sure you have a closed casket funeral before the week is out."

"You can't threaten me."

"I don't threaten, Mr. MacNeal, I merely supply people with life choices."

Sinclair shook his head. "Don't worry, this Aryan thing will stop now."

"In a pig's eye it will." Darius MacNeal stood up and tugged at the hem of his jacket. "I own Build-more, I make policies."

"If you continue paying Heinrich, I'll quit."

MacNeal looked at Sinclair the way an exterminator looks at a cockroach. "You can't quit, you're fired."

Sinclair's face brightened. "Good, then I don't feel bad about kicking your ass out of my home."

"And as your landlord I won't mind evicting you. You have a week."

"One more thing, Mr. MacNeal," I growled, "you were paying to have Lorica given some trouble. How much would you pay for the Witch's head on a platter?"

MacNeal's eyes narrowed. "Name your price."

"$1,000,000, payable to the Sunburst Foundation."

"$1,000,000! That's seven years of bedevilment by the Aryans."

I smiled. "You get what you pay for."

He nodded. "How will I know when you've done it?"

"Oh, don't worry," I laughed, "it'll be in all the papers."

As we left Sinclair MacNeal's suite, Bat saw one of the diners and got the man to retch by making a simple "gulp" sound. We laughed about that as we took the elevator down and used the maglev train to take us back to City Center. I accompanied Bat down into Eclipse, but he went off to earn some pocket change in a pit fight, and I headed back to Coyote's stronghold.

I spent the next two hours getting voice samples and burning vox response chips for the explosive detonators. I double-checked all the equipment that Bronislaw had sent over, made modifications to some of it, and arranged it in discrete piles and color-coded it for everyone. All they had to do was come in, suit up and we'd be good to go.

I returned to Marit's home a little after midnight. When the door to the transversor opened I thought, for a moment, that something was wrong. Every light in the place was out and had been replaced by a multitude of candles glowing in the darkness. My recollection of the house outside Sedona flashed before my eyes, but evaporated as I saw Marit walking toward me from the back.

The diaphonous gown clung to her like a white fog and stretched to taut invisibility against her flat stomach. She moved forward and, in the flickering half-light, looked more a ghost than a real person. I caught a hint of flowers as she stopped and candlelight reflected gold in her blue eyes. She folded her bare arms across her midriff, and her right hand bunched the fabric on her left hip.

"Tycho, if we attack Lorica, we'll die."

Her words came quietly in a tone befitting such a dire

and final prediction. I saw gooseflesh pucker the flesh of her arms, and her nipples became erect. Her eyes never left mine, but the shifting of the candle flames made it look as if a thousand little demons danced within her skull. Her face remained blank, as if it had been composed for viewing by a mortician.

"If you are that certain of death, Marit, take a pass. Don't go."

She shook her head in a motion so slight that had her hair not moved, I might have thought it a trick of the light. "No, I will go. I must. I owe it to the others." She blinked her eyes and some life returned to her face. "It's just that I wanted to let you know what I am feeling. I want you to understand why it is so very important for you to be with me tonight. There is only one way to defeat death, really drive it away."

She turned back in the direction from which she had come, but held her left hand back out to me. "Come with me, my love. Let us laugh at death together."

The next morning Marit and I walked into Coyote's stronghold hand in hand. Jytte was there before us. Bat and Natch arrived soon after we did, and I set about briefing them as I put the equipment for Crowley and Loring into a pair of large, canvas dufflebags.

"Your equipment is color-coded with a small piece of tape on it. Bat, you've got red; Marit, blue; Natch, green; and Jytte, gold. I'm black. Get your body armor on first, then suit up in the rest of this stuff. If you need any help, sing out."

Natch frowned. "I know this is Eclipse, but won't we look a bit conspicuous going into Lorica with all this on? I mean, shouldn't we get it in to Lorica first, then put it on once we get inside?"

I nodded. "Good thinking, but things have changed a bit. After I left Bat I spoke with Nero Loring and El

Espectro."

Bat shivered. "Crowley? I shouldn't have let you within 50 miles of Sedona."

"Right. Loring told me that the woman running Lorica is not, in fact, his daughter. He says the real Nerys was kidnapped and this new Nerys was substituted for her. He came to that realization recently, yet was ousted from Lorica before he could act upon that knowledge. He would have done something, in fact, but his daughter's captivity made that impossible. We're going to rescue her and then put and end to the Witch."

Everyone accepted my explanation with a little more ease than I would have expected, but life in Eclipse was weirder than I found myself comfortable with anyway. Clearly the folks near Boxton had known the tenement through which Marit and I had returned to Eclipse was the seat of some weird stuff. They'd set up barricades against whatever came out of it. Likewise the Indians had come up with a very effective way to deal with creatures like Leich. Instead of worrying about the grander implications of these inhuman things and other places, they just handled them.

I suited up. I put on my radio headset and settled the earpiece over my right ear. The main body of the box I clipped to my belt. I turned it on, heard static, and shut it off again. The earpiece, which also served as a microphone by picking up sound through the eustachian tube in that ear, fit snugly over my ear but did not wholly prevent me from hearing sounds other than the radio.

That in place and working, I pulled on my combat harness, buckled the web-belt around my waist and tightened up on the shoulder straps. Across my stomach I had three ammo pouches, each with two clips for the AR-15-A2. At the small of my back I kept another pouch that contained six blocks of Semitek with radio/vox detonators attached. A holster on my right hip contained the Wildey Wolf and on the left hip, to balance it, I had three clips of ammo for the gun. Under my left arm I wore my Bianchi shoulder holster with one of the Colt Kraits and on the right three clips for it helped balance me out.

Including the carbine and spare ammo pouch on my left hip, I had better than 30 pounds of equipment on me. Because the harness helped distribute it properly, it felt like much less and would not hamper me if I had to run fast or get out of the way of something. Live weight is much better and easier to handle than dead weight, yet too much live weight could catch up with me and make me all dead weight.

Bat and I helped the others get into their stuff. Everyone had the same amount of equipment and our provisions differed only in that Bat and I carried the plastic explosives while Natch, Marit and Jytte had been given some basic first aid trauma kits. Jytte, despite the unnatural lightness to her body, seemed to stand the weight of the material better than Natch or Marit. Marit checked her own weapons to make sure they were functional, then quickly acquainted Jytte with the deadly tools we'd given her.

All of us piled into the Vanagon Marit and I had rented that morning. I drove us over to Crowley's and around to the side. The gate there opened automatically and we pulled into a small parking area off the street. A wooden fence shielded the house's backyard from the street, but the gate there opened as we approached it.

Crowley and Loring greeted us in the backyard. Loring looked dressed for a weekend of fishing, but his tan fatigue pants had enough pockets to let him redistribute some of the supplies on his combat harness. Marit helped him get into his gear, and they started a pleasant conversation about Lorica before Nerys had assumed control of it. Loring seemed thankful for her attentions and pleased to have a new ally.

Crowley looked at the equipment I'd brought him and smiled. "Carbines are a good choice because, if what I have read is at all accurate, fighting will be in close. You might as well pass out my ammo and that gun because I prefer these." He dropped to one knee and zipped open a blue nylon bag. From it he pulled two small, boxy guns with short barrels that had a bore only slightly smaller than my Wildey Wolf. He handed me one, and I smiled.

"Ingram Mac 10, .45 caliber, fires from the open bolt. Nasty little gun." I turned the gun over in my hands. "Old, but still deadly. They look like they've seen a few wars."

"Relics of a misspent youth, my friend." Crowley pulled on his radio, then donned the combat harness I had brought. He stripped out the CAR-15-A2 clips and replaced them with clips for his Mac 10s. He put one of the small guns in the pouch at his back unloaded, then let the other dangle by its shoulder strap from his right shoulder. Both he and Loring already wore body armor, so his CAR and their vests remained in the duffle bag.

"If you'll follow me," Crowley announced, "We can get started."

His house's rear yard was remarkable in that it had fully leaved trees and bushes. White stones covered the earth everywhere except for the patio on which we stood and had been raked into a zen ocean pattern. As he spoke he waved us toward a koi pond toward the rear of the property, then he squatted down near a big, mechanical statue that looked like the offspring of a steamroller and a Harley Davidson motorcycle. He flipped a switch and the fluttering thump of a pump came from inside the machine.

Crowley stood and wiped his hands off on his thighs. "One of the owners of this house put in a bomb shelter shortly after World War II. Before the turn of the century, when I bought this place, it had served as an avant garde art gallery, which is when the koi pond went in, covering the shelter's opening. I reclaimed the shelter, though I have put it to a different use. Before it was meant to keep things out. Now, in many ways, it keeps things in."

As he spoke the water level in the koi pond dropped, revealing a small island created by a submarine bulkhead hatch. Bat twirled the wheel on top and the hatch hissed open, spraying water out of the water-tight seal. Bat descended the ladder built into the wall first, then the rest of us followed, with Crowley coming down last. The hatch clanged shut above, and I heard the clicks of another couple switches being flipped.

One, I have no doubt, reversed the pump to cover the hatch. The other apparently turned on the lights, because fluorescents flickered to life and filled the moderately sized room with light. Aside from some battered swords, shields and similar archaic weapons of war mounted on the white walls, the room appeared empty to me. Then, as I shifted to the left, I saw a black box in the far corner. It remained visible for a moment, then vanished until I changed my position.

"What the hell is that?"

Crowley made a beeline for the corner in which it appeared to exist. As he walked to the space where I had seen it, he reached out and jerked back slightly as if he had gotten a static shock. His touch seemed to "ground" the device for a moment, and I got a chance to get a good look at it.

To me it looked to be of very fine hardwood construction. Half again as tall and wide as a phone booth, it had a depth of approximately four feet. It stood flush against the far wall of the room, and I could not see a seam at that end. It almost seemed like the box had grown out of the wall, and I would have remarked about that aloud, but I was very much afraid Crowley would confirm my speculation.

Over on the far side he seemed to be playing with

controls, but as I moved over to see what he was doing the center of the box started to sizzle with the gray static of a television getting no signal. Blue and red sparks played through the gray and white, but I heard nothing coming from the display. As nearly as I could tell the box had just become a giant TV screen with no sound.

The old man stepped away from the control surface. "Let me explain this quickly. We are going to be traveling to another place, another dimension which actually lies fairly close to our own. It is called Plutonia—thought I doubt the natives think of it as such. It is a place where all the natural laws seem to apply, save some area-specific time flow fluctuations."

Jytte cocked her head to the side. "Explain please."

Crowley sighed. "I don't know if I can. Dimensions often have their own special properties. Ah, the Underworld of Greek mythology, for example, has an area called Tartarus. It is, in reality, a small collection of pocket dimensions in which the physical laws have been grossly warped. Sisyphus is always rolling a stone uphill because *any* direction of travel, in that specific dimension, is *uphill*. The giant Tityus has vultures eating him alive during the day, but during the night he regenerates—as do the birds, so his torment can go on forever. The regeneration is not a property of him, but of the place he has been trapped in.

"In Plutonia, as nearly as I can determine, there are 'holding cells' where time does not pass in a normal way. I think these are really food storage areas, and they inherently retard aging, spoilage and decay for obviously beneficial reasons."

He jerked a thumb at the control panel which, to my eyes, looked like an opal screen with lights pulsing all over it. "I have set this thing to take us as close as is safe to the place where Nerys Loring is being held. It is another dimensional gateway, so we may encounter hostilities almost immediately."

I shook my head. "Wait a minute. Why can't you put us down in another area?"

Crowley sighed heavily. "Dimensions have boundaries. A gateway is a simple place to go through. If I were going alone, I would not be using this device. I would go through by myself and pick out the most beneficial route. I cannot bring all of you with me, so this is it. While the creatures in Plutonia are sentient, they do not really have anything to counter the weapons we're bringing in." He fed a clip in through the Ingram's handgrip. "Besides, hive mind entities are only dangerous if you really make them angry."

"Great." I stepped up to the box. "Just walk through?"

"Just walk through."

"Okay, folks, radios on. Sound check, black." I heard everyone else identify themselves by color, then I smiled. "See you on the other side."

At first touch the static wall felt cold. Numbness nibbled up through me as I moved forward. I felt goose bumps rise on my skin, and my scrotum tightened. I crouched a bit as I moved ahead, then I felt a flash of heat as I came out on the other side. My head swam for a second, then I jumped up and rotated forward to land outside the dimensional gate.

The gateway on the Plutonia side was shaped like a hexagon. It had taken on the identical look to that of the box in Crowley's shelter in terms of the color playing through it. The major difference was that while the static on Crowley's machine appeared to be heading into to a central nexus point, here it sprayed out to the edges.

The other difficulty with the gate on the Plutonia side is that it was set in the floor of a large chamber. Bracing myself on the edge of the gateway, I held my hand out to Bat when his head poked through the surface of the static pool. It took him a moment to orient himself, then he leaped up like I had, and I pulled him home.

The two of us crouched side by side, and I heard him whisper some Polish oath through the radio. We both pulled back the charging slides on our assault rifles, then covered the only exit we could see in the weak, mossborn luminescence in the cavernous room.

Bat looked around the room, then shook his head.

"What?"

He shrugged. "I used to have an ant farm when I was a kid."

"And?"

"I used to dream about being shrunk down and visiting the nest." He frowned. "I was a dumb kid."

"Why?"

"I called 'em dreams." The big man circled the room with his rifle. "They were nightmares."

The others came through, and only Nero Loring seemed to be unable to see anything. Jytte held his hand and got him to crouch down as we waited for Crowley to come through. When he did, he took on the black-shroud form I had come to recognize before I met him in Eclipse.

Bat took one look at him and scowled. "That's it. When I get back, I torch Sedona."

Crowley laughed heartily. "I'll give you the matches." He pressed his left hand over Nero Loring's eyes, and the man started looking around the room. Nero's face slackened a bit, then he blinked away tears as he imagined his daughter having spent so many years in this place.

Loring charged his carbine. "What are we waiting for? Let's go."

Crowley held up a hand. "A moment." His other hand came up, and his fingers splayed out. I saw them tremble as he moved them around. The gold ring glinted on his right hand as Crowley worked through a series of eerie and complicated gestures. Finally he lowered his hands and pointed toward the doorway. "We're two levels below where she is. Up a slant corridor, first hard right, then second left. She's in the third room on the left."

Marit frowned at him. "How do you know?"

"Nero gave me a locket his daughter used to wear. I matched the emanations from it to those I feel above. We have to hurry. Something is wrong."

Bat and I took up the lead and moved out into the corridor. Starting at the doorway's round frame, glistening lines of mucus ran along the walls and ceiling of the circular tunnel. In the darkness I could not make out any difference between them, but as I got close I noticed a heavy mixture of scents, almost as bad as being caught in a bar during perfume wars between the women nearby. For a half second I wondered if they were some sort of biomechanical circuitry, then dismissed them as bizarre decoration.

Jytte touched one of the lines. "Scent marking. These are the same as painted lines along the walls of a hospital. I would guess this thick central one leads to something important, like food or the queen."

I crouched a bit further up the corridor and took a plastic-bomblet from my pack. "Bat, set a red one opposite me here on the wall." I pressed mine against the rough stone and flipped the small switch, arming it. A small, red LED came on to let me know it was ready to go.

The hard right turn Crowley had mentioned took us from one upward-slanting corridor to another, then leveled off into a large gallery. Going forward slowly I could see little more than patches of green luminescence floating in an ocean of darkness. In the distance I could hear some chittering and clicking that sounded like drumsticks being hammered against each other by a very agitated musician.

"Caine, stop!" the radio hissed in my ear

At Crowley's warning I came to a full stop. I felt the breeze from something moving past from right to left. Clicks and pops sounded closer, then stopped. I heard a creaking sound, like old leather being stretched. Two sharp clicks, like rocks being struck together to make a spark, exploded above my head. I started, then refroze.

Crowley's voice sounded in my earpiece. "Easy, Caine, easy. The one near you is only a worker. You won't smell like food to him, so don't worry. Stay calm. Don't shoot."

Like a ventriloquist, I subvocalized, which the earmike

picked up with ease. "You can see these things? You can see in the dark?"

"It is a skill you can develop if you survive this. Stay still."

I drew a quiet breath in through clenched teeth. A thick, bitterly sweet odor like that of dead flowers washed over me and grew as the clicking became closer. I heard the sound again and again from up above me and to the right, but as I tried to see what it was, all I could make out was a shadow eclipsing distant patches of green moss.

A bead of sweat started at my right temple and slowly started to crawl down the side of my face. My right bicep started to quiver as the weight of the carbine began to vampirize its strength. The bulletproof vest I had on became clammy, and I found myself starting to overheat. More sweat appeared on my brow and one droplet coursed down between my eyebrows, along the edge of my nose, to sting my right eye.

The way my heart pounded, I felt certain the thing must have heard it. Because of Bat's remark, I imagined it as some huge ant, just waiting to catch me in its mandibles. Two huge scythe-blades mounted on its jaws would snap me in half. *Not the way I expected to go at all.* I knew if I could just shift the carbine's muzzle around I could pop the thing.

Then, suddenly, in a series of clicks and crunches, the thing went away. I let my breath out slowly. "Crowley, what the hell was that?"

"A Plutonian, I would imagine." His voice stopped for a moment and, in that pause, lost all the whimsy it had contained. "I don't like this. Forward 12 steps, turn left."

I followed his instructions to the letter and found myself close enough to another corridor that the mosslight let me see my team as they came in. "Crowley, what don't you like?"

The green light did not reflect from his black form.

"That worker was in a classic search pattern with its antennae, but it backed off before it touched you."

"Our luck."

"Or something called it away." He pointed further down the tunnel.

Marit took over the point position and led us to the third opening on the left. She produced a knife from a boot-sheath and started digging away at the wax-covered web-fiber panel blocking the hole. "It's six inches thick. It's like carving clay. There's some light, real light, on the other side."

Bat pulled a knife of his own and stabbed the eight-inch blade in at shoulder-height. Wrapping both hands around the hilt, he started tugging backwards and walk-ing from one side of the hole to the other. The wax-web peeled down like whale blubber being flayed from a humpback. Natch pulled the thick membrane back and Nero Loring ducked into the room first.

He wailed so loudly that I tore my earpiece out of my ear. I stooped below the cut Bat had made and found myself in a tiny chamber. Candles stood in a number of alcoves around the room, filling it with a normal golden light. If not for the room's irregular shape, the furnishings, which included two bookcases full of novels, would have caused me to believe it was a rather spartan dorm room at some paramilitary private school. It hardly seemed a horrible prison and, dozing on the bed with a novel on her stomach, Nerys Loring hardly seemed in distress.

But then, from where I was standing, I could not see what had driven her father to his knees. He reached out for her and pulled her to him. Because she did not react when her father screamed, I knew something was wrong. I thought maybe she had been drugged, but when Nero reached out and hugged her 14-year-old body to him tightly, I saw and understood his anguish.

Like a bad toupee, her black scalp flopped back to

hang at her neck like a hood on a jacket. The whole back of her skull had been ripped away and her brain had been stolen.

"No, no! She's not dead. Her body is still warm," her father moaned.

I turned toward Crowley and pointed at the bed. "This isn't possible. She had her brain removed and there's no blood? Can't be done."

"Of course it can." He snatched the knife from Bat's hand and grabbed my right wrist. In a slashing motion he drew the blade across the back of my hand, and I felt the sting of the blade. Looking down I saw the cut. It wasn't deep and wasn't particularly long, but it wasn't bleeding either.

"How?"

"I told you, this room, this area is special. Look at the candles." He pointed at one, then went close and tried to blow it out. The flame wouldn't even flicker. "They burn without being consumed. It is an aspect of this place."

Crowley bent down and hauled Nero Loring to his feet. When Loring resisted, Crowley slapped him once, hard, then clawed his hands away from the girl's body. "Let her go!"

"No, she is my daughter!"

"She *was* your daughter. You said you encoded a pattern in the software driving the maglev circuit's functions, right?"

"Nerys!"

Crowley slapped him again and lifted him by his shirt-front until Loring's feet left the floor. "Listen to me, Nero Loring. They have your daughter's brain. They will use it to trigger the circuit. Can you stop them?"

"I don't know." The man shook his head while tears streamed down his face. "I think so, but I don't know."

Holding him there with one hand, Crowley turned and pointed at Jytte. "You, you're Coyote's computer empath.

Can you stop the machine?"

"If I am able to obtain access, possibly."

"You'll have access. Caine, come here."

Before I could take a single step forward, a thunderous click and the sound of tearing fabric echoed from the doorway. I spun, bringing my carbine up instantly. Discarding the rest of the room's seal with a shake of its head was the biggest antlike creature I'd ever seen. Chocolate brown in color, I made it just slightly smaller than a bull of the nearly extinct elephant species of Africa.

Instinctively my finger tightened on the carbine's trigger. Flame shot a full foot from the muzzle while the stream of duplex bullets slashed a dozen holes across the thing's face. They snapped off one of the huge mandibles, and it clattered to the ground like a black ivory tusk. The creature reeled back and slammed into the opposite side of the corridor, then scrabbled back up to its six legs before Bat's broadside burst blew a hole the size of a pumpkin through its thorax.

I had expected some sort of death scream, but the creature had remained silent. Instead a brutally pungent scent flooded the room. The first wave of it made my head spin. Marit dropped to her knees and retched. I started to collapse but caught myself on a table. Crowley let Loring fall to the floor, then staggered over to me as the air began to clear.

"Listen to me. You've got to get Nero and Jytte into Lorica. You have to stop Nerys and Fiddleback." He raised his right hand to my forehead and touched me. As he did so I saw a vision of the opalescent control panel for the dimensional gateway flash into my head. "Control sequence is Roy G. Biv—each time you touch a light it will shift to the next color in the mix. The pattern I projected to you will get you to the base of the Lorica Tower. I know it works. I've been there before."

"When you helped Coyote get Nero out of there, right?"

Crowley's head came up, and he looked at me. I could almost see his eyes through the shadow. "You are very perceptive, Caine, but we do not have time for this. Go. Go back the way you came. Use the dimension device to get to the tower. I hope you're in time."

"You must come with us."

He shook his head. "Can't. Fiddleback's out-thought us here."

Bat shouldered his rifle and fired two bursts down the corridor. "They're massing, Caine."

"Go, take Loring. There is a chance he can still get through to her." He glanced over at the body. "I've got to see if there is another way out of this."

"You'll be okay?"

I heard Crowley laugh lightly. "I'm an old man, but Fiddleback and I haven't filled up our dance cards yet."

"Okay, let's go." I reached back and pulled one of the plastique explosive packets from my pouch and armed it. I hunkered down next to the opening on the side opposite Bat. "How far?"

"Thirty feet. It's a low ceiling, be careful."

"I have a better idea." I reseated my earpiece, then pressed the plastique into a little ball with the detonator in the middle. "I don't know if I used to bowl or not, but…"

I stepped out through the doorway and rolled the ball down the middle of the corridor. The circular tunnel's concave floor kept the bomblet sailing right down the center. The little, blue LED blinked on and off as the ball rolled deeper and deeper down the corridor. When it got as far as I thought safe, I pressed my earpiece to my ear and said "Bluegill."

The bomblet detonated right beneath one of the Plutonians, vaporizing its thorax. The creature's abdomen cartwheeled back over a line of the creatures, spraying them with its vital fluids. The head crashed to the ground, with the antennae still twitching in a search pattern and the mandibles clicking together.

Bat stepped into the corridor and triggered off two more bursts. "Clear, move it."

I let Natch and Loring head out and sent Marit and Jytte after them. I waved Bat forward and heard more shooting. I turned around to wish Crowley luck, but I found myself alone in the room. "Good luck to you anyway, old man. I hope like hell Fiddleback doesn't get either one of us."

The brilliant backlight of the muzzle flash from Bat's carbine made him a marble statue at the juncture of the short corridor and the large gallery. He stood in the center of the passage and sprayed the gallery with gunfire while the others ducked behind him and secured the slant tube down. "Move it, Caine."

I reached back and pulled out another bomblet. "Go, Bat. I'm following close. Guard your eyes when I give the word." I sprinted forward, guided by the light from his gun as he fired in bursts and retreated. As I reached the mouth of the corridor, I hunkered down beside one of the dying creatures and saw two of our people at the slant corridor's mouth open up.

Giving myself a second to size up the situation in the light of their gunfire, I noticed that the Plutonian protecting me was not really a giant insect. A thick, leathery flesh covered over bony armor plates making it much more like an armadillo than anything else. It felt warm to the touch and a thick tuft of hairs ran along its spine. If a rhinoceros had been formed in the image of an ant, it would be a Plutonian.

The Plutonians had arrayed themselves in a staggered line and were advancing steadily toward my companions. A blast in their midst could disorganize them. Crowley had called them a hive mind, so I looked for one with longer antennae in a vain attempt to locate the mobile equivalent of a comcenter.

"No such luck." I rolled the Semitek into a ball and armed the chip. The LED glowed with a yellow light. Steadying myself with my left hand pressed against the Plutonian carcass, I arced the bomb at the highest point of light I could see in the main gallery. "Cover!" I waited a second, then added the mnemonic trigger for the blast. "Yellowtail."

The bomblet exploded fairly close to the ceiling with considerable force. A number of the large, lumbering Plutonians crashed to the gallery floor, their six legs splayed out as if they were roadkill. Others blundered into their compatriots and began fighting them, locking these elephantine ant-things in mortal combat. A few whose antennae had been broken in the blast just spun and spun where they stood.

The explosion ignited the cocoonish web covering the upper part of the ceiling. Starting at the point of the blast, the flaming fabric peeled down from the roof and blanketed the Plutonians with fire. The sticky material clung to them like a second flesh and roasted them alive. The choking deathscent combined with smoke and burning flesh to fill the gallery with a venomous fog.

The roaring inferno made vision much easier than before. Pushing off the corpse, I ran to the slant-tube and shot past Jytte and Marit. They triggered off two more bursts, then ran after me as we sprinted down. We caught Natch and Loring at the turn, then saw Bat waving us through the doorway into the gateway room.

When we were all in, I nodded to Bat and he said, "Red snapper." The floor jolted as the first explosives we'd set detonated and blocked the passage we'd run down. I pointed to the dimensional gate and told everyone to sit on the edge. "I'll get this set. Reload now because we'll probably be going in hot."

I ran over to the control console set near the hexagonal gate. The controls had no buttons or knobs, but seemed to be divided into a 10-by-10 grid that, at the moment, had a few reds, blues and greens amid a sea of white. All of the colors were pastels, yet they flashed with light much as colors shift within an opal.

I touched the very first panel in the grid. It went from white to red and, at the same time, I caught a light, airy scent. This made sense, as the Plutonians seemed to work more from olfactory stimulus than visual clues. I hit the panel again and the light became orange along with another sweet scent being offered as a clue.

I quickly discovered that after violet came white again—with no scent—so I set about changing the colors to match those of the image Crowley had implanted in my mind. As I hit the finished pattern, the gateway began to display the static pattern, with it flowing inward instead of out.

"Go!" I pulled a Semitek packet from my pouch, armed it, and pressed it to the console. Standing on the edge of the gateway I said, "Count five, green sword." I stepped off into the static and felt the numbness swallow me alive.

Coming out on the other side, I fell face first into a viscous, sticky fluid. It felt cold and gelatinous on my hands and face, but as I pushed myself upright, it popped free of my cheek without leaving a residue. Getting my feet under me I stood slowly and found the mucuslike substance clung to the walls and, while somewhat elastic, snapped back in place when stretched beyond a foot or so.

"Where are we?" I saw, obviously, that my companions and I had come through into a huge cylinder. The flooring beneath the slime vibrated slightly, and I heard muted rasping sounds that seemed to rush toward us, then recede away again. I matched my mental image of the control panel with the one Crowley had given me, and they were identical. "Either we're in Lorica, or Crowley made a big mistake."

I turned around and started betting on the latter possibility because Bat stood on the ceiling of the tunnel and shrugged. Halfway between the two of us, Nero

Loring knelt on one knee and pressed a hand down through the slime to the concrete below it. The rest of us, like spokes on a wheel, stood on the interior of the cylinder with no proper regard to the orientation of gravity.

"I think, Caine, we're in the central cylinder around which the main elevators in the Lorica Citadel are built." Loring pulled his hand free of the muck and stood. "I had envisioned a private elevator in here just for me. With this space 20 feet in diameter I could have driven in and been brought all the way up to the penthouse."

He pointed back over his shoulder. "In a conventional sense, that's down and we're facing up. I don't know how gravity is being manipulated here, but it seems to be concentrated by the slime, perhaps as a mechanism to make food fall toward it. As long as we're careful and this stuff goes all the way up, we've got roughly a third of a kilometer between us and the imposter."

A distant and loud boom caused all of us to drop down on our bellies. "An attack?"

Natch shook her head. "Thunder. It always sounds like that in Eclipse."

"Thunder? I thought the storms don't start until evening, when the city cools enough to let the clouds drift in."

"They don't." Marit looked at her watch. "Hold on, this is weird."

As she spoke, I glanced at my own watch. The analog dial read 9:15 a.m., which felt right for the amount of time I've been awake so far. The digital said 8:30 p.m., which was about the time the storms would be starting. "Time moves very slowly in Plutonia, it seems."

Loring pointed up. "It doesn't matter what time it is, there is a storm brewing. We must stop the Witch."

Working our way up along the cylinder felt very strange, especially with Bat persisting in what looked like, from my vantage point, his hanging by his feet from the ceiling. We advanced slowly and cautiously, but saw no opposition. Nowhere did the slime break or fail to secure us.

At the far end of the cylinder a smaller passage opened up. It was about half the diameter of the main tube and that the slime grew only on the sides and floor of the tunnel. It spiraled out and down from the main tube, but because of the twist in it, I could only guess at its length. It seemed, as nearly as I could determine, to be a transition point through which the tube's gravity could be aligned with that of the external world.

Loring said he knew nothing about it, but confirmed my suspicions on its purpose. "This is new construction as far as I know, but it should come out in the penthouse."

"I'll go first and signal when it's clear." I put a new clip into the carbine, then started down the tributary tunnel. I started on a side wall but found myself channeled onto a narrow pathway. By the time the slime ran out, the passage had been squared off and opened into the white silk world of Nerys Loring.

I paused in the doorway and looked both ways, but with the shifting walls billowing and snapping, seeing anything was impossible. "Looks clear, I think," I whispered into my radio. "Come up slowly in case I'm wrong."

One step through the doorway, and I found out how very wrong I was. Two feet hit me in the right shoulder as someone jumped me from above the doorway. I rolled beneath the impact, but before I could come up and turn around, a solid kick in the ribs sent me flying even further. My carbine went skittering across the floor and sunk in one of the streamlets off to my left while I came up short against a low wall and smashed into it with my shoulders.

Mr. Leich, dressed head to toe in black, stood in the middle of floor and laughed mildly. He rubbed his hands on his thighs, then balled them into fists. Behind him, like squashed bugs on the pristine white of the walls, I saw twin slime handprints above the door, which explained how he had hung there until I arrived.

"Hope I didn't leave you hanging too long, Mr. Leich."

His dark RayBan sunglasses hid his eyes, but I imagined no mirth in them, nor did I hear any in his voice. "You've been a very bad boy, Mr. Caine. I owe you, and she said I could have you." He licked his lips lasciviously, then smiled and showed me his fangs.

I gathered my feet beneath me and stood. "If you want me, come get me." I dropped a hand to the Wildey Wolf's butt.

He shook his head. "You still don't understand, do you, human? You've shot me four times. You've caused my flesh to be scraped off in a skid. When you hit me with your car you fractured my leg in eight places. The paramedic said I'd never walk again, then I drank his blood and danced away from the accident site. You can no more fight me than cattle can fight against the slaughterhouse."

Leich pointed at my pistol. "Go ahead. Take your best shot. You've learned nothing."

I pulled the Wildey and snapped it off safety. "On the contrary, Mr. Leich, I have learned a great deal."

The first shot I triggered hit him in the right shoulder with enough of a punch that his sunglasses bounced off his face. Leich twisted his torso back toward me to show he could take everything I could dish out. Then his head turned to the right as he suddenly realized that the thing lying on the floor back beyond him was, in fact, his right arm.

"Don't go to pieces over this, Mr. Leich," I chided him, "or should I call you 'Lefty'?"

Pure suprahuman loathing blazed in his eyes as he turned back to me. He started to snarl something, but my second shot pinned the words in his throat and blew his larynx back out through his spine. Blood splashed over the silk sheets snapping like sails in a gale. His body flopped back into the watery grave that took my carbine while his head did a triple somersault in the air, then hit the ground. It bounced once and rolled back off his nose. Lying on his ear, Leich gnawed at the air for the next five seconds, then he lay still in a pool of blood.

Bat and Jytte appeared at the doorway with their carbines at the ready. "Trouble?"

"No, Bat, it's under control." I holstered the pistol. Behind him Natch and Loring caught up and Marit played rear guard. "He's the only one she had waiting. Either she's very stupid or…"

"…or there is nothing you can do to stop me!"

I heard her voice echo throughout the penthouse and a thunder strike punctuated her statement. I spun around to face deeper into her domain, dreading the effort necessary to hunt her down in her silken labyrinth. *She is a spider in her web.*

The bloody splotches on the sheets to my left slowly began to expand and grow. They spread out until they consumed the whole white cloth, then they infected the next sheet and the next. Those silken curtains filled with blood, and it dripped over marble, staining it, then down into the streams. The streams themselves began to overflow, washing across the floor and whirling Leich's carcass away.

The liquid soaked through my boots and felt warm and sticky just the way blood should.

Then, suddenly, every sheet ignited in a stark burst of magnesium light like they were made of a magician's flash paper. I shielded my eyes as best I could and coughed as the acrid smoke choked me. Heat spiked in the room, and I waited for the nauseating scent of singed hair and boiling flesh, but the sensation passed in an instant.

I opened my eyes to a new world. What had been white

before was now black, as if it had absorbed the soot or the heat had seared it. Now that the sheets were gone, I could see countless little alcoves. All their furnishings looked intact except for the change in color from the other evening when I saw them. The lights had dropped from bright to dim, taking the penthouse down into darkness and, by contrast, allowing one thing to attract our attention.

Off to the west, looking over the city, stood a series of three arched windows. The central one rose half again as tall as the two flanking it and together they provided a breathtaking view of the city. Through it I saw City Center and three brilliant lighting strikes off to the northwest. Angry clouds filled the sky and eerie white flashes edged them with silver.

The others followed wordlessly as I moved toward that site. Standing in front of the windows on an altarlike dais, I saw Nerys. She wore a white gown styled on classical Greek lines, yet cut short to reveal her long legs. Golden cords wrapped round the bodice and snaked between her breasts. In her hand she held the cords' tasseled ends, pulling the cords taut around her body as if they alone could contain her exuberance.

I reached an aisle that led directly to her. As I moved down it I had the disturbing sensation of a supplicant approaching a deity to ask for a boon, but I banished it with a snarl. "It's over, Nerys. We know everything."

"You're wrong, Caine, it's just beginning," she laughed throatily. "There is nothing you can do to stop it, and you owe that fact to Nero Loring himself."

She gestured languidly at a display console that slowly rotated into view. At first glance, as it slithered through shadows and was backlit by lighting, I thought it a polished and chromed prototype from the finest neotech laboratories in Japan. When it locked into place and I got a better look at it, I knew no human could have ever have created it.

The black cables running from one edge to another could have been optical fibers sheathed in shiny plastic, but they flared out at either end in psuedopod receptors that clung to the box like leeches. The cables pulsed as power ran through them and light shifted within panels to which the cables had fused. The panels themselves looked, in the beginning, like complex LCD compilations but I quickly saw, in fact, they were scaly flesh that changed colors with a chameleon's ability to camouflage itself.

A lucite post rose from the center of the device while I stared at it, then fanned itself out like a peacock's tail. Narrow at the base and almost a foot wide at the peak, I saw strange shapes imbedded in the lucite. Then, a second before I realized what medium the artist had used to create the organic designs, I saw they were really thin brain slices trapped between two layers of the clear synthetic.

The Witch looked at the machine with rapture on her face. "Say hello, dear."

A black membrane on the front of the machine quivered like a drumhead to produce a little girl's voice. "I'm sorry, Daddy. I don't want to do it but I can't stop."

"Nerys!" Loring shouted. He pointed at the Witch. "What have you done to her?"

The Witch's eyes narrowed. "Only that which you forced me to do, foolish man. You sought to thwart me and my master. You used her brainwaves, I have used her brain. What has been done is your doing." She turned and glanced at the maglev line and the St. Elmo's fire begining to play along its length. "It cannot be stopped."

"We can blow the line." I pointed back the way we came. "Let's go, Bat."

The Witch laughed at me. "You're going nowhere."

"You're going to stop me?"

"No." She shook her head. "Now, my *pet*, you may reveal yourself. You have done very well."

Marit stepped back away from the rest of the group, but kept her carbine level. "You all know, at this range, I won't miss and your vests won't help. I don't want to have to kill you. Just put your guns down."

Our collection of long guns and pistols clattered to the floor.

The Witch folded her arms across her chest. "You see, Mr. Caine, Fiddleback is not alone in keeping pets. I would kill you for what you have done, but it is not my place to discipline another's toy. I will leave that for when Fiddleback arrives." A close lightning strike turned her face into a mask of silver. "That, by the look of things, should not be long at all."

I looked at Marit and shook my head. "Marit, how could you?"

"I didn't mean to hurt you, Tycho. I didn't."

I heard her words, but the plea for understanding in her voice died in the black hole at the center of her eyes. "Stop now, Marit. Shoot her. Redeem yourself."

"I can't, Tycho, I can't." Marit winced. "I have come too far to be cheated now."

The Witch chuckled lightly. "Your mistake, Mr. Caine. You can offer her nothing more than a warm body in the night. I, on the other hand, can offer her immortality. I can offer her eternal beauty and wealth. I can give her all the things she hungered for as a child in Eclipse. In return, I asked for her to deliver Coyote to me. She has failed in that task, but you are a prize that is, at the moment, far more valuable to me."

She opened her arms wide like a mother welcoming children. "All of you have been resourceful. I appreciate and respect that more than you know. Come to me. Embrace me. Become my servants and, through the grace of Fiddleback, I will see to it that your every dream is fulfilled beyond imagining.

Bat folded his arms. "You mean I get to kill you more than once?"

The Witch shook her head. "How droll, Mr. Kabat." As Marit circled around to stand beside her patron, the Witch pointed at Bat. "When I give the word, my precious, cap him, so he dies in pain, and slowly."

"As you wish, mistress."

"What of the rest of you? Nero, you have been a thorn, but I will let you live. You, Feral, you can have anything you want. And you, Jytte Ravel, I can make you at home in that body. I can make you whole again. It is your choice."

Outside the sky exploded with jagged slivers of pure energy and static crackled through my radio. The storm rolled in over Squaw Peak, thunder rumbling like a growl in a wolf's throat. Multiple lighting strikes walked their way down the side of the mountain. They struck the numerous lightning rods protecting Frozen Shade from storms and for a brief moment, a sizzling energy rope tethered the clouds to the ground. As each line parted, darkness again flashed over the landscape, but the glowing purple ring of the maglev circuit brightened.

Natch chewed her lower lip, then shook her head. "I wouldn't join you even if you were as smart and powerful as you think you are. No sale, Bitch-witch."

The Witch's eyes sparked. "Ravel?"

"You and your kind steal humanity. The only way you could make me whole is to steal from another." She shook her head once. "Void transaction."

"Idiots! Can you not see what she sees?"

"Nope, we can't." Bat shook his head. "But then, we have our eyes open."

"Marit," I whispered sadly over the radio.

She looked at me. "Tycho?"

"I'm sorry."

"Sorry? For what?"

I tried to remember the person she had been the night before.

I failed. "For this. Salome."

A second after I said the word, the Semitek embedded in the main body of her radio exploded. The lead shot nestled at the point of the shaped charge burst free of the small plastic radio case, shattering the clip she had used to fasten it to her harness up by her right shoulder. Plastic fragments and metal shot shredded the harness and blew through the body armor. Recoil started her spinning back and to the left as the shot tore through her chest, punctured her lung and opened her pulmonary artery. Spinning uncontrollably, she brought the muzzle of the carbine up and whipped it across the Witch's face.

The Witch reeled off the back of the dais and fell from sight. I dove for the floor and came up with the Wildey Wolf. Bat dropped to one knee and recovered his carbine. Natch grabbed Nero Loring and started pulling him away from the dais while Jytte headed straight for the computer. Suddenly something moved over near her, and Jytte came flying back to bowl Natch and Loring over.

The Witch came back up in her true form. She still wore Nerys' face over her own, though the pale flesh had been stretched to the point where green showed through from beneath it like an infection. Likewise the flesh of her hands had become corpse-white cellophane gloves that ended in tattered strips at her wrists. Sharp black claws pierced the skin at the end of the fingers and glistened with venom.

As she slithered forward she slid free of the rest of the flesh she had worn in her time as a changeling. A black tongue, forked like that of a serpent, flickered through Nerys' ruby lips. From her throat, all the way down between very mammalian breasts and along the full 20 feet of her snakelike body, yellow ivory scales covered her. Green scales armored the rest of her and gathered into barbs on the backs of her elbows and the points of her shoulders. She blinked away the membranes covering her eyes, showing the elliptical pupils of her amber eyes.

"I need this deception no more! The coming of my lord is nigh!"

Bat and I opened up at the same time. He burned through his clip before I finished mine. His duplex bullets ripped a line across her torso starting at where her left hip might once have been and ending at her right shoulder. My five shots centered on her head and throat. One nailed her dead center in the forehead, shredding her human mask and helping knock her back off the dais.

She ducked from sight for a second, then rose up again. I could see broken scales where Bat had hit her, but as I watched they repaired themselves. "You cannot kill me! Your weapons are too puny! I am invincible!"

Somewhere behind me Nero Loring started laughing.

Bat, Natch and Jytte all concentrated their fire on her. Bullets ricocheted from her head and chest, shattering the windows behind her. Immediately the storm's howling winds whipped through the room, lashing her face with the hair she had worn as a human. Huge chunks of rain-slicked glass whirled out into the night as I jumped up onto the dais and pried Marit's carbine from her dead fingers. Water washed over the back of the Witch and ran off her scales like the bullets we shot at her.

Loring's laughter cut through the thunder and his ridicule seemed to hurt her more than our bullets. She coiled up at the base of the shattered window and hissed at him. She set herself to strike at him, then twisted her head around and glanced at me with the corner of her eye. Her hands twitched, and she came for me.

As she lunged in my direction, the broken shards of wet glass beneath her coils provided her less than optimal traction. Half her serpentine body shot back out through the window as her torso launched toward me. Even in mid-strike she realized what had happened, so her raking claws shifted from me to the dais and sunk in through the formica top and the particle board beneath it.

She looked up me and her snake-tongue flayed the last of the human flesh from her face. Clinging there, with her arms outstretched, she hissed menacingly. "This is not over!" A green coil appeared at the edge of the building, but a burst from Jytte's carbine knocked it back out into the night.

"It is over."

I jumped back off the dais and without my added weight, it slowly slid back toward the broken windows. I leveled Marit's carbine at it and burned the clip. The duplex bullets blasted it into so much kindling and Formica dust. The wind sucked the debris out, taking both the Witch and Marit in the bargain.

I ran to the window and steadied myself against one of the window frames. Falling further and further through sheets of rain, I saw a black whiplike shape undulating through the air. Then, amid a bright flash of light, it hit Frozen Shade. A lightning strike tore into the damaged panel, more sparks shot up and an S-shaped fire begin to burn at the base of the Lorica Citadel.

I turned away from the window and shouted over the howling wind. "Nero, Jytte, what about that computer?" The light around the maglev line continued to build and seven spiral rainbows rose from the local maglev lines to link each citadel with City Center. "Whatever she started, it's continuing."

Jytte looked at the machine and shook her head. "I am unable to assess what I can do. Given time, I could piece together the neural links that make this thing work." She pointed at the two thick cables that touched the base of the brain-fan. "All input and output is going through here, being filtered through Nerys' brain. Deciphering the mind of a 14-year-old girl is not possible."

I turned to Nero. "How did you code the brainwave data?"

"Her patterns in doing one thing would trigger an effect and in doing another would stop it." The stormwind pulled at Loring's vest and whipped the long strands of his hair through the air. "She hated math, so that's what

I used as a trigger. It was the pattern from a series of math problems!"

"And the stopper?"

"Singing a song. Her favorite Christmas hymn, 'Silent Night'!"

A particularly strong and close bolt of lightning silhouetted Bat at the window. "Get her singing, Loring, or we'll all be doing a Requiem! Jesus, Caine, look at this!"

The rainbows broke loose of their citadel moorings and began rotating above City Center like a helicopter blade. As they spun faster and faster they blurred together into a flat disc that slowly began to arc down into a bowl that covered the city. The light show continued to whirl at a frenetic pace and lighting strikes increased, skewering the luminescent dome for a second or two, then being sucked up into its maelstrom.

Then the bowl's edge touched the maglev line. It continued to spin for a moment, then instantly stopped. Pressure built within the dome, and my ears popped. Below us, in the citadel, windows imploded. I heard my heart begin to pound inside me and I found breathing difficult. I tried to step back away from the window but the very air felt thick as wet cement.

Suddenly the center of the bowl blew upward, and the whole funnel-shape began to spin again. I fell backward and lost sight of the sky for a second. When I came back up it had all changed, and I felt liked I'd dined on razor blades and ground glass for the last three days.

The whole brilliant funnel had vanished, leaving in its wake a green and red neon latticework that might as well have been the funnel's bones. Around it and through it I could see the storm clouds, and though the center seemed to go up through the clouds, I saw nothing but a void in the heart of the funnel. Lightning strikes from outside it only hit the lattice, making it glow golden-yellow at that point for a second, then it returned to the red or green color it had been.

I shouted over at Jytte and Loring. "You better do something. This is really weird."

Jytte's fists knotted in frustration. "The Witch knew what she was doing. Most of these brain slices are from the left side of the brain. All math and logic, very little language."

Loring knelt next to the machine. "Come on, Nerys, you have to do it. 'Silent night, holy night...'"

The machine's membrane answered him with, "I can't, Daddy. I can't."

"Think of something!" I stood and watched the first blue tendril hook itself over the edge of the funnel. "Bat, get the hell out of here, take Natch with you. I don't know how far you'll get but...."

Bat shook his head as a second tendril appeared over the event horizon. "I don't run." He slapped a new clip into the carbine and worked the charging lever.

The tendrils solidified as the creature hauled itself up through the hole dug in the sky. The creature's outline hardened into a carapace studded with hooks and bumps and claws. Whereas before it had been smoky gray and insubstantial, it was now a light brown that was his true color. Like the Plutonians he had doubtlessly fashioned in his own image, a leathery flesh covered his body. His head and face were pure arachnid, with compound eyes and sharp mandibles which could have taken the top off one of the Goddard Towers were he inclined to crane his neck toward it.

The creature hung on the lattice with one hand while reaching out with the other. The arm telescoped out to extend from its shoulders, near the center of the city, to the base of the Lorica Citadel. With one of its triform fingers it nudged the burning body that had been the Witch, then brought the finger to its mouth and it tasted of the ashes.

A buzzing, popping voice sounded in my head. "Thiz one never underztood. Inferior, with pretenzionz."

"Jytte! Do something!"

"There is nothing to do, Caine. The parts of the brain we have can't sing!"

The creature's head rotated around to focus on me. "My pet, you oppoze me?"

"I am not your pet!"

"Defianze iz powerful. How to break your rezolve and leave your mind intact?"

"Please baby, just sing it for me," Loring begged the black box.

"I can't, Daddy."

The creature reached out for me, but as it did, lightning struck the lattice in two places. The talons grasping at me flashed into their blue outline form and sparked from the metal window frames. They passed through them and left the stink of ozone in their wake as I jumped back, and Bat ducked beneath them.

"He's still vulnerable! Sing the song!" I shouted.

"I can't," the machine wailed.

Not knowing if the machine had visual sensors or not, I pointed at the creature. "You have to. If you don't, Fiddleback will kill your father."

"No, not my daddy!"

I was staring at the machine, but the voice that answered me came from my left. As I glanced over in that direction a little girl in a Plutonian silk tunic ran across the room and hugged Nero Loring. "Daddy, I won't let him hurt you. I won't."

"Nerys!" Loring held her out at arm's length, then hugged her to him. "'Silent Night,' you have to sing 'Silent Night.'"

"Silent night, Holy night," the girl began obediently.

I looked out at the funnel. It looked as bright as ever. As I watched a helicopter lifted off from one of the landing pads on City Center and climbed toward Fiddleback.

"That's Scorpion," Bat assured me.

"Jytte, this isn't working."

Fiddleback reached down and contemptuously swatted the chopper from the sky. It exploded when his talons moved through it. Flaming debris fluttered down through the air and another Frozen Shade panel died with a flash.

Bat looked over at the computer. "Jytte, this really *isn't* working!"

Natch pointed at the black box. "Nerys isn't hitched into the machine."

Jytte reached out and took hold of the two cables attached to the bottom of the brain-fan. She tugged once, and they didn't come lose. Her perfect lips peeled back away from even white teeth, transforming her babydoll face into a mask of fury. She pulled again and one came free, then a third yank ripped the other one loose.

A little line of yellow lightning arced between the two receptor pads. "This will sting, Nerys, but it won't hurt you. Sing, child sing!"

Two little puffs of smoke went up as Jytte pressed the electrodes to the girl's temples. Nerys stiffened, her head jerking backward, then she craned her head down and stared straight out at Fiddleback. "Silent night, Holy night," she sang in a trembling voice.

Every note she sang started the funnel's lines quivering as if they were guitar strings or piano wires. The light dimmed behind the ripples running along lines and burned white-gold at the peaks. Sparks ignited at the juncture points and teased lightning strikes from the thunderheads.

"All is calm, all is bright."

Fiddleback's outline flickered and wavered. Blue light pulsed along his outline. The lines on the funnel to which he clung began to melt like ice beneath a blowtorch.

"Round yon virgin, mother and child. Holy infant so

tender and mild."

Fiddleback's image began to stretch and fade. The funnel lost its rigid shape, and the rainbow lights began to make their return. They started swirling through the sky and twisted Fiddleback around and around until it he looked more like a piece of rotelli than he did a Plutonian. His arms, which had become little more than blue lines, twisted about him like razorwire coils.

"Sleep in heavenly peace, sleep in heavenly peace."

Fiddleback's grip on the vortex failed, and the rainbow whirlpool sucked him up and out of the world like a cockroach being flushed down a toilet.

Awakening at the heart of a lightning storm, with thunder shaking the very earth with its violence, is not a pleasant experience. Glass crunched beneath my feet as I stared out through the penthouse's broken wall. I let my left hand rest on one of the metal supports, and I dared the storm to strike it and consume me, gambling that it would not.

The thunderstorm we had witnessed so far was but an overture to the elemental fury that lashed the city. Mother Nature reshaped and released all the energies that had been stored up in the funnel. Repeated and nearly constant lighting strikes lit the building in stark, skeletal colors. It almost seemed to me that the Earth, having been left so open to assault from another dimension, wished to scour the wound clean and ensure that no vestige of the infection remained.

Captain Brad Williams had been on duty that night and arrived with a contingent of security people shortly after the funnel dissipated. Williams recognized Nero Loring and accepted Nero's story of an electrical short that caused all the damage. I could see in his eyes and sense in his being that he didn't truly believe what he was told, but he desperately wanted a rational explanation to let him deal with what he had seen. He took Nero and Nerys off and Coyote's three aides with them, leaving me alone with the storm and my thoughts.

So much had happened in such a short time that I really did not know how to assess all of it. Ten days ago I was a null. I did not know who or what I was. Over the next week and a half I discovered, apparently, that I was an assassin who had been hired to kill Nero Loring. In a

180-degree turnabout, I worked with him to destroy the creature that had supplanted his daughter and ordered me to kill him. Along the way I had killed a pair of traitors in Coyote's organization and helped defeat an extradimensional creature bent on the domination of humanity.

Pet had turned against master and, just this once, the pet got away with it. I labored under no illusion that Fiddleback had been destroyed. A creature capable of crafting the sort of intricate and long-term plot that would culminate in creating a city-sized dimensional gateway would not venture everything on attempting to break through. I had been instrumental in his failure, and I knew his retribution would be both direct and cruel.

Lost in thought, I wandered through the Witch's shattered domain. As things in the Lorica Tower began to return to normal, power flooded back into the penthouse and I found a wall-projection television playing in the back. On it I caught a news special concerning the happenings in the Lorica Citadel and above the city. The newscaster reported things straight—though Fiddleback did not image well on video—then showed a clip with the head of the Phoenix Skeptics commenting on what had taken place. Their executive director dismissed it all as a combination of St. Elmo's fire, an unusually bright and southern display of the aurora borealis and mass hysteria.

He was very convincing—wrong, but convincing. I could imagine a whole host of people—people like Brad Williams—denying the evidence of their own eyes in favor of his description. In an odd way I knew I had functioned like that throughout my life. I had seen all the signs of what was going on with Leich, but I denied the evidence of my own eyes because the explanation—that he was regenerating after crippling and fatal wounds—stood incredibly far outside the possibilities I'd been taught to accept.

I had seen Leich. I had seen the Witch in her true form. I'd been to dimensions outside the one in which our world existed. I had experienced things that forced a redefinition of the term "normal." And yet, were I to tell the Skeptics what I had seen and done, I would have no corroborative evidence of my claims, and they would dismiss me as being deluded or delusional.

Suddenly I understood part of what had to drive Crowley and Coyote. They were men who realized that things existed outside the normal realm of human experience. Crowley had said Coyote would be blind to the dimensions, so he limited his work to Earth, while Crowley himself worked elsewhere. Instead of trying to explain the nature of the universe to a populace unable to accept or understand it, they took on the responsibility of responding to and resolving problems that most people refused to acknowledge as existing.

"I think you understand things very well, Tycho."

I turned around as a young man about my height, with dark hair, moustache and goatee casually strolled through the devastated penthouse. He smiled as I held my hand out to him. "Tycho Caine. You must be Coyote."

The man laughed, and I caught familiar notes in his voice, but I could not place where I'd heard it before. "This is the second time you have made that assumption." He pulled off a gray glove and offered me his right hand. A gold ring flashed on it.

"Crowley? But you're so young. You can't be…"

"Perhaps not in the logic of this world, but it *is* possible." His grip was firm and he pumped my arm with strength. "It was a decidedly distasteful experience."

I narrowed my eyes. "You took Nerys's body to the dimension of Tartarus where Tityus regenerates everything the vultures have eaten in a day."

He nodded. "Because of the way the storage areas

worked, Nerys was not really dead. I took her there directly, which was not an easy journey. Because enough of her brainstem had been left behind, she regenerated her brain. It took six months, but I am pleased to see the effort was worth it."

I stared at him. "Time, I take it, moves a lot faster there than here?"

"In reality it does, but when there it hardly seems so. She regenerated her brain, and I regenerated the damage of my infirmity—old age. If it were not for what it did for Nerys, I would think it a hideous place. Nothing to do but shoot vultures and listen to a barely literate Titan bellow curses against Apollo all day and night."

"You brought Nerys here? I didn't see you."

"You were a bit occupied. I left quickly because I needed to cover my tracks. I also made contact with Coyote." The man's green eyes narrowed. "If you are willing, I will take you to him."

"Please."

Crowley grabbed a hold of my combat harness. "Blank your mind. Concentrate on perceiving nothing and yet everything. Control your breathing. You want to open a portal between you and the dimensions outside this one."

"I understand." I took in a deep breath and let it play out slowly. I forced my mind to forget the aches and pains I felt, and I took myself deep inside. I imagined the wall of reality to be like a theater curtain, and I gently probed it for the slit that would let me pass through it.

"Good."

I felt a tug on my belt as Crowley and I moved forward. Tantalizing flashes of color strobed past, each a window into a different dimension. Some, perhaps those closest to and most like what Earth had once been, felt warm and buoyed my spirits. Others we brushed by kindled bloodlust or visions of depravity I never would have imagined unaided. As we moved on things became darker and yet more warped, but the only way I can describe them is to note I felt colder and colder as we progressed.

Finally we came to a bare, arid landscape that looked at once to me to be the red planet where I had seen Nero Loring. As my eyes adjusted to it, however, I realized that it was red only in a circle that centered itself on Crowley's shadowform. Outside that sharp line the world was rendered in white, black and a varied array of gray shades. Though a sun burned in the black sky, I still felt cold.

Outside the circle I saw a man. He seemed small, but I knew that was more than a function of his appearing as if projected on a screen, instead of actually standing there. He looked fortyish, with a full head of hair and strongly chiseled features. His dark eyes had a depth to them that I could see in spite of the flat image. A nervous tic tugged at the corner of his right eye, but I would have expected a man who had done what all he had to show some effect of the stress.

He smiled openly, erasing some of the worry from his face. "You've had a busy evening, Mr. Caine. You have my sympathies concerning Ms. Fisk, and my awe that you had prepared yourself in case Pell was not the only traitor. I had not considered that possibility. So the code word for Marit was Salome. I assume the others had similar biblical mnemonics."

"Yes." Even though it had had gone dead, I checked to make sure I had switched my radio off. "Bat was Sampson, Natch was Delilah and Jytte was Lilith. Loring was Adam."

A meteorite died in the sky behind him. "And Crowley? Was he rigged to explode, or did you trust him?"

I glanced over at the shadow man and shrugged. "Lucifer."

Coyote paused for a moment, then nodded. "You are

very much the man I thought you were. You deserve answers, and you shall have them, finally."

"I would like that very much. Who am I?"

The small man folded his arms across his chest. "I must apologize to you for having manipulated you as grossly as I did. As Crowley has told you, I am unable to go freely through the dimensions to deal with problems. I knew I would need someone like you who could do that, but to get you to work for me I needed to have something you wanted. In your case, it was your identity. I apologize because I have known who you are since before you awakened, and I have known this because I stole your memory in the first place."

My jaw dropped open. "You what? All of this has been a sham?"

"Yes, but a necessary one, I think." Coyote's face hardened. "I'll give you the thumbnail sketch, then Jytte can provide you with a file that will confirm all I am telling you. You are, as you have surmised, an assassin. You are one of the best in the world, probably in the top seven, definitely the top ten. This I know because, well, I know it. You have an impressive record, especially against targets that must be hunted down. You are one of Fiddleback's favorites, and this is the reason you were brought to Phoenix to kill Nero Loring. You have never missed a target, to my knowledge, and your record still holds. You are an impressive and terrifying man.

"In researching you, however, I did discover two flaws in you. You have very expensive taste in rental cars, which allowed us to get a line on the identity you used here. *You* chose the name Tycho Caine, which I find interestingly symbolic: Tycho—derived from the Greek *tychon*, 'hitting the mark.' And Caine, of course, was his brother's slayer. Everything else you know about Tycho Caine is a fabrication that I have created because, as you have been known to do, after your hit you engaged in a bout of gambling. I suspect this is because, after you murder someone, you want to give the universe a chance to get even with you. My agents found you, drugged you and after we built up the Tycho Caine we wanted you to search out, they released you."

"Wait, wait, wait." I turned to Crowley. "How much of this did you know?"

He gave me an enigmatic shrug. "Enough. Coyote confided in me he would be turning one of Fiddleback's tools against him, and he asked for my help. I gave it to him *and* to you."

I looked back at Coyote. "But this doesn't make any sense! If you knew who and what I was, why didn't you kill me and be done with it? Given what you do, given what Crowley does, I can't imagine either one of you wanting me alive."

Coyote looked down. "I had my reasons."

"Then they were flawed reasons. Flawed, just like your statement that I've never missed a target. I've met Nero Loring. I missed."

Coyote started a slow circuit around the circle of color. "I wanted you to deal with my traitor problem and with Nerys Loring. The first was a task I could have handled, but I thought it better left in your hands. In that group the only person I knew I could trust was Jytte. Beyond her, anyone was suspect, and I was not certain I could deal with the problem in the only way feasible. You could do that.

"The problem Nerys Loring presented was one that required someone with unique skills and abilities to handle. Your success in stopping her proves to me you are the individual of whom I can make the following request:

"I want you to replace me."

"Replace you? I don't understand."

Coyote stopped moving. "I have a rare disease of the

brain, Gerstmann-Straussler-Scheinker syndrome. It causes nerve degeneration, dementia and death. I was diagnosed with it only a month before you arrived in Phoenix, and this caused me to shift my plans. My doctors did not give me very long, so I had to make arrangements. They included you."

I glanced at the shadow man. "Why don't you take him to Tityus' dimension? He could be cured."

"No." Crowley ruefully shook his head. "GSS is *genetic*. Once it starts it is natural. Regeneration would have exacerbated the disease, not made it better. He might have regressed physically, but his brain would have deteriorated even faster."

The shock of Coyote's request and the story of his condition stunned me. "This is, ah, a lot to handle." I held my hand out toward him. "Come with us, we can discuss it further. I need some time."

The little man shook his head. "I'm afraid I have no time to give you."

"What do you mean? You're still sharp. We can work this out."

"It's too late for that." Coyote squatted down on his haunches. "I knew that you would only leave yourself open to my people after the completion of your hit on Nero Loring. That is when you would fall into my grasp, but I could not sabotage the effort against Nerys by allowing you to kill him—and I knew I could not fool you into believing you had succeeded were I to employ some sleight of hand to whisk him away and out of danger. For that reason I took Nero Loring's place, and I filled your sights the day you saw Nero Loring die."

I stared unflinchingly into the dead man's black eyes and recalled the vision on the bluff when I met Nero Loring for the first time. I *had* succeeded in killing him. I had shot Nero Loring through the head, but I had no way of knowing it was someone else in disguise. The idea that a human being would allow himself to be knowingly shot to death did not exist in my world.

"You're dead?"

A thin smile graced Coyote's lips. "I could never fool you in life, so I had to do that in death. Jytte managed to create a Coyote synthesizer program that, with the proper input, was able to provide you with vague but apparently meaningful messages. I was able to guess ahead of time how much of this work would go, so we scripted up conversations, and I prerecorded them. The computer cut and spliced as necessary. As long as you believed I was alive and working to solve the mystery of your identity, you worked with me. You have seen how I work, and my files can offer you more cases to study than you could ever desire."

He shook his head and looked, for the first time, hopeless. "I apologize that this elaborate charade was necessary, but only by forcing you to see the world through the eyes of a normal person could I communicate to you how desperately I need someone with your skills to replace me. If you take up my mantle, you will have the resources to build where you previously tore down. You may create where before you have destroyed. You may not be able to leave the world a better place than it was when you found it, but you can slow its descent into the depths of hell."

I spoke around the lump in my throat. "I can pay forward."

"Precisely." Coyote pressed his hands together. "I took your life, and you took mine. Jytte has an injection for you that, if you so desire, will unblock your drug-induced amnesia. You may return to your old ways and, with this explanation, Fiddleback may even accept you back again. If not, I am certain there are other Dark Lords who would be happy to take you into their stables."

I shook my head. "I don't know, I just don't know."

"Jytte can tell you more, much more, but it's your choice, Tycho Caine." Coyote shrugged and the world began to darken around him. "My time as Coyote is up."

"Wait, answer me one question: Why Coyote?"

The fading phantom laughed. "The Dark Lords—things like Fiddleback and worse—consider us varmints and seek to exterminate most forms of life on Earth. When varmint extinction programs were tried before, in the 19th and 20th centuries, the coyote not only refused to die, it flourished. Coyotes moved into cities and bedeviled those who sought to destroy them. What other totem animal could I chose?"

The world outside the red circle collapsed into blackness. I turned to Crowley and saw lights begin to play through the dark. As the color slowly drained from our circle, the light built behind him, and I found myself back in Phoenix, on Camelback Mountain, looking southwest over Frozen Shade and the rest of the city. Looking behind me I saw we had returned to earth near one of the vast mansions built on the side of the mountain.

The occultist silently pointed toward the stairway carved into the rock. He followed me as I climbed up to the front door and opened it. Crowley closed it behind me, then led me in and down to the basement level through a steel door hidden behind an oaken wall panel in the study.

The hidden rectangular room had been simply furnished. I entered at the narrow end and saw, all the way across from me, a large screen projection television. Off to the right stood a bank of Hitachi computers and opposite it a row of 10 file cabinets lined the wall. In the center stood a long conference table with an even dozen chairs distributed about it. Nearest me, filling the walls, were workbenches with equipment that ran the gamut from chemical analysis units and scanning electron microscopes to electronics construction stations and gunsmithing tools.

A single tear rolled down Jytte's perfect face as she stood beside the table. She set a silver tray with a full syringe on the table next to a cellular phone. A single droplet of liquid glistened at its tip. I looked up at her and wondered what was going on behind that plastic mask of a face.

"Coyote said you had information for me, to help me make my decision."

Jytte nodded. "According to an agreement Coyote made with Nero Loring, you will be acknowledged as his nephew, Michael Loring. You will become the CEO of Lorica Industries, with all the rights and privileges that entails. Nero has handpicked a board to run the company for you, so the burdens of day-to-day activities are limited to those you personally choose to assume."

"Or," I noted, "the ones allowed by the rigors of becoming Coyote."

"As you wish. Lorica has facilities throughout the world. Your legitimate resources will be vast, and those assets that Coyote has prepared for his work will allow you to work in secret with unparalleled ease."

I felt a shiver run down my spine. "Who was he, Jytte? Who was Coyote? What was his real name?"

She blinked her eyes once. "That information is unknown to me. He was Coyote. I do not know if he was the first, was the only or will be the last Coyote. What you have seen is who he was."

Coyote. He was a man who set a trained killer on his own people to find out who among them was betraying him. He was a man who coerced others into working for him. He stole my identity and led me on a wild chase that not only put my life in danger, but caused me to kill a number of people—including aides he had trusted in the past. He also caused the deaths of innocent people, like Hal's wife.

I looked at the syringe. Were Coyote and I that different, really, at the core of it? I killed for rewards that brought me satisfaction, and he did the same. That he let himself believe he was making the world a better place meant nothing.

Or did it?

He caught a bullet in the head to take a chance that his crusade would not die.

I reached my hand out and picked up the phone. I punched up a number quickly and waited for someone to pick it up on the other end. I smiled as a sleepy voice answered.

"Hello, Mr. Sinclair MacNeal?" I smiled as he cursed at the time. "I understand you are at loose ends at the moment. I think we could work well together. Listen, it doesn't really matter who I am, but just for the sake of simplicity, you may call me Coyote."